Are You Compatible With Your Boss...
Partner...
Coworker...
Clients...
Employees?

Lynne Palmer

Published by
Lynne Palmer

Are You Compatible With Your Boss..Partner..Coworker..Clients..Employees?

ISBN 0-9652296-9-6

Library of Congress Catalogue Number 00 090 592

Published by:

Lynne Palmer
Toll Free: 1-800-615-3352
Web Site: www.lynnepalmer.com
Email: lynnepalmer@lynnepalmer.com

Printed and bound in the United States of America

Books by Lynne Palmer

Astrological Almanac (Annual)

Do-It-Yourself Publicity Directory

Astrological Compatibility

Prosperity Signs

Is Your Name Lucky For You?

Your Lucky Days and Numbers

Nixon's Horoscope

Horoscope of Billy Rose

ABC Chart Erection

ABC Basic Chart Reading

ABC Major Progressions

Pluto Ephermeris (1900-2000)

Money Magic

Astro-Guide to Nutrition and Vitamins

Gambling to Win

The Astrological Treasure Map

Contents

Introduction

How Astrology Works For You

You have an inner power that, when applied, allows you to control your outer environment. This inner power is represented by your Sun and/or *dominant* side when used on the positive side.

Your Sun sign is the sign that the Sun is in at the exact moment you are born. A little more astrological knowledge is needed to understand what your *dominant* sign is. Your horoscope is based upon the day, month, year, time, and place of your birth. There are eight planets — Mercury, Venus, Mars, Jupiter, Saturn, Uranus, Neptune, and Pluto — and two luminaries — the Sun and Moon —in our solar system as we know it. These planets, as they appear to us in the sky, are located in one or more of the twelve signs of the zodiac, which are situated in the various constellations.

Each of these ten elements — eight planets and two luminaries — will occupy a sign. Thus you may have different signs of the zodiac in your horoscope. If a sign is close in degrees to the other signs in the horoscope it may be considered *dominant* and if there is more than one planet in a sign, that sign may also be considered *dominant* in your horoscope and, thus, is the key to your character. In other words, if one sign is close in degrees to the other signs, or if more than one planet is located in a sign than you will act more like this sign than any other in the zodiac.

If your Sun sign is NOT your dominant sign, you may not behave at all like it. If your Sun sign doesn't have many aspects (the distance in degrees and minutes that two planets are apart) with the other planets and/or if it's the only luminary (or planet) in a particular sign, it can be considered weak. Perhaps you have more planets in another sign and therefore that sign is more *dominant* than your Sun sign. If this occurs, you may be aware that you are constantly expressing the characteristics of this *dominant* sign and *not* your Sun sign. It's very possible to have several signs that are *dominant*. When this happens, you act and think like the traits representative of each sign. It's all up to you, as to how you express these astrological energies that are part of your nature.

Once a horoscope has been cast, you must also consider your Rising sign (also called Ascending sign). As the earth turns on it's axis, a particular sign appears on the horizon at the exact hour, minute, and second of birth — it is "rising" or "ascending" in view. You may be more like your Rising sign than your Sun sign if the Rising sign is *dominant* in your horoscope — that is, if it makes *many aspects* to the Sun, Moon, and/or planets as they appear in your chart at the time you were born.

When you recognize and use the harmonious side of your Sun and/or *dominant* sign, you'll be halfway up the road that leads to the top .Part of the secret to success involves knowing your talents and using them to the utmost. The other part and our concern here, deals with getting along with others — *specifically*, an employer, employee, coworker, partner, client, or customer. This can be accomplished if you know how to treat others according to their Sun and/or *dominant* sign or planet. If you are not financially independent you can't afford to make enemies or create discord with your business associates. In fact, it's unwise to make such waves even if you are wealthy.

Without knowledge and understanding of astrology you may flounder indefinitely. Why waste valuable time when you can get there much faster, and with less stress and strain, by using astrology as a tool? This book will assist you in understanding yourself and others, knowing your capabilities and how to handle them in a way that's going to pay off, as well as learning how to deal with people in business who may or may not be compatible with you. By adhering *today*, to the methods outlined in this book, *tomorrow* you'll be better off. You may go even higher than your wildest expectations — maybe you'll be one of those millionaires we'll be reading about!

Chapter One

Astrology and Compatibility

You've all heard statements like "The boss and I fought constantly, so I quit." "That guy I worked with bugged me so much I walked off the job." "My partner and I couldn't see eye to eye, so we ended up in court to settle our differences." "My client was so indecisive, that I asked her to take her business elsewhere." You must be aware that compatibility plays a major role in business success. The above complaints are all typical of incompatible Sun and/or *dominant* signs.

What about those people who get along well with each other? You're probably also familiar with an employee who remains with a firm until he retires, or an employer who manufactures her employee's invention, and both reap the rewards, or partners who strike it rich together.

What is it that makes you get along with one person and yet cross swords with another? In terms of astrology, the signs of the zodiac, like our bodies, are composed of electromagnetic energy. As any student of physics knows, certain elements and compounds blend, while others produce a jolt like an electric shock.

The ancients assigned four elements — fire, water, air, and earth — to the signs of the zodiac. All elements, including those in chemistry such as sulfur, radium, carbon, and mercury, are composed of electrons and protons. Electrons carry a unit charge of negative electricity, and protons carry a unit charge of positive electricity. Therefore, some elements, like some signs of the zodiac, produce a charge in the atmosphere when mixed together that results in combustion. Other elements, like some signs of the zodiac, when combined, charge the air with harmonious and positive energy.

You've heard people say "We just didn't have the right chemistry, so we parted," or, "We get along great — the chemistry's right." They just may be speaking of these elements (Fire, Water, Air, and Earth signs) which are composed of electrons (negative charges) and protons (positive charges). Each element blends best with it's own kind: Fire signs (Aries, Leo, Sagittarius) with Fire signs; Earth signs (Taurus, Virgo, Capricorn) with Earth signs; Air signs (Gemini, Libra, Aquarius) with Air signs; Water signs (Cancer, Scorpio, Pisces) with Water signs.

As everyone knows, "Water puts out fire." Water and fire signs do not tend to mix well together — nor do some combinations of Earth and Fire or Earth and Air. However, Earth and Water or Fire and Air blend rather well with one another except when they are in opposition, that is 180° apart.

A horoscope wheel has the same number of degrees as a circle — 360 — and the twelve signs of the zodiac are located therein. Therefore, six (half of the zodiac, or half of the circle) of these signs are opposite (180° apart) each other and their traits often are opposite too. The signs' basic traits can be seen in this simple breakdown:

4

Aries is opposite Libra: Aries loses his temper quickly and enjoys a good argument, while Libra can control her temper and will give in rather than quarrel.

Taurus is opposite Scorpio: Taurus moves slowly, whereas Scorpio moves fast.

Gemini is opposite Sagittarius: Gemini doesn't always keep his word, whereas Sagittarius will go out of her way to fulfill a promise.

Cancer is opposite Capricorn: Cancer is emotional and changeable, whereas Capricorn is unemotional and constant.

Leo is opposite Aquarius: Leo likes to lay down the rules and dictate, whereas Aquarius believes everyone should live their own lives, and do their own "thing".

Virgo is opposite Pisces: Virgo is orderly, critical, and gets bogged down by details, whereas Pisces is messy, overlooks faults, and neglects details.

Despite the differences in opposite signs, they're often attracted to one another. You've certainly heard the adage "opposites attract" — in many instances this applies to opposite signs. Often what one person or sign lacks the other has: for instance, Aries doesn't weigh the pro's and con's of a situation while Libra does. Libra isn't aggressive but Aries is. In a business partnership the combination of these two signs may be an asset; especially when Libra holds Aries back from spending enormous amounts of money on things that aren't needed. Besides, Libran's need partners who have the nerve (Aries has) to drum up business.

When planets are in opposite signs they are said to be in an Opposition aspect to one another. An aspect is the distance in degrees that two signs are apart. Although these signs may complement one another, in most cases, they bring about a separation of ideas as well as a separation between two people who fall under their influence. For example, if you are a Leo and your employee is an Aquarian, the two of you may disagree so tremendously that the Aquarian walks off the job. An Opposition is considered the worst aspect in astrology and is followed by the Square, Sesqui-square and Semi-square.

The Square aspect is found when two planets are 90° apart. It results in obstacles between two people who have their Sun (or a planet) 90° apart. For example, Taurus and Leo, both stubborn signs, will refuse to budge and cause constant obstacles in their business together. The Sesqui-square — two planets 135° apart — aspect will cause aggravations and the Semi-square — two planets 45° apart — aspect causes friction.

The ancients discovered that when two planets are 45°, 90°, or 180° apart a unit charge of negative electricity is released. Therefore, if you are an Aries and contact a Cancer (90°, Square aspect), a negative field automatically sets up between the two of you. The relationship may involve stormy emotional scenes that may bring about a loss of business or employment. The same type of situation may also occur under the Semi-square and Sesqui-square, but instead of a barrier being created friction or aggravation may result.

The harmonious aspects in astrology are the Semi-sextile (two planets 30° apart), the Sextile (two planets 60° apart), and the Trine (two planets 120° apart). The ancients discovered that when two planets are these distances apart a unit charge of positive energy is released. Therefore, if you are an Aries and come into contact with a Gemini (two signs 60° apart) a positive field automatically sets up between the two of you. The relationship may involve a brilliant exchange of ideas that can bring about a business gain, a salary raise, or higher position for the Gemini who is in your employ.

To use the information contained herein, you do *not* have to calculate the aspects; by reading the text you'll gain the perspective you need. All signs, planets, and aspects, contain energy straining to be released either on their negative or positive side. You, as an individual, have the power to control them and make them work to your advantage. However, if you choose not to do anything to prevent problems, they are as likely as not to manifest their destructive side and cause a loss of money, employment, and create disharmony between you and the people you deal with.

Once you understand this, life is not as complicated as it's made to be. It's really very simple: either you blend with someone or you don't — and if you don't, you can try to do so if you wish to put forth a little effort in that direction. Not only can you channel your thoughts and actions into positive outlets in every-day activities, but also toward those you come into contact with, regardless of whether it's by mail, telephone, or in person.

Since 1957, I've been an astrologer, I've seen the wonderful results achieved by people who convert disharmonious energy into harmonious energy when they come into contact with someone who is really incompatible with them. In fact, I do it myself every time I give a consultation to someone whose horoscope doesn't blend well with mine. This has aided my business because these very same people refer my services to others. Therefore, when you control negative forces by being positive and not allowing anything to disturb you, success can be attained.

What about those individuals who refuse to change, adapt, or get along with others? I've noticed that they either get fired, quit, break with a partner, or dump a client and cost themselves enormous sums of money. These are the people who are either stubborn (Taurus, Leo, Scorpio, or Aquarius) or who just want to be themselves and if someone doesn't like it, that's just too bad! Of course this attitude makes it more difficult for them to be successful.

The aspects, signs and/or planets represent your attitude toward everything in life. Those individuals with whom you are compatible can help you achieve success mainly because *your attitude* toward them is harmonious. Those with whom you are incompatible can hinder success mainly because *your attitude* is disharmonious. Of course you can say that the opposite holds true — *their attitude* toward you is either positive or negative with like results.

Compatibility in Business can be used in various ways depending upon your relationship to others — are you a partner, employer, employee, coworker, or client? The strategy used to reach the top will be different in each case not only because of the position you are in but because each sign of the zodiac represents a certain way of acting and thinking, remember?

If you are an employer and must choose between several applicants, whom would you select? Wouldn't it be to your advantage to hire someone who not only is stable and productive, but is also compatible with you? Or if you had to lay off an employee, knowing an individual's Sun and/or *dominant* sign and how it blends with yours can help you make a decision. However, if you blend well with two people, you are choosing between, it may be a toss up. But the qualities of one sign may outweigh those of another — that is, as far as you are concerned.

If you have someone on your payroll who does excellent work but the two of you clash, do you realize that if you understood this employee better the strain between you would be lessened? If you and your employee are compatible it makes for harmonious vibes. When harmony exists between people, especially in the working environment, business tends to flourish.

If you are an employee you may be fearful of losing a job when you don't get along with the boss. Perhaps business has slowed down and you are afraid of being the next one to get the ax. To avoid being caught in this type of situation, perhaps you should work for someone compatible with you. If you understand your employer and how to *really* please her or him, you may enhance your possibilities for moving up the corporate ladder not only through your business abilities but also because of the way you handle job relationships.

If you don't get along with your coworkers it's possible you could lose your job. Sooner or later the boss will discover she has an employee whose antagonism interferes with his work. Most people dislike laboring in a hostile environment. Wouldn't you prefer to perform your tasks in peaceful surroundings? Or if the two of you could understand each other better, wouldn't this help both of you do your work? Compatibility improves your chances and getting to the top becomes that much easier.

Before you tie yourself up with a partner, discover whether the two of you are compatible or incompatible. If you don't blend you may be in for disagreement, money can be lost, tempers can fly and havoc become part of your daily routine. Not only will the two of you notice friction between each other, but also your customers and employees will see how you behave toward each other. This could adversely affect sales. If this discord could be avoided because you chose the right partner, wouldn't that be a relief? If it's too late because you're already in a partnership, at least you can learn to understand one another better and know how to handle your differences.

Wouldn't it be to your advantage to know what makes your client tick? Isn't it important to know how to appeal to him to consummate a deal? Wouldn't it hasten a business transaction if you are aware of his needs right away? If the two of you are compatible, it stands to reason that you'd be beneficial to one another. But what if you have to deal with one another and have difficulty because you do not get along? By learning how to appeal to his best side you can continue to do business with him. That's one way to keep the cash register filled, isn't it?

How would you like to do a fantastic business with everyone, regardless of a person's Sun and/or *dominant* sign and, still, maintain a friendly relationship? This can be accomplished quite easily if you have knowledge of the zodiac signs, how to handle them and whether the two of you are compatible or incompatible.

And, just think, if the person in question *does* blend with your Sun and/or *dominant* sign, you two will enhance your chances to have tremendous success!

Now that you understand the basics of astrology and compatibility, I will go one step further. As I mentioned in the introduction, success can be achieved quickly by using astrology as a tool. Suppose you know someone's Sun and/or *dominant* sign — you may ask, "How can that help me?" Not only does it give you the clue to the individual's personality, it also provides a tip on how to deal with that individual. But there are many instances in business when you don't know the sign the person in question was born under or has *dominant*. What then? There are certain giveaway traits that can help you recognize that individual's Sun or *dominant* sign right away. Once you know this, you are better equipped to handle any situation that may arise. You are also one step further along the road to success. So read on...

8

Chapter Two

Recognizing Someone's
Sun or Dominant Sign

Picture twelve people in a room, each representing a sign of the zodiac. This is the office you might see: Aries performing her tasks hurriedly. Taurus appears strong and solid while he sits as still as a Buddha statue and slowly, but efficiently, does his job. Gemini walks back and forth from her desk while she talks on two phones simultaneously. Cancer aloofly, and dutifully, performs his chores at a snail's pace. Leo appears like she's sitting on a throne while those who surround her are waiting for their orders. Virgo has his nose buried in the accounts receivable books. Libra's all dolled up and smiles as she saunters across the room. Scorpio is intense and lost in concentration while engaged in his job; however, he suddenly glances up and you swear he's seen right through your soul. Sagittarius cracks a few jokes while quickly performing her job. Capricorn's seriousness puts a damper on the scene while he calmly and stiffly tends to business. Aquarius seems to be a free spirit, and a comrade to others, while she erratically tends to her chores. Pisces appears to be daydreaming until a customer walks in, then suddenly he's wheeling and dealing.

Now that you've seen all of the signs together, here's how you can recognize them when you're alone with them.

ARIES SUN AND/OR DOMINANT SIGN

Did someone just dash past you as if she was on fire? If she stopped at all, did she talk fast? Was the conversation centered around her? Did she seem to know where she was headed and what she wanted to accomplish? Was she all bubbly and excited over her projects? Did she snap at you, interrupt your speech or get fidgety if you tried to talk? Did she appear busy, impatient, and aggressive?

If you answered "yes" to these questions, you probably had a brief encounter with an Aries or someone who has Aries as a dominant sign.

TAURUS SUN AND/OR DOMINANT SIGN

Did you pass someone plodding along like it was an effort for him to pick up his feet? When you stopped him, did you do most of the talking? Did he respond to your inquiries with only a few words or a nod? Did he seem bored by or even uninterested in the conversation? Were you impressed by his patience?

If you answered "yes" to these questions, you probably met a Taurus or someone who has Taurus as a dominant sign.

GEMINI SUN AND/OR DOMINANT SIGN

Are you aware that a woman just breezed by; it wasn't just the wind? Did you try to catch her? Did she maintain her quick pace while the two of you chatted? Did she talk with her hands? Was she all wound up with nervous energy? Did she skip from subject to subject without seeming to pause for a breath of air? Were ideas just pouring out of her mouth? Was it difficult for you to get a word in? Did she finish your sentences for you?

If you answered "yes" to these questions, you probably were yakking with a Gemini or someone who has Gemini as a dominant sign.

CANCER SUN AND/OR DOMINANT SIGN

Is that person ahead of you moving so slow that you caught up with him in no time at all? Did he appear cool and detached when you spoke to him? Was his speech guarded, even crabby? Did he seem to absorb every word you said? Were his replies carefully considered rather than spoken spontaneously? Did you notice that within minutes his moods changed?

If you answered "yes" to these questions, you probably came into contact with a Cancer or someone who has Cancer as a dominant sign.

LEO SUN AND/OR DOMINANT SIGN

Are you aware that the woman who just glided by you is not really a queen although she appears to carry herself like royalty? When you caught up to her, did you notice that she appeared haughty? Did she take command of the conversation? Did she name-drop or show that she was in an authoritative position? Did she exude a certain elegant charm while stealing center stage? Did you gather from the discussion that she doesn't waste her energy on petty things?

If you answered "yes" to these questions, you probably encountered a Leo or someone who has Leo as a dominant sign.

VIRGO SUN AND/OR DOMINANT SIGN

Did you almost miss that man who passed you by because he was moving quietly as a mouse? If you stopped him, did he appear shy? Yet once engaged in a conversation, were you stunned that a man who appears so unassuming could have that much knowledge? Did he point out flaws in your ideas? Was he overly critical? Did it take him a long time to reach a point because he was busily engaged in filling in all of the preliminary details?

If you answered "yes" to these questions, you were probably having a discussion with a Virgo or someone who has Virgo as a dominant sign.

LIBRA SUN AND/OR DOMINANT SIGN

Does that woman alongside of you seem to be walking on clouds? When you stopped to engage her in a conversation was she what you might call a real charmer? Did she discuss the pros and cons of an issue? Did she seem just and fair when expressing an opinion? Was she refreshing and, yet, confusing? By the time she finished with her explanation were you as indecisive as she?

If you answered "yes" to these questions, you probably were speaking to a Libra or someone who has Libra as a dominant sign.

SCORPIO SUN AND/OR DOMINANT SIGN

Does that man a few feet ahead of you walk briskly, with a determined gait? When you caught up with him did you notice he looked at you suspiciously? When you spoke to him did you realize that he really was trying to avoid a conversation? Did he have a poker face? Did he volunteer little or no information? Did he seem to be in perfect control of himself? Did you feel that you'd better obey his bidding or else?

If you answered "yes" to these questions, you probably came into contact with a Scorpio or someone who has Scorpio as a dominant sign.

SAGITTARIUS SUN AND/OR DOMINANT SIGN

Is that woman way ahead of you darting about so fast that you have to run to catch her? Once you reached her did you have to continue walking fast even when conversing? Did she speak rapidly as she walked? Was she friendly? Was she all bubbly? Did her eyes light up like a Christmas tree? Did she openly talk about herself? Did she seem optimistic? Was her attitude confident? Were her words to the point?

If you answered "yes" to these questions, you probably encountered a Sagittarius or someone who has Sagittarius as a dominant sign.

CAPRICORN SUN AND/OR DOMINANT SIGN

Is that man walking beside you dressed conservatively? Is his face grim — seeming almost gloomy or melancholy? Does he respond evasively to your inquiries? Does he speak slowly and deliberately as if every word were carefully thought about? Did he use logic and sound like he had good old-fashioned common sense? Does he seem practical? Is he pessimistic about some fantastic scheme? Does he seem patient?

If you answered "yes" to these questions, you probably conversed with a Capricorn or someone who has Capricorn as a dominant sign.

AQUARIUS SUN AND/OR DOMINANT SIGN

Is it difficult to keep up with that woman walking beside you? If the two of you stopped and talked, did you feel an almost electrifying magnetism? Does she seem to want your friendship? Does she monopolize the conversation? Is she a know-it-all? Does she constantly interrupt you? Was she abrupt? Were her views radical? Was she contrary to your opinions? Was she obstinate when it came to her beliefs?

If you answered "yes" to these questions, you probably became friends with an Aquarius or someone who has Aquarius as a dominant sign.

PISCES SUN AND/OR DOMINANT SIGN

Did you just pass a man who ambled along as if he didn't have a care in the world? Did he have a faraway look in his eyes? Did he reply vaguely when you spoke to him? Was he sympathetic to your problems? Did he offer aid? Did he tell you about his overnight get-rich ideas? Were they impractical? Did his dreams seem too unbelievable to be true?

If you answered "yes" to these questions, you probably met a Pisces or someone who has Pisces as a dominant sign.

With these tip-offs you can key into a person's sign and behave accordingly almost from the moment of your first meeting.

In the following chapters, you will learn about the personality of each sign, how to handle everyone and how your sign blends with all of the other zodiacal signs that may, or may not, be compatible with yours. This information can be used to improve a relationship by helping you to understand your boss, partner, employees, coworkers, or clients better, and thus ultimately lead to your becoming successful. It's all up to you! So good luck on your way to the top!

Chapter Three

Aries Compatibility In Business

If you were born between March 21 and April 19, your Sun is in the sign of Aries. However, you may also express Aries traits even if it is not your Sun sign if Aries is dominant in your horoscope (refer to the Introduction, Page 1). If this is the case, you should read this chapter just as if your Sun sign is Aries.

ARIES PROFILE
Getting Acquainted With The Aries Personality

The Aries man is easy to get to know. Once you understand what motivates him, it'll be a cinch to deal with him whether he's your partner, employer, employee, coworker or client. There will never be a dull moment when an Aries is around. He is energetic and can wear most people out by running circles around them. In fact, you may think you're on a roller coaster ride if you try to keep up with him.

Because Aries is bursting with so much energy, he needs lots of activity to keep him busy. Sitting around and doing nothing makes him feel like jumping out of his skin. An Arien thrives on a hectic schedule and an electrically charged atmosphere. Pressures and deadlines are normal, everyday daily occurrences for him. Every hour must be productive, otherwise he becomes dissatisfied. Nothing elates him more than accomplishing a difficult task. In fact, it spurs him on to even more complicated work.

Aries is always on the lookout for any newfangled gadget that comes along. This man is a gambler who delights in taking chances on new ventures. Unfortunately, he has a bad habit of leaping first and thinking second. An Arien is honest, loyal, direct — a person hell-bent on doing *something,* even if it destroys the office furniture or a client relationship. But with the right treatment, he's as gentle as a sleeping ram (his sign's animal symbol). Treating him right is a step toward your being successful with him in business.

IF YOU ARE AN ARIES

Because you're always in a hurry you may ask, "What can I do to get to the top quickly?" Success can be achieved faster if, when you deal with others, you adhere to the following advice.

When dealing with your employer you must realize that you are beneath him or her in status. It's difficult for you to be subordinate, but in a work situation it's necessary to a certain degree. Rather than making decisions that are out of your department, let those who are supposed to make them do so. Don't try to handle the boss's job unless asked.

If you disagree with your employer, tell him about it calmly and diplomatically. Avoid temperamental outbursts.

If you aren't advancing as quickly as you think you should be, avoid being impatient. Continue working extra hard so superiors will notice you. Your promotions will come when the time is ripe.

When you deal with partners, employees and coworkers be on guard against resentment because of your competitiveness. It's important to you to be the best in every task you undertake, but if you behave in a manner that makes others feel inferior, you'll attract enmity.

Slow moving or slow talking people drive you up the wall. If it's necessary to keep them on the job, or to work with them, you must develop patience. Everyone isn't a dynamo like yourself. The way you whiz through everything so fast, you are rightly called a "cyclone." Help others by kindly encouraging them to be a little more speedy. However, if it's against their nature try to be understanding. When you speak to them make sure to avoid being too bossy and attacking their egos.

When dealing with clients your main problem is impatience, especially if you are involved in a transaction with someone who takes a long time to make a decision.

Control your temper by talking slowly. Are you aware that it's usually when you speak hurriedly that a quarrel ensues? If you want to be successful in business, you are one sign that has to learn to control your temper.

To go one step further, once you as an Aries know or can recognize the sign your partner, employer, employee, coworker, or client is, read his sign's chapter to learn how best to deal with him as well as to understand his compatibility with you. If you wish to know what he thinks about you, read the Sun-Sign Compatibility section starting on Page 22. The remainder of this section deals with how others relate to you as an Aries, what they can expect of you and how they should handle you. So now let's go on an interview with your sign, okay?

AN INTERVIEW WITH AN ARIES

When an Aries employer interviews you, your resumé will be glanced at quickly. A few questions may be thrown at you. Answer them as fast as you can. An Aries employer will want to see if you're alert. You may be asked whether you are available to work overtime, especially on weekends and holidays. If you're not, don't expect to get hired. She may inquire why you chose to work for her company. She's testing you to see if you are really interested in her business or just a paycheck. She'll be impressed if she thinks you are fascinated by the nature of her enterprise.

You may be hired on the spot and asked to go to work right then and there. Keep in mind that this woman will fire you just as fast as she hires you. Promotions happen in the same manner. If you're performing your job well, you'll be advanced sooner than you had anticipated. However, if you're also an Aries, you'll expect to get ahead by leaps and bounds, so sudden promotions won't be a surprise.

If you're interviewing an Aries applicant: If you keep him waiting too long, he may be gone by the time you get to him. However, if you get a chance to interview this man, it won't take you long to discover that he's a person who's interested in your business. He may ask you all sorts of questions (later you may wonder who the interviewer was) about your company. You will notice that he speaks right up and isn't afraid to say what he thinks. Perhaps he'll surprise you by giving you a suggestion that could improve your business. Maybe it's that remark that leads to your hiring him. He's restless and impatient, so rather than risk losing him, ask him to start work when the interview is over. He'll be most cooperative. However, you should keep in mind that he is as likely to walk off just as quickly as he walks on the job, especially if a promotion isn't given him when he thinks it's due.

Now that the interview is over, let's *first* go to work for an Aries, and then see how Aries is going to fare as your employee, okay?

YOUR ARIES EMPLOYER
What Does Your Aries Boss Expect Of You?

Your loyalty is a must. An Arien wants you to be interested in your job and the prosperity of her business. If you have any ideas about improving monetary or working conditions, she'll be pleased to hear your suggestions. She expects you to be daring and willing to take chances, especially if it's something that is profitable.

Aries appreciates you initiating projects on your own rather than waiting for her okay or taking up her valuable time with an endless array of questions. She expects you to be as independent and enthusiastic as she is. The Arien boss want you to work and move as fast as she does. If you try to outdo her, you'll really be in with her. The rat race makes her thrive because it keeps her on her toes and makes her accomplish more than she otherwise would. Aries beams when you are busy doing your job without taking time off to rest. She likes you to be creative and to be continually coming up with fresh approaches.

This woman appears to be in command, and is. However, she still likes you to tell her that she is doing the right thing. When you react enthusiastically to her ideas, she's glad you're on her payroll.

How To Handle Your Aries Boss

She will not put up with any nonsense or idle gossip on the job. A real no-no is joking or wasting time. If you are shiftless or irresponsible, expect a temperamental outburst from her — you may even get fired. Don't let her darting around fool you into thinking that she isn't paying any attention to you. It's the nonmovement that she notices — that she can't stand. Don't be lazy. Put your heart into your work and be busy at all times.

This is one boss who can get angry quickly with employees who sit around doing nothing while they are waiting for her to give an order. Aries expects you to have enough sense and initiative to do things on your own. Let your creative talents out. Be daring. Take chances. Don't be afraid to speak up and give her your ideas. She welcomes them with open arms. This type of action can help save, rather than lose, a job.

If you want to be unemployed suddenly, balk at putting in overtime or working on a holiday. An Aries tends to be selfish and puts her needs first. Your personal life means nothing to her. Business is her number-one concern. Forfeit some pleasures in your private life if you want to continue getting a paycheck from your Arien boss.

Adapt to your Arien employer's schedule and demands. Expect emergencies to come along and disrupt your duties. She doesn't understand routine; it's continually changed when you work for her. Go along with her. If she wants you to quit a project or abandon it in midstream, do just that. If you think it's unwise, though, give her a logical reason for going against her decision. Aries wants employees who are not afraid to stand up to her.

When you speak up it makes her believe that you are 100 percent in her corner and interested in your job. If Aries feels that you don't care about either, don't be surprised if you're out pounding the pavements looking for employment elsewhere. An Arien will not tolerate anyone to be on her payroll who shows an I-don't-care attitude, which to her implies that you don't give a darn whether her business thrives or not.

To really show Aries that you are on her side, the next time her bluntness and rudeness makes her lose a customer, get her aside and tell her tactfully that you've got a plan that might help her keep her clients. Explain that when she's talking to a customer, you'll signal her if you notice she's getting too impatient or being too outspoken. Let her know that she should avoid saying things that can make her lose a business deal and that you want to help. An Arien appreciates your thoughtfulness, that is, if you tell her about it kindly, without bruising her ego.

Try to keep up with her if you can. Be competitive because she thrives under it. Challenge her with new ideas, new projects, new developments. If she wants to jump into a deal impulsively and you disagree with her action, stop and briefly explain your reason. Long explanations make her nervous because she could be working while having to stand there and listen to you ramble on and on. Don't be surprised if she performs her tasks while you are conversing. Skip those details that bore her. Don't attack the Aries ego or put her ideas down without using diplomacy. Tell her that you respect her for her ingeniousness. However, a certain move could result in a loss or may not be wise at this time.

Encourage her worthwhile ideas and projects and give her ego a boost by praising her for all her wonderful attributes. Be sincere because she's not gullible. This woman loves to hear and talk about herself. Never discuss *your* plans or accomplishments— only hers. Give her the attention she craves. When you do, you can depend upon having a job with her. Aries won't let you down.

This boss is not cheap and doesn't hold back from a salary increase on purpose. Aries is so heavily involved in such a multitude of activities that she forgets about others. Don't be afraid to ask for a raise. If she thinks you're deserving, you'll most likely see her generosity in action the next time you receive a paycheck.

If you make a mistake, admit it, apologize, say you'll try not to repeat it, that you'll do better next time. An Arien will give you many chances to prove your talents. She does not look back so do not remind her of past errors, even if they just happened yesterday. Forget it as soon as you've been reprimanded for it because that's how quickly she's forgotten it.

Don't get upset when Aries throws a fit. Stay out of her path when she's displaying her temper. It's best to say nothing unless absolutely necessary. Get busy with your job and block out her rages. Maybe her anger is not directed at you but is merely her way of blowing off steam when she temporarily can't handle a situation to her satisfaction. If you're drawn into a conversation, don't do or say anything that will make matters worse. Try to be objective and pleasant. It's just a matter of time when she regains her control and is off and running again as if nothing ever happened.

Because an Arien doesn't allow illness to stop her from working, she expects you to do the same. If you call in sick every once in a while, she won't get too vexed. However, if it becomes a habit, you may be tossed out on your ear permanently. And that's not the way to get ahead in the business world. So if you want to become successful, think about the possible consequences before you decide you're not in the mood to go to work today.

YOUR ARIES EMPLOYEE
What Can You Expect From Your Aries Employee?

If you have a slack period, the restless Arien just may take it upon himself to clean or reorganize the entire office from top to bottom in nothing flat. You'd better move fast as he scurries by carrying a heavy machine. If something gets knocked over in the process, just consider it a typical action of his sign. This man's a real eager beaver who goes out of his way, not only to please you, but to gratify himself. He's alert, versatile, and peppy. Aries may talk loud because he wants to make sure everyone hears him.

When given a free hand he discovers new methods to speed up production in his department as well as everyone else's. He's got nerve and thrives on gutsy jobs. Aries does not dillydally nor is his work sloppily done — he gives it his all. This male moves so fast that he disappears and reappears before you've hardly blinked an eyelash.

A heavy work load is how an Arien keeps his sanity. A noisy working environment increases his vivacity and vitality — this adds excitement to his world, When he's talking on several telephones simultaneously, and hopping back and forth to the phones, he's at his happiest. An Arien is not afraid to talk to people or enter risky ventures in connection with his vocation. He's a hard to equal go-getter.

If business appears to be sliding, expect this man to be direct and tell you how to improve it. He won't desert you if he knows you're having a rough time making ends meet. The Aries loyalty shows when he courageously sticks it out until you're back on your feet again.

How To Handle Your Aries Employee

Give him a certain amount of authority. Let him give orders. Give him a title, even if you have to make up one. He needs to feel he's in charge of something. Aries wants a job where he can advance; if he feels held back, he'll leave you in a jiffy. An Arien is impatient and has his eye on your chair. When he fills it he expect you to be one step higher up.

The Arien is an aggressive employee who shows an interest in the company he works for. He is bossy and may want to run the entire show. Delegate some of your work to Aries; this will leave you with more time to make bigger and better improvements in the overall business of the corporation.

Give him important duties and responsibilities. He likes to have an incentive so he can outshine everyone else. Make sure his job is challenging. Tell him what a great worker he is and how proud you are to have him as part of the team. Make him feel that he's personally involved with the company's success. If an Arien thinks he's an important cog in the organization he'll do everything in his power to make the corporation prosper.

If Aries enjoys his work and his position, he is about the best unpaid press agent you'll find anywhere. In his private life he may praise his company's product to the skies, or perhaps tell about how wonderful it is to work for your company. An Arien's enthusiasm is genuine and the ravings are not done for any ulterior motive — he really is *that* excited!

Don't confine Aries by sticking him behind the scenes. He likes to deal with people. Give him freedom to move about and make some decisions. Keep him busy and offer lots of variety. Don't bog him down with detail because that's not for this man. Avoid looking over his shoulder while he's working; he needs to have space without you breathing down his neck. Don't dictate to him; he'll rebel if you are overbearing.

Give your Aries employee a certain amount of independence. He dislikes schedules and punching clocks. Most of the time he's not aware of the hour and may eat lunch as late as 3:00 p.m. If he is late to work, he may make up for it by skipping coffee breaks, missing lunch, staying late, coming in early the next day or taking work home at night. Aries is so dynamic that he can do the work of two people, which you may discover if he ever leaves you.

If you have a new task for Aries (hopefully it's something novel and daring), tell him that he's the perfect person for it and that you have complete faith in his ability to do an excellent job. Once these words are spoken, an Arien will rush enthusiastically into the chore. If there's a deadline connected with it, so much the better. He thrives under pressure and turns out some of his best work while under stress. When he's bored or gets in a rut, you may lose him. Don't ever tell him to slow down. Try to be considerate of his speedy ways. Be thankful that you have such a conscientious employee.

Allow the Aries to express his creative and innovative ideas. Don't dampen his spirit by saying that they are too impractical. Let this man show you that they are practical — that is, if it isn't a costly point to prove. You might be surprised when he comes up with a profitable venture.

Never criticize him in front of anyone. Tell him about his mistakes in private. Be tactful. An Aries will usually apologize when he's wrong. If he makes hasty and wrong judgments, try to help him avoid making the same error twice.

Explain how it is better to consider a situation from all angles before making a decision, and that, in most cases, it's wise to delay action until everything has been carefully thought through.

Praise the Aries for his fruitful ideas and you'll see even more amazing feats performed. Those innovations which helped your business should be rewarded by giving him a bonus. If you can't afford the extra dough being spent at this time, tack up his achievements on a bulletin board so everyone in the company can read about his accomplishments. This ego boost is more important to him than money.

As a rule, an Arien doesn't ask for a raise because it expects it automatically. When Aries asks, you had better believe it's because it's deserved. So don't be cheap. After all, you are getting two people for the price of one, remember? And that's one way to be successful, isn't it?

YOUR ARIES COWORKER
What Can You Expect From Your Aries Coworker?

There are just a few basic facts to keep in mind when working with this fellow: he's competitive, moves fast, is bossy and temperamental. The Aries man is a real dynamo and accomplishes more than most people. So don't be fearful that you'll fall by the wayside. He will not tattle on you if you're slow. Instead he'll try to do your job also. But he won't try to take your livelihood from you; he calls it "helping you out." An Aries has to keep everything moving at a quick tempo and he expects you to do the same.

An Arien craves excitement, the novel, and may be as creative as the Arien-born playwright, Tennessee Williams. He may try to involve you in one of his new and innovative methods to speed up job tasks. With an Aries as a coworker, you should be prepared for all kinds of spur-of-the-moment ideas. He may talk you into working overtime — and for free yet! Or, because he hasn't stopped for the day, you may not realize that you're laboring past quitting time.

Expect Aries to blow his top quite often. It's his way of letting off steam and is really a part of his nature. It doesn't disturb him so he can't imagine how anyone else is affected by a few angry words. He doesn't realize that you may take him seriously by thinking he's directing his vehemence in your direction. So if you don't mind that sort of package wrapped up in one individual, you've got nothing to worry about. But if any of these traits bother you, then changes may be in store for you. If you don't want to quit your job and you want to go to the top, change your mental attitude toward your Aries coworker.

How To Handle Your Aries Coworker

If you can learn not to be annoyed by anything he says or does, you'll avoid upsets and clashes. For instance, you know he blows his top easily so if he starts to drop, spill or bump into things, he may yell and scream about everything. This is his way of blaming someone, or something else, for blunders due to his rushing around. When these rages occur, don't make things worse by agreeing with him. Keep quiet and go about your business as if nothing happened. Don't argue with him because if you try to defend yourself, he won't even hear your side of the story. Don't worry, he doesn't hold a grudge, cools off quickly and will have forgotten the entire incident within the hour.

When Aries tries to dictate to you, even though he doesn't have the authority to do so, you can either go along with him or speak up. The former keeps peace in the environment and the latter may start violent arguments. Try to understand that when an Arien gives orders it's his nature to be a commander. He's not doing it to insult, belittle or harm you in any way. You may think he's bossy because he feels superior to you, but even that doesn't enter his mind. He takes over because it seems natural for him to do so. If you have an ego problem than you'll resent his demanding attitude.

If you mention that he's equal to you in position and has no right to tell you what to do, Aries may get irritated, sparks may start to fly and the battle is on full blast. To avoid this type of scene, and to boost your ego, give him a challenge — like something that's difficult to do. Don't be demanding; keep everything light, cheerful, and pleasant and he'll jump right in and follow your suggestions. If you use force and lay down the law to him, then you'll have an enraged Arien on your hands to deal with.

Do you like to run in a race? If so, Aries and you can vie for the lead spot. If you're a slow worker — Taurus, Cancer, Virgo, Capricorn, Pisces — you may not want to increase your speed. However, if you're the type who enjoys a contest, enter it with Aries and see who can finish his job the fastest. This man absolutely loves to compete and will think you're wonderful if you can keep up with or even go faster than him. Watch out though! If he has to wait for you before he can do his duties, be ready for Aries. This man will be such a nervous wreck that either he'll leap in and help you, or start yelling, "Hurry up!"

If the preceding becomes a pattern for any length of time, Aries will either quit or ask to be transferred. If your boss thinks you are holding up progress you could be out of a job and Aries may be "in like Flynn." Maybe in the long run this will work out for the best, especially if you climb up the ladder of success elsewhere. But, before you risk anything, wouldn't it be better if you tried to do your very best? Then if you get fired, you can tell yourself that either you weren't compatible with your coworker and/or employer, or you should try to improve your job performance. Maybe taking special courses offered at night school or a college would be to your advantage. The brighter you are, and the more you use your brain, the easier it is to reach the heights with a career.

YOUR ARIES CLIENT
What Can You Expect From Your Aries Client?

This guy is likely to come on like gangbusters. He may fidget, pace the floor, even have difficulty slowing down enough for you to understand what he's saying. An Aries won't hesitate to speak his mind. If he doesn't agree with you, he'll let you know right away. This man wants everything in the open. He is honest with you and expects the same from you. When he feels that you are being dishonest or holding back the truth, he'll unleash his fury so fast that you'll wonder what rubbed him the wrong way.

He's eager to learn about anything new. In fact, the latest "in" thing makes him perk up. You'll know he's an Aries the moment you see him get excited about something that you are mentioning. If he seems willing take a risk, and tells you that he wants to be the first in his area with your product, you can bet you have an Arien on your hands. Further proof is a quick decision and a dash out the door as sudden as his arrival.

How To Handle Your Aries Client

How do you deal with someone who has so much energy? He hardly gave you a chance to explain anything and you should know that he never will. Ariens can't stand details and long, drawn-out discussions. If you want him to be a regular customer, talk and act fast. The moment you see him start to fidget, skip the details. If he paces the floor, that's a giveaway that the time he's allotted you is coming to a close. In fact, at this point, if you don't speed up your conversation and/or action he may get quite irritable and walk out the door while you're still yakking away. So, get to the point at the very beginning of the meeting.

Appeal to his pioneering instincts. Make your sales spiel *personal* so he can identify with it. Get Aries carried away by telling him how great your product is for *him* and how it will save *him* time. Bolster his ego. Tell him how great it looks on him and how he'll perform better with this gadget. Once he seems optimistic about it, you've got the sale wrapped up.

If you work in a department store and you're waiting on another customer only to be interrupted by someone who seems impatient, she's probably an Aries. If you don't stop immediately and give her attention, she'll move on. However, if you do wait on her, it'll be a quick sale because this woman knows what she wants.

If you're a waitress in a restaurant and your customer walks in quickly, sits down, glances at the menu and beckons you to the table, it's almost a sure thing you've got an Aries on your hands. Ask him if he's in a hurry. If he says, "Yes" push his order through fast and serve him fast. If this guy's in the mood to take his time with a meal, don't rush him. However, don't expect him to take forever to eat. When he dawdles, he's still eating faster than most people.

By now you should have gotten the message that regardless of whether you work in a beauty salon, a grocery store or run a manufacturing corporation, your Aries client knows what he wants and expects you to expedite it right away. If you don't want to lose his business, you should give him your undivided attention and hasten all of your actions when serving him. Your wallet will get fattened and you will maintain the good customer relations that are so essential to a business. Doesn't making a buck, rather than losing one, indicate that you're headed in the right direction toward becoming successful?

YOUR ARIES PARTNER

What Can You Expect From Your Aries Partner?

You may think you made a smart move when you teamed up with this woman because she's bright, innovative and never seems to run out of new ideas. At times you may swear she's a female Charlie Chaplin, Harold E. Stassen and Houdini all rolled into one, (they were all Ariens). So what do you do with a talented person who can give and take orders like a general, jump into hot water and get out of it like an escape artist — and to top it all off, may have your company solvent one moment and in debt the next?

With all of her outstanding traits (faults too), is the Arien worth putting up with? Only you can decide that. However it's easier to make a decision when you understand her personality. You can expect an Arien to try and outdo you. She will keep you on your toes, especially if she discovers you're lagging behind.

The office may be chaotic most of the time. Aries can't keep things that neat or orderly, but she knows where everything is and can find anything immediately. If you bug her one time too many, expect an explosion. This is not a timid lady you are partners with — she's dynamite! If you are going to remain in business together, it's important that you work well together so you'll both benefit financially. If you don't understand and know how to handle your Aries associate, you could lose money on a deal. And that's not the way to satisfy your dreams of success, is it?

How To Handle Your Aries Partner

Risky ventures are her thing. She enjoys taking a chance in life. She's ready to hunt whatever it is she's chasing. Maybe it's a rainbow with the pot of gold sitting there waiting just for her and because she's bubbly, it's easy to be won over to her side. How can you avoid falling into the same trap with her? The moment you see her eyes light up with excitement, watch out!

Once she's given you the overall picture, excuse yourself and quietly disappear. Get the details (Aries would have overlooked them) from the other people involved in the project. Weigh all the pros and cons. Once you've analyzed everything, discuss it with the Arien. Keep your conversation brief and to the point, giving her your logical reasons for not going along with it. However, if you agree with her, that this is a fantastic transaction for the both of you, then you have nothing to worry about — just be as impulsive as she is and plunge in all the way.

Your Aries partner believes that when the money starts to roll in, you should expand. Her impatience to do an even greater landslide business often gets her into hot water. Don't be surprised if she starts things without consulting you. And, furthermore, Aries doesn't shop around for the cheapest way to do things because she's in a hurry. This woman is likely to spend a fortune (hers and yours) on this sudden whim of hers.

Try to understand that Aries gets so caught up in the excitement of an idea that she doesn't stop to think about anything other than making it a reality. Often this woman gets so busy that she forgets about what she did from one hour to the next. So by the end of the day she may have forgotten to tell you who she called in relation to business. Also an Arien is so positive that she's doing the right thing that she never believes anyone, especially her partner, will ever oppose or question her.

If you want to curb those surprising moments — like when someone shows up suddenly with blueprints — draw up and sign an agreement with Aries that all future transactions must bear two signatures before anything is decided upon. An Arien is usually quite congenial and may think you have a terrific idea.

Your Aries partner is out to make a success of the business. You can count on her to be aboveboard, open, direct, and honest. The thought of stealing or trickery does not enter her mind. An Arien finds it stimulating to make a buck, even if it is the hard way. When obstacles are thrown into her path, she comes alive and can't wait to defeat them all. Usually victory is hers. Compete with her if you've got the energy. Aries accomplishes more with a sparring partner than with a gutless, placid, and quiet one. So bandy those ideas about and see what new enterprises may develop.

Do you know that Aries has a temper that when lost can frighten quite a few people away? Like the Fire sign she was born under, she may flare up as quickly as a match when lit. Flames may rage, but they also can be calmed down and go out by themselves. So don't be hostile by adding fuel to the fire. Let her be and soon you'll have a delightful partner back to normal again — and you'll see that pot of gold in front of you. Some of the Arien enthusiasm will rub off when those profits come rolling in — that's when the two of you can celebrate victoriously.

Sun-Sign Compatibility

This section deals with each sign of the zodiac in relation to an Aries Sun sign. Knowing how your sign blends with an Arien, you go one step beyond understanding his personality, and one step closer to knowing how to handle him in any business situation. Greater insight is invaluable— it not only helps a business prosper, but it also encourages peace of mind on and off the job

The following Sun-Sign compatibility summary with the exception of Aries/Aries, *are from the point of view of the person dealing with Aries. Note:* for the Ariens point of view, see the Sun-Sign chapter of the person Aries is dealing with, i.e.; Leo — refer to the Leo chapter explaining how Aries thinks about Leo.

ARIES/ARIES

Both of you are pioneers; you start new things that no one else ever thought about. But because you are usually leaders, you need others to work beneath you and complete the tasks you initiate. You are both impatient and have to refrain from jumping impulsively into anything.

Deals are discussed and consummated quickly. All decisions are made instantly by both of you. The ideas, plans, or projects that you each have are expressed with such enthusiasm that it seems like you both are "high" on something. You are both doers and accomplish goals; thus, you can rely upon one another to get any job done.

Most of the time, the two of you work well together. But when one of you tries to outshine the other, the competitive spirit you each possess is likely to emerge. However, it's this constant challenge that you both thrive on — and this adds zest to a working relationship.

It won't take long to finish a task because you both like to get it done as quickly as possible. Every job is met with enthusiasm. To accomplish desired goals, you push one another. You will have to toss a coin to see who is going to be the boss, because it's anyone's guess. Both of you are temperamental, thus quarrels could easily occur — but they subside just as quickly.

TAURUS/ARIES

Your Plodding style is difficult for an Arien to adjust to. However, this woman likes a challenge, and may compete with you just to see who will get to the top first. You dislike it when Aries ruins your carefully laid plans by leaping in impulsively. This female is sometimes too much of an eager beaver for you to handle.

If the Aries pushes you one time too many with an order to get the lead out of your pants and do it right now, you may try to show her how obstinate you can be. However, your not budging doesn't last long because your practical side comes out. If you think your going to lose money by being bullish, you'll be subservient to the Aries

You admire the Arien for her brilliant mind and creative talents. In fact, you relish improving and perfecting her creations. You shudder when she leaps into things without thoroughly thinking them through. And you are amazed at how she still manages to accomplish her goals.

When she tries to involve you in her many varied pursuits, your obstinacy shows. But if you try to hold her back, the Aries temper is unleashed. Once you lose your patience (and it will take a while before you do), a hot quarrel follows and could end with the Aries going out the door so fast you wonder how anyone could possibly move so quickly.

You are opposite personalities; thus what you lack, Aries has. But the main difficulty with you two, is that your slowness and cheapness, does not blend with the Aries speed and generosity. Otherwise, you two could make a go of it.

GEMINI/ARIES

You don't mind if the bossy Aries is in charge. He's easy for you to get along with. This guy doesn't put you down for new ideas. In fact, he encourages you to contribute your knowledge to current projects. Luckily you go along with one another's proposals for modernization.

His mental and physical quickness reminds you of yourself. Transactions are speedily executed. There are no dull moments with you two. It seems as if you are just as busy as the Arien. You are well aware that you both have too many fingers in the pie, but if it doesn't bother him, it certainly isn't going to disturb you. Somehow the two of you manage to accomplish most of your goals , in spite of your both flying off in so many directions. For some unknown reason they all seem to come together at the right moment.

When Aries gets angry at you because you didn't do something you were supposed to, it makes the day more interesting. His temper doesn't faze you in the least. Rather, it breaks up monotony, which isn't such a bad idea every now and then.

You can't quite figure out how the Arien manages to stabilize you, but you find it happening more and more as each day passes. It's something you know you need and are glad to have this guy around you in business.

CANCER/ARIES

It bugs you when Aries piles his work load on your desk. Neither one of you likes to finish tasks, but it seems like you are always stuck with the detail Aries leaves behind. You wouldn't mind doing him favors if you thought he appreciated you, but all he does is drop a batch of files on your desk and runs out the door as if he's on his way to a fire.

When he returns and still doesn't say "Thank you" it really hurts your feelings. You want sympathy and Aries doesn't give it to you. It would be nice if he'd take an interest in you, and say how great he thought you were doing, but not one compliment. It's as if he expects you to know he's grateful. You are just too sensitive for this guy .

You dislike Aries rushing you to work faster. He doesn't understand that if you don't go slow, you'll make errors. It just seems you can never please this guy. Your entire body shakes when he starts ranting and raving. Loud noises and harsh words just make you sick.

Aries is just too impractical for you to be with in business. He's always spending money on new equipment, processes, advertising or some crazy idea. When you try to explain that the company can't profit by his method, he's likely to throw a temper tantrum and tell you how behind the times you are. What is the solution to this dilemma? Simple! The two of you just shouldn't work together.

LEO/ARIES

Because Aries is a doer, you are pleased to work with him. Those quick decisions of his, are helpful in all that you undertake. This guy is as conscientious as you when it comes to work that has to be done. You are glad that he's not lazy.

Now and then it might disturb you when Aries gives you orders to do something. Generally you won't take them from anyone, but this guy does it in a way that's not offensive. Of course, he's fast on the praises, which makes up for any bossiness on his part. You feel things are evened up when he obeys a few of your commands.

It seems like the two of you are competing with each other all the time. The Aries is constantly challenging you. This spurs you on so you'll outdo him. Instead of presenting a problem, you've probably noticed that his action improves the quality of your work, which is tops to begin with.

You are thrilled with the large-scale projects the Aries gets you involved in. It's satisfying for you to be involved with someone who isn't afraid to spend money.

Somehow you are confident of his abilities and know that the two of you are going to be successful. And when those dollars start rolling in, your hunches prove correct. The Aries loyalty through thick and thin is something you admire. Lots of money can be made by the two of you when you join forces, if you can work out the competitive element.

VIRGO/ARIES

You are mortified when Aries exclaims, " Who cares if this isn't *exactly* as it's supposed to be?" When you answer, "I care" it may startle this woman. Your belief that perfection is necessary with all labor performed is the opposite of the Aries view, so expect to clash.

The Arien's lack of interest in details causes extra work for you. However , she does realize your attention to detail is valuable. If she tends to the overall picture and you to the pieces, things may work out. However, her lack of neatness is yet another problem for you.

You can't stand it when the Aries messes up your desk by haphazardly throwing down papers and files wherever they happen to land. Her own working area is so disorganized that you can't see how she is able to accomplish anything. And when you offer your services to put everything in tip-top shape she throws a fit.

You are not about to be rushed by Aries. It's a waste of her time to even try. Her impatience drives you up the wall. You are shocked by how gutsy she is when she leaps into new ventures without analyzing them first. And then when she doesn't count the cost of anything, you cringe. For some reason you don't share her enthusiasm for the chances she takes in business.

LIBRA/ARIES

The energy Aries possesses amazes you. The way this guy tackles the most complicated tasks is something you admire, and you know he appreciates your telling him so. Aries is someone you enjoy working with because when you get snowed under, he is so great about helping you get caught up.

Difficulties on the job occur when you take forever and a day to weigh all the pros and cons. Your indecisiveness could be costly in business. However, you can always count on Aries to save you when he comes to your aid and quickly solves your problems: another reason why you are proud to be associated with him. When Aries takes on more than he can handle, his temper flares up easily. It's almost impossible for you to work in an environment where bickering takes place. He seems to calm down when you flatter him. Those compliments are easy to give, especially when they bring peace and harmony so you can do your job properly.

Your energy comes in spurts. You can work at a hectic pace for a little while , but can't keep it up like Aries does. This guy does seem to understand that you need to take it easy after a rough period and you appreciate it. You help him when he argues with others by getting everyone to apologize and be friends again.

The two of you are opposite signs, but have opposite traits that can compliment one another. Libra, your charm, when combined with the Aries executive ability, is an asset to any corporation.

SCORPIO/ARIES

When pitted against each other, you two may clash head on , and you usually know that Aries doesn't have your staying power to win the race. This competing against one another is a daily occurrence that you both seem to thrive on.

Nothing Aries does escapes you. You notice everything and file it away for future reference. Aries gets upset with you and may try to cause a scene when she starts to rant and rave. However, you keep quiet and continue your duties as if you didn't hear her. You believe that her loud babbling only makes her look bad and you good. One thing you can't stand is witnesses. But you are not afraid of Aries and when alone will let your venom loose.

You are both impulsive. However, you know that you are one step ahead of Aries because you will, at least, investigate and do thorough research on a project before getting involved. When Aries leaps in before you've had a chance to discuss or explore possibilities, you see blood-red and are ready for the kill, especially when a large sum of money goes down the drain. But Aries can see the fury in your eyes, and knows enough to get out fast. However, when you do catch up with the Arien, you may have severed all business relations legally.

It's a shame that the two of you have your differences because you are both quick and work hard. Everything could be done twice as fast if you would cooperate with each other, but who can put up with all of the stormy scenes you two create?

SAGITTARIUS/ARIES

It's a joy to work with this guy because he knows he works as fast as you do. Aries is as willing to take chances as you when something innovative pops up. And when you lose a few bucks on some risky venture, you're glad it didn't faze Aries anymore then it did you.

This guy is so dynamic that you never tire of encouraging him to take on more projects. Aries goes along with all your plans. It's wonderful he is so easy to get along with. Seldom do you ever have a run in. If he blows off a little steam, it doesn't disturb you in the least.

The productive endeavors that you two enter are so stimulating that you both get high just talking about them. It doesn't take long for the Aries enthusiasm to envelope you to the point that you believe the two of you can move mountains and accomplish more than most mortals. And perhaps you can.

You don't mind Aries getting bossy with you. If he wants you to do something. Why not? You know that he has your best interest at heart. Besides, you don't mind taking orders from someone as knowledgeable as Aries. And what about all those times when you told him what to do? He went along so agreeably. The Arien's actions never upset you. You will make the best of all situations, and are thankful Aries has the same positive outlook as you do.

CAPRICORN/ARIES

You respect Aries because he's gutsy and takes a chance on new and risky deals. When he courageously attacks these undertakings with a zest you wish you had, you admire him even more. But his impatience to see a project through to fruition drives you nuts. You just don't understand how anyone could dump something good in midair.

You watch Aries like a hawk and know his job inside and out. In case this guy decides to walk off the job for good, you want to be prepared to take over his desk. Your judgement of character is usually fairly accurate. You know , therefore, that Aries is either going to be promoted or leave the company if an advancement doesn't come as fast as desired.

Of course you are aware that this guy has a bad temper too. When Aries tries to push you to hasten your speed, you just go slower. If he screams his way out of a job, that's no concern of yours, although it may be to your advantage if you are next in line for his position.

Problems eventually arise when you two work together. You each take a different approach to reaching the top: Aries is openly competitive, whereas you are inwardly and quietly competitive.

AQUARIUS/ARIES

You get along great with Aries because she, like you, is searching for the quickest way of performing a job. Once found , this woman keeps up with you. You don't mind it at all when she races you to see who will finish first. Dealing with her is the adventure of the mind that is needed with any work you perform.

You can't bear to have anyone breathing down your neck. The Arien gives you freedom and independence to do the job your way. It's a relief to be involved with Aries because she doesn't have any difficulty in comprehending your innovative ideas. In fact, she throws in a few additional ones herself.

Her impatience doesn't upset you. When she abandons a task you are quite happy to finish it. She's very complementary with the way you handle everything. Seldom if ever has she quarreled with you. However, the Aries temper doesn't disturb you because you can see that it's not aimed directly at you. Luckily you're tuned into her and know that when she does get angry, it's just her way of blowing off steam. You realize that she means no harm by her outbursts.

You are not overawed by anything that Aries does. Her off-the-beaten-track methods are just as wild as yours. The Arien's interest in the new and different fascinates you. It's as if you two are on the same wavelength, which makes all work seem like child's play. You make an excellent team!

PISCES/ARIES

You feel left out of everything when working for , or with, an Aries. It's impossible for you to keep up with her because she moves too fast for you. Most of the time this female says things that are over your head, or they are said so quickly you can't fathom what she means.

The Arien's demands to accomplish tasks " right now" are more then you can cope with. Aries always manages to hurt your feelings, especially when she screams at you. This just makes you withdraw more, so half the time you don't even hear what all the ranting and raving is about.

Headaches or heartache occur with the two of you because your temperaments are so opposite; you move slow, Aries fast; you're a dreamer, she's a person of action; you're evasive and tend to be deceptive; Aries is open and tends to be honest. There's a lot left to be desired in this relationship.

Chapter Four

Taurus Compatibility In Business

If your were born between April 20 and May 20, your Sun is in the sign Taurus. If Taurus is dominant in your horoscope (refer to the Introduction, Page 1), you may also express Taurus traits even if it's not your Sun sign. If this is the case, you should read and treat this chapter just as if your Sun sign is Taurus.

TAURUS PROFILE
Getting Acquainted With The Taurus Personality

This woman is not easy to get to know. Once you understand what motivates her, it will facilitate dealing with her regardless of whether she's your partner, employer, employee, coworker, or client. Taurus may appear stodgy, but don't let that fool you. She's bright and alert in her own quiet way. This woman is as strong as a bull (her sign's symbol) and can outwork and outlast most people. This isn't obvious because she plods along slowly until a task is completed.

Taurus is even-tempered — it takes a lot to make her mad. This woman can work, and work, and work to get a job done. And, she won't let you rush her. Inwardly, Taurus is suspicious and uncertain of new ideas. Her views are carefully considered, her responses slow, and once she's said no, nothing will make her change her mind. But if you're patient, she'll eventually open up to something new and once she's agreed to go along with you, you can't find a better ally.

Taurus loves success — it's not an ego trip with her — she labors mainly for the money and prestige that goes with being on top. Her persistence, efficiency, exacting perfectionism, dedication to a project, and ability to endure hardships, make her a sure-to-win candidate for the high position she longs for. Taurus is an asset to anyone in business, especially if you understand her nature.

IF YOU ARE A TAURUS

Because you are extremely ambitious you may ask, "What can I do to get to the top?" Success can be achieved faster if you adhere to the following advice when you deal with others:

When dealing with an employer be more open. Your unresponsiveness makes the boss think you're not interested in your work. Speak up, state your views, instead of keeping quiet., Then, your employer will know that you can think for yourself and that you care about the company. Remember, bosses aren't mind readers and hidden grievances can turn you into a mad bull on the rampage. Because you dislike change, you'll stay in an unhappy situation, fretting and fuming, rather than quitting.

You are a painstaking but self-effacing worker. Staying in the background may keep your promotion from coming along. Loosen up and be a little lively rather than so stiff and formal. This change in your personality may be all that stands in the way between your present position and a higher one.

When dealing with partners, employees and coworkers be on guard against arousing hostility with your stubbornness. You dislike change, but if you refuse to go along with new concepts you may lose out in the long run. You can lose a job, money, or position.

Fast-moving, fast-talking people utterly confuse you. If it's necessary to keep them on the job or work with them, you have to realize that everyone is not as slow or thorough as you. If they are competent, isn't it to your advantage to finish a project quickly? Try to understand that it's their Sun sign that makes them rush.

Because you are neat and expect everyone else to be the same, you are disappointed when someone does second-rate or sloppy work. However, your employee doesn't know how this disturbs you because you fail to mention it. You are just sitting there trying to be tolerant and waiting for him to improve. Then if you can't stand it any longer, you fire him. You should speak up and tell him your likes and dislikes. Not only will that make him try his best to please you, but it will save you a lot of stress-filled hours. Give others a chance — their success leads to yours.

When dealing with clients your main problem is your slowness, especially if you are involved in a transaction with someone who is in a hurry. If this occurs, speed up or let someone else wait on the customer. If you are forced into making a quick decision, listen to your inner self (you can't go wrong) and follow your intuition. You can accomplish almost anything you set your mind to. However, if you don't get the lead out of your pants, you may find yourself lagging behind.

Try to think about the ways you can save your client money and still make a profit yourself — an easy thing for a financial whiz like you. You're the type who believes you have to spend more to make more. You're always busy wining and dining your customers.

Avoid being too stubborn about your opinions. If you're more flexible, you'll increase sales. If a client is interested in you handling something new and untried, don't ruin the deal by saying "no" immediately. Keep an open mind and tell her that you'll give her your answer after you've investigated it thoroughly. Your main downfall in business is your refusal to adapt to sudden changes and progressive ideas and products. Often your set ways are an asset; however, you'll discover that you can get to the top much easier if you are not so dogmatic.

To go one step further, once you as a Taurus know or can recognize the sign your partner, employer, employee, coworker, or client is, read his sign's chapter to learn how best to deal with him as well as to understand his compatibility with you. If you wish to know what he thinks about you, read the Sun-Sign Compatibility section starting on Page 40. The remainder of this section deals with how others relate to you as a Taurus, what they can expect of you, and how they should handle you. So now let's go on an interview with your sign, okay?

AN INTERVIEW WITH A TAURUS

A Taurus employer interviewing you: Your resumé will be carefully scrutinized. He may test you with a few questions. This employer will want to see if you make logical deductions. You may be asked to solve a hypothetical situation. Take your time (this will impress him) before answering. Be calm, cool, and collected. Use reasoning and common sense. Explain your conclusions as sensibly as possible. He's looking for careful consideration and sound judgment.

Don't expect to be hired right away. Taurus has to go through a lengthy deliberation and decide between you and the other applicants. This may take days or weeks. Don't let this bother you. Remember, this man will keep you on the payroll as long as you continue to be valuable. He won't suddenly fire you because he believes in giving you a chance to prove yourself. Discard thoughts of quick advancement; promotions may take a while in coming. However, if you're a Taurus you don't anticipate getting ahead very fast anyway.

If you're interviewing a Taurus applicant: If you keep her waiting, she won't get upset. Taurus is there to get a job regardless of how long it takes. When you interview this woman you'll discover that she's got excellent business know-how. Her questions about the corporation let you know that she wants to work for a company with a growing future. And her practical side shows when she asks about the medical, bonus, and profit-sharing benefits she will be eligible to receive. You can tell that she wants security — a cue that she's a money-oriented person. This combination of business know-how and practicality should make you hire her. Don't ask this woman to start working immediately; give her a little time to get accustomed to the idea of change before she starts work. Keep in mind that Taurus will stay on the job as long as she's treated with respect and given a chance to prove her worth. She'll wait patiently for a promotion.

Now that the interview is over, let's first go to work for a Taurus and thus see how Taurus is going to fare as your employee, okay?

YOUR TAURUS EMPLOYER
What Does Your Taurus Boss Expect Of You?

If you're being transferred from one department to another, regardless of the reason, Taurus is suspicious and will watch your every move. Don't let that fool you; this man wants you to be as efficient as he is.

Taurus enjoys molding you like a clay statue. Once he's trained you his way, he'll go out of his way to keep you in his employ if you abide by it. He expects you to be dependable and reliable, so don't upset the apple cart.

This man wants you to succeed because that means his business will also be on top. If you are going to school nights to improve yourself, he'll admire you for this, especially if your studies can benefit his company.

Taurus is disciplined and won't tolerate your procrastination, leave a project in mid-steam or fool around on company time. He expects you to do your duties and obey his rules and regulations. If they aren't strictly adhered to, he will weigh it against you. This man will give you enough rope to hang yourself. However, if you live up to his expectations you've got a job that may last a lifetime.

This man is in command despite his quiet and unassuming manner. His lack of enthusiasm and compliments may throw you for a loop, but your being in his employ for any long length of time implies that he's glad you work for him.

How To Handle Your Taurus Boss

Don't wear loud or garish apparel; stay away from jeans. The Taurus boss leans toward conservative dress; the blue-collared look for men and the suit that shows authority for women. The neat, scrubbed, and businesslike appearance is his favorite. Good manners are important.

Taurus is so set in his ways that he balks if the furniture is moved. Don't mess up his desk or office. Keep it tidy at all times. If you're his secretary or maid, don't change anything around. Keep your own working area orderly if you want to stay in his good graces.

Avoid coming in late. If you get away with it once, don't keep thinking that it's okay to repeat the offense another day. Just because he didn't say anything about your first offense doesn't mean he approved. If you want to make a good impression on him, come in early and stay late. By being punctual and competent, you've got a permanent job. Don't bed too cozy with Taurus. Be on guard, stay alert, work hard, and tend to your business; his quiet and kind manner may fool you when you least expect it.

Before you show him your work, check it over thoroughly. He's a perfectionist. Misspelled words or other errors go against his grain. Perhaps he will let you get by with a few mistakes, but don't get lax because of it. If you are careless once too often that's it with him.

Don't rush so fast on a new job that you make errors. If you don't catch on right away Taurus will give you a chance to learn. He moves slowly and understands that you have to be sure of yourself before you gain speed.

This man rules with an iron fist. Follow his orders to the letter. Pay attention to detail when performing a job. Finish tasks and don't balk at the schedule he wants you to maintain. When giving an explanation, leave out the frills — keep it simple. Avoid both being too brief or long-winded,

Don't become so relaxed that you goof up. His even-temperateness may make you think he won't mind if you have a little fun on the job. Taurus wholeheartedly believes that he's paying you for working, not playing, so don't even try to sneak in a few laughs. Be serious and tend to business. If he catches you in action and appears grumpy, that's your first warning sign. If you continue, you'll be thrown out on your ear.

Avoid laziness. Be ambitious. Let him see this side of your nature and watch how fast you'll move up the corporate ladder. Because he's a builder of money — bank accounts, dollars — cater to this world of business he loves.

This man's not a generous boss. However, if he's 100 percent sold on you, he will see to it that you get the increase in wages and special bonuses you deserve. If you want to ask for a raise, review your past job achievements with him. Don't be afraid to speak up and remind him of your past record but to get more money out of this man, you've got to really be deserving in his eyes. If Taurus gives you his word that your salary will be boosted on the next paycheck, you can rely upon it. He keeps his promises and expects you to deliver in the same way.

Generally this man is unresponsive to new ideas. However, he will listen to you if you approach him quietly and calmly. (He can't stand emotional scenes, loud noises, or arguments.) Taurus doesn't have much imagination, so appeal to him by being logical, sensible, and practical. Don't expect him to crack a smile or react immediately to any proposition. Never rush him into making a decision or goad or push him into doing anything.

If may take him a day, weeks, or months to consider your proposal. Taurus is an old-fashioned fuddy-duddy. He isn't progressive or desirous of experimentation. Give him weekly reports about the progress of others (especially his competitors) are making with a new machine. You must convince him thoroughly that this latest gadget or equipment will speed up production. Taurus thinks that if he's making a good living now with the old, why change to the new?

Once the product has been researched, tested, and proven over a prolonged period to be more effective than anything else on the market, he will jump on the bandwagon and put his order in. But until that day arrives, just keep him up-to-date on the headlines it's making in the business community.

Avoid trying to make him change his routine or way of doing things. Taurus likes to run his own affairs so don't make the mistake of telling him what to do. If he's decided that the outdated but proven method works for him then he's going to continue with it. Don't argue with him because if you push him too far, this gentle man will slowly get angry enough to fire you.

Try to encourage Taurus to build up his business gradually. Give him ideas to enlarge his operations that aren't exorbitant. Appeal to his materialistic instincts as to why he should expand. Don't try to con him — he's hard to snow. Keep in mind that you won't see him leap into anything, but help make him the tycoon he years to be and you'll never regret it.

This man is not the retiring type (although he may be if his Sun sign is weak rather than dominant). Taurus is possessive and will keep you on his payroll forever if you live up to his standards. (He dislikes change and quick turnovers of employees, remember?) Just give the job your all, be sincere and honest and not only will you be a success sign, you won't have to job-hunt!

YOUR TAURUS EMPLOYEE
What Can You Expect From Your Taurus Employee?

Taurus may ignore family life for a career. This woman's determined to succeed. She may be quiet as a mouse but don't let that fool you — she's got her eye on the top spot (it might be your job too). However, she's in no hurry to move up the corporate ladder.

Taurus seldom takes sick leave. Usually she's the first one to arrive in the office and the last one to leave. Her lunches are short; often coffee breaks are skipped. This woman is a workaholic and doesn't believe in taking unnecessary time off. You won't find her gossiping or meddling in the affairs of others. Her motto is that you're there to work and that's all you should be doing. Taurus can be counted on in business and be trusted with confidential matters.

Don't expect her to be a Speedy Gonzalez. She works at a steady pace. It seems like the job won't be finished on time but somehow it always is. If you think she's going to make overnight changes, think again. This woman has difficulty breaking set patterns, making alternations gradually.

If Taurus is in charge of the office it's not going to be a madhouse; it'll run smoothly. She doesn't get hysterical in a crisis or over an emergency. This woman takes everything in stride. She's calm, unemotional, and handles everything with tact and diplomacy while everyone else is running around in a dither. Taurus can shoulder responsibilities. If she runs a department or service, you can depend upon her doing a great job.

She demands your respect and gets it. Taurus is interested in making money so she's not going to do anything that will jeopardize her income. Expect her to do her best.

How To Handle Your Taurus Employee

If she things that there's a bright and financially rewarding future with your company, she'll stick it out. Salary boosts and peaceful vibrations will help her to stay.

Taurus doesn't like anyone to look over her shoulder while she's working. Once you've explained everything thoroughly to her, leave her alone to do her job. Don't push her. Deadlines and pressures as a daily routine are out for this woman. She refuses to hurry for anyone. Isn't it better to have a perfectionist in your employ rather than someone who sloppily rushes through everything?

This is one woman who won't make any suggestions voluntarily. If you want her to express an opinion, you'll have to ask her. However, there is an exception to this: when you've made a fool of yourself over some business deal, Taurus will quietly step in and tell you what you should have done. Perhaps she's been patiently waiting for you to goof up so she can get your job. This is known as "the Taurus waiting game." If you're the overly aggressive and impatient type, this woman knows she can win because you'll make a hurried decision that winds up as your mistake and her gain.

Taurus appears to have a never-ending patience. Don't fool yourself. This is one woman whom you shouldn't push too hard. She will only put up with disturbances for so long and then — watch out! When you go one step too far you'll know it. Taurus resentment shows when her face is emotionless and she moves like a robot. The next time you step out of line, the bull will no longer look like a gentle lamb. Taurus will tell you off or just solemnly walk off the job.

Before Taurus gets upset enough to quit, heed the first warning signals. This woman does not make spur-of-the-moment decisions to quit; it's built slowly for a long time. All the while she expects you to change or conditions to improve. There is no use running after her and pleading — not even an enormous pay boost will get her to return. Once she's made up her mind, that's it! She's unyielding, remember? But before this stage is reached, talk to her and see what it is that she dislikes.

Taurus is not that picky or demanding; therefore, the difficulty may be an easy solution to solve — like your lowering your voice or refraining from prodding her to work faster.

This woman is obedient because she respects your wishes and knows that she's on the payroll to follow your orders. She doesn't hold it against you either. Taurus considers it to be part of your job. She's a great respecter of those in high positions. There are times when she'd like to tell you that she disagrees on an office procedure but she remains silent. When you are in doubt about something, why not ask Taurus what she'd do? Perhaps she'll save you from making a terrible mistake.

Taurus is against mixing business with pleasure. The office is her job area and is separate from her private life. She's not about to sleep with you to get ahead. This woman knows that her work speaks for itself. She may have a policy of not dating men from the same office. Her job is her security and she wants to remain there until she has accumulated a nice nest egg. Taurus isn't about to jeopardize all she hopes to gain just for a romance that could ruin all her well-laid plans. So, if you're a woman chaser, leave this one alone, especially if you want to be successful.

If this woman is in your employ as a salesperson, give her freedom to handle a client and the expense account as she wishes. Taurus is a natural charmer, especially when she entertains customers in restaurants. She's not dishonest so you don't have to worry about any bill padding or her using the account for personal reasons. Taurus can shoot the bull in a low-keyed manner that rings up sales. However, if you tighten the purse strings or tell her how to handle a client, she becomes disgruntled because she believes that you don't trust or believe in her abilities. Therefore, if you want a larger bank account, leave her alone.

You don't have to give Taurus a title just to placate her ego. However, when she's earned one, you'd better take action before any problems develop. Success is her goal and she wants to be simply rewarded. And why not? She's been an asset to you, hasn't she?

YOUR TAURUS COWORKER
What Can You Expect From Your Taurus Coworker?
There are just a few basic facts to keep in mind when working with this fellow: he's dependable, moves slow, is stubborn, and resists change. The Taurus man is highly motivated and wants to get to the top. However, he won't compete with you and it won't disturb him if you bend over backward to get a promotion. The Taurean knows that his being a workaholic will pay off at some future date when the time is ripe. He's not in a hurry to get ahead. This man likes to accomplish what he sets out to do with the least amount of time and effort. A Taurean works hard for worldly goods and may wind up with as much money as Taurus-born tycoon, Henry J. Kaiser.

This is one person who won't meddle in your business and, furthermore, he doesn't want you to get nosy with him — familiarity turns him off. Don't expect him to gossip or discuss anything except the business at hand. Also, dismiss the thought that he's going to be part of any office frolics. Taurus believes he's working to get a paycheck, not to have fun on company time.

This man is uncritical; he won't boss you. He will leave you alone to do your tasks. You can rely upon his helping you whenever necessary. However, don't expect it to be right then and there — Taurus has to first finish his job before he's able to concentrate on anything else.

With a Taurean for a coworker, you should be prepared for quiet moments and congeniality. Nothing seems to shake him up or catch him off balance or off guard. He takes everything as if it's the normal order of the day. So with this type of person working beside you, nothing should interfere with your plans to move up the corporate ladder.

How To Handle Your Taurus Coworker

If you're new on the job, don't expect Taurus to be very talkative. It takes him a while to become accustomed to you. Do your work and leave him alone to do his. Don't engage in unnecessary conversation. If you do he will either nod or softly give you a yes or no answer or none at all. You may think he's jealous, has a chip on his shoulder, or doesn't like you. However, it's his personality; he wants to concentrate completely on his chores. So why don't you do the same? If you are as diligent as the Taurean, you'll have your foot on the road that leads to the summit.

If you need to give Taurus instructions, don't expect him to understand it immediately. It has to be thought over and practiced until it becomes routine. Be patient and realize that this is part of his nature. Once this fellow is confident, you'll realize what a painstaking coworker you have. However, if you're working side by side with an inert Taurean (and they do exist), expect to handle most of the workload — this type shies away from responsibilities and doesn't exert himself the way he should. Eventually, he'll be fired; seldom does a Taurus quit.

The industrious Taurean thrives when given a schedule to abide by. He'll even make believe he has one when he doesn't. This man will pitch in and help you if you lag behind. Taurus is loyal and will not rat on you. Be kind even though he's serious and seldom laughs. Never forget that he has a goal of a better salary and higher position. He believes that you think like he does. Don't worry, he's not competitive. This man will not step on, or use you, to get a promotion. He relies only upon his own hard working efforts to get a better job.

Avoid being bossy; he knows what to do and resents anyone other than a superior giving him orders in an overbearing manner. If you notice that he doesn't respond to you even with a grumble, that's a sure sign you've been put on his bad list. When this point has been reached, just stay out of his way and perform your duties as if nothing is wrong. This fellow holds a grudge but will get over it in his own slow way.

Don't pile documents on top of other papers that are on his desk; place them to the side. Taurus doesn't want to wade through two sets of papers; he likes order. If you remove anything from his desk, put it back in the same spot or you'll have a disturbed bull on your hands. He will not tolerate a mess; so don't spill coffee or cake crumbs on his desk. You can be secure and sure of Taurus, but never abuse it. Do your job well and he'll do the same — that's the only way the two of you can work happily side by side.

What if Taurus lags so far behind that you have to wait for him to complete his job before you can do yours? And what if you are blamed for it? There are several alternatives: you can slow down and improve your work; help another department; offer several suggestions to the Taurean.

Sit down on your coffee break and discuss it with him. Explain your situation. Let him know that you haven't tattled and told the boss that he's the one responsible for holding up production. Mention tactfully and diplomatically, without bruising his ego, that maybe he'd be happier working in an entirely different field — one that pays better wages (that's always music to a Taurean's ears). Suggest he reevaluate the type of career he wants, and that maybe a personnel counselor could help him.

Don't expect a quick answer; he need time to mull it over. Of course, he may tell you that you should mind your own business. However, keep in mind that this *is* your business, especially when you are being blamed unjustly and are being held back from a promotion and raise. Remember, you cannot allow a coworker to hold you back from reaching the pinnacle of success.

YOUR TAURUS CLIENT
What Can You Expect From Your Taurus Client?

This man is inconspicuousness when he walks nonchalantly through a store. If he stops at a counter, you may notice that his body appears to be rooted to the spot. If he handles everything carefully, asks the price of each item and continues to scrutinize a particular object without saying one word, you can bet that you've got a Taurus customer.

If you ask him, "How do you like ...?" he may grunt, mutter something unintelligible. The most you may hear is, "It's too expensive." Don't expect any questions or statements; he's too busy thinking about it and comparing the price with the same item he's seen elsewhere. This man is looking for a bargain. He likes something that is inexpensive but has value. If he doesn't buy anything, don't be surprised. Taurus is never in a hurry to make a decision.

Next time you see Taurus he may purchase the object he looked at on a previous occasion. However, even then he doesn't seem to be excited about it. The transaction is all a matter of fact. The moment he opens his wallet and pays you, that's about the closest you'll come to seeing this man express an emotion. However, it's not one of glee because Taurus dislikes parting with his dough.

If you're a salesperson and call on Taurus, don't expect an eager beaver; you'll get the reverse. This man is not interested in modernizing. He is not about to take a risk and, most likely, he'll be the last in his field or area to try something new. These actions are clues that you are probably dealing with a Taurean. After a little practice you'll be able to spot him right away. And when you do, you're on the first lap of the journey upward; the second lap comes next.

How To Handle Your Taurus Client

How do you deal with someone who has a poker face and appears conservative and uninterested in your product? First, take him out to eat — he enjoys gorging on good food and imbibing alcoholic spirits. Use a realistic approach with him; he can spot a phony in a minute. Discuss business so he will believe that you are interested in him and his success. Appeal to his desire to make money and get ahead. Realize that this fellow lacks imagination, wants to have the facts broken down in detail from A to Z and wants to know about the proven results of what you're selling.

Impress Taurus by slowly explaining how your product can be used to cut down on time and consequently employees, thus speeding up productivity. As a result, his business can expand gradually (never tell him it will happen overnight because he's leery of get-rich-quick deals) and, thereby, profits can increase considerably. Give him a complete rundown on costs, value, use, longevity, repair time, and how others have benefited.

Don't ask Taurus to commit himself right away. This man is afraid to break away from established customs and take a chance on anything new. If you rush him, you'll lose a sale. Be understanding. Give him time to think. Call him at a later date and remind him of your product. If he says no, avoid wasting your time and energy in trying to convert him to a yes answer. Accept him as he is. Let time lapse and visit him again with more proven results. He will budge if the practical side of the situation is shown.

The moment Taurus turns around, goes away, or back to work, you know he's through with you. This is a hint for you to leave because he's had enough. Make a gracious departure and tell him you'd be pleased to answer any further questions at his convenience.

If you're in a business where customers come to you, keep your office orderly and neat. Taurus is impressed with tidiness, kindness, efficiency, good manners, and someone who handles things with ease. Avoid getting personal with him. If he decides to open up, he will; but don't hold your breath for it. Avoid becoming impatient with this man; if you do, he'll ignore you, walk out or deal with someone else. If you want him to be a regular customer, speak softly and slowly and don't talk about yourself — just tend to business. If you're a waitress, avoid rushing him through a meal.

By now you should know that Taurus is a hard sell. If you want to keep those dollars rolling in, it's necessary to maintain good customer relations. Do the best you can to handle Taurus effectively and you'll discover that you're on the right road to becoming successful.

YOUR TAURUS PARTNER

What Can You Expect From Your Taurus Partner?

You may be glad you joined forces with this woman because she uses common sense, shows good judgment and is determined to succeed. She's got the energy of El Cordobes (the bullfighter), the charm of Rudolph Valentino and the brains of publisher William Randolph Hearst, Sr., all were Taureans. So you've got a real winner with this woman.

Your Taurus partner will not invest a dime in a business, until she has carefully considered every aspect of it. She wants her money to come back a hundredfold. This woman is patient , and will wait years to accumulate a fat bank account, and along the way she never loses sight of her dreams. Her financial advice is excellent. Taurus is practical, but you may call her cheap. She wants value for the funds spent, and will not waste it on foolishness. This woman does not trust new inventions or machinery and uses outdated methods unless you prove their usefulness. And then it will take her time to buy them — she hates to part with even a penny.

Taurus has the ability to deal smoothly with people, especially those who will help her promote her plans or reach her goals. She can shoot the bull, and sell you, and others, on her ideas. This woman works hard because she wants to live comfortably. She's a loyal partner and will stick by you through thick and thin. Taurus expects you to be as ambitious as she is. So don't let her down. After all, you do want to be successful, don't you?

How To Handle Your Taurus Partner

Business is this woman's number one priority. If you expect a fun loving partner, think again. All you are going to get from her, is work and profits. If you want to stay in her good graces, join her workaholic program. She appears sweet and docile, but don't let that fool you; she's firm and business-like.

Let Taurus be the treasurer, because she can handle funds of others, as carefully as she handles her own. This woman believes in spending money to make money. Don't stand in her way, she knows what she's doing. Taurus entertains grandly, and has need for a large expense account. Don't be surprised if she loans an out-of-town client her car! Her feet are always on solid ground, even as she slowly steps up the ladder to reap larger financial rewards.

This woman puts herself wholeheartedly into a job , she is dedicated to a task and won't stop until it's right. Taurus can't stand to leave a chore hanging in midair, it's got to be completed before she'll rest. So don't interfere with her, and be understanding of her desire to be busy at all times. The Taurean is realistic and accepts responsibilities, but she wants you to take care of your share too. If details are not your cup of tea, give them to Taurus — she loves handling them.

Your partner doesn't care whether she works behind the scenes or directly with people; she's capable of both. Taurus likes an atmosphere where she can think. If you are busy yakking about personal affairs, she'll have difficulty in concentrating on her work. She doesn't show her feelings so it's difficult to know whether she likes, or dislikes something. If you get a cold shoulder and a blank stare, you'll know she's bugged. So get back to your job. Your idle chatter is a waste of valuable time, and will attract problems in your business relationship with Taurus.

If you want to please this woman and get ahead, be more productive and do less talking about private matters. If you are an Aries, Gemini, or Sagittarius, you are able to work and chitchat simultaneously. Avoid doing this around Taurus. If you don't you'll soon see her fret and fume. However, that's just a tip-off to what's coming next — a vexed Taurean blowing her stack!

If your work is dependent upon waiting for your partner to complete hers, don't rush her. Nothing will make this woman hurry. Her slow-but-sure manner is all she knows, and she's not about to change her routine. And whatever you do, avoid shocking her with sudden changes. Taurus gets tense and agitated when she's forced to alter her work pattern. It takes her a while to become adjusted to a new schedule. And it's equally a strain on her to adjust to conditions, or situations, that are not to her liking, even though she knows they are all for the best in the long run.

It's of value to express your ideas for expansion. However, Taurus needs time to reflect upon the pros and cons, before a decision can be made. When asking this woman to give you her opinion, don't goad her into a quick response. She has to let suggestions and proposals jell before making a commitment.

Help her with new equipment or methods. Encourage her; explain the procedure slowly, clearly, and use logic. Let her see the practical reason for it. This will make the transition much easier and more agreeable than if she was just shoved into something new, especially if it's something you bought without her knowledge. Sometimes, if you want to make progress, you have to purchase modern machinery on your own, and then let her slowly get used to it; otherwise, she'll be behind the times , and so will you! And that's not the way to be successful, is it?

Sun-Sign Compatibility

This section with each sign of the zodiac in relation to a Taurus Sun sign. By knowing how your sign blends with a Taurean, you are going one step beyond understanding his personality and one step closer to knowing how to handle him in any business situation. Greater insight is invaluable — it not only helps a business prosper, it encourages peace of mind on and off the job.

The following Sun-Sign compatibility summary (with the exception of Taurus/Taurus) *are from the point of view of the person dealing with Taurus. Note:* For the Taurean's point of view, see the Sun-Sign chapter of the person Taurus is dealing with, i.e., Virgo — refer to the Virgo chapter to see how Taurus reacts to Virgo.

ARIES/TAURUS

The slow ways of the Taurean agitate you until you realize that you can't push a stubborn bull into moving faster. However, before you come to this conclusion you have exploded a few times, said a few nasty words, and built a silent wall between the two of you.

Because Taurus is a thorough thinker, you find him a stabilizing influence, someone who can save you from hurried mistakes. What you start, the Taurean completes perfectly. However, you dislike having to wait for the end results, perfect or not.

At times the Taurean's lack of enthusiasm toward your ideas, plans, or projects is more than you can bear. He just can't understand that your incentive is lost when he doesn't get as carried away as you do. Because you overcome all obstacles when inspired, it's difficult for you to understand that Taurus must have concrete results before any emotion is expressed.

Your anger shows when Taurus refuses to become involved in more than one enterprise at a time. You feel that this holds you back from entering and being challenged by, many fields of endeavor. Your impatience really shows when Taurus takes seemingly forever to make a decision. And worse than anything is his cheapness, and not wanting to spend the money on new equipment that could speed up productivity and increase business, thereby bringing you both financial gain.

However, notwithstanding all of the problems between the two of you, Taurus can help you in many ways — to save money, to make and stick to plans, and to curb your impulsiveness.

TAURUS/TAURUS

Both of you are ambitious, and each can work hard, which is an asset to any business relationship. The two of you must achieve goals even though it may take a while to do so; both are patient and understand that " Rome wasn't built in a day" You don't interfere or hold each other back from attaining your aims. Both of you make plans and stick with them regardless of the obstacles you have to confront.

Both of you are practical; you both prefer keeping the same workable equipment or methods to buying the latest machines out on the market. Both believe in spending money to make money; therefore, the clients will be entertained lavishly. Both like potted plants in the office as well as paintings on the wall, but neither of you is going to splurge on office decoration.

You get points in your favor because both of you are slow-working and slow-moving. And you know better than to rush one another. The two of you persevere at a task until it's completed. Projects are carefully considered, therefore there are no clashes in this direction.

Honesty is expressed by both parties; "Shooting the bull" goes on mainly when you deal with clients rather than each other. However, if you are in a customer-dealer relationship , then there's some wheeling and dealing taking place on both sides. In a boss-employee relationship, you'll be strict and the other will be obedient.

GEMINI/TAURUS

In business there are setbacks because the Taurus' immobility opposes your mobility. He likes the old and familiar whereas you are attracted to the new and unfamiliar. And it seems there's nothing you can do or say, that will convince him to go along with your ultra-progressive ideas. He is stubborn and won't budge for anyone. Luckily, you are adaptable and for the time being can give in to him. However, when your desire for change sets in again, you'll try one more time to approach him with avante-garde equipment or methods. Eventually you'll tire of this never-ending conflict of opinions.

Often your impulsiveness gets you into hot water. But good old reliable Taurus certainly is appreciated when he helps you solve a problem. And what about those times when he completed those tasks you left unfinished? Taurus is a stabilizing influence, but he really annoys you when he can't keep up with your fast mental and physical pace.

The telephone, business deals, and new projects consume most of your time, therefore you let the bills slip by. Aren't you thankful that Taurus pays the creditors and keeps the collectors away from your doorstep? Also, you are glad that he pulls you out of the red and keeps you in the black, although it's nerve-racking for you to have to sit still while you listen to his advice. But, when followed, you are glad you did.

If the two of you are going to be a team, you have to learn patience. If you can learn to wait, you'll discover that nine out of ten times it's well worth the effort. You are a dreamer, and Taurus is realistic. So give him enough time and he'll turn your dreams into reality — just don't expect it to happen overnight.

CANCER/TAURUS

You admire the Taurean's drive to be on top. She sets a good example for you to follow: working hard to achieve her aims. She is dependable and won't let you down. Because your moods vary, it's difficult for you to finish a task; however, the Taurean's disciplinarian influence makes you complete all projects.

The two of you are similar; quiet and peaceful surroundings are essential. In a noisy atmosphere Taurus can't think, and you get upset due to your extreme sensitivity. Seldom will the two of you argue. Taurus is easygoing, even-tempered, and gentle. She won't even complain when you are capricious. This woman is so considerate and understanding of your needs that it makes you work harder to please her. Now and then she may hurt your feelings when she gets gruff, but it doesn't last long.

You are reassured by her daily actions that she's the right associate for you. Her methodical and thorough work habits — something you lack — are impressive. Taurus doesn't rush you, which is a relief because you get frustrated when pressure is exerted. Both of you are slow because you are anxious to avoid making errors. Carefulness and efficiency go hand in hand with the two of you.

Taurus doesn't say much but when she does speak, she's direct. This woman follows through on everything. You don't mind her ruling with an iron hand. Taurus glows when you are conscientious, thus inspiring you to do even better. The two of you are a great team because you have so much in common.

LEO/TAURUS

The Taurean's lack of enthusiasm for your ideas and current projects makes you lose the spark that spurs you on to accomplish great tasks. He curbs your impulsiveness when he puts his heavy but firm foot down. Once it hits the ground it stays there. No amount of persuasion will make him change his mind. This infuriates you both since both are stubborn and determined — two set people could lead to a stalemate.

When you are running ahead, Taurus is lagging behind. You find this exasperating, don't you? But you may as well realize that he's not about to rush for you or anyone else — not even a fire. But this man seldom makes a mistake because he is so thorough. Let him plod along and take his own sweet time — everything will be finished on schedule. If you are to work together, patience is a necessity; however, it's something you're a little short on.

Two plus points in your favor: both of you are dependable and loyal. However, you like modernization and Taurus likes to stick with the old and tried; so you clash in this area. Both of you agree that you must spend money to make money. It's just that you overdo it and pile up the debts. Taurus frowns upon this. You call him cheap and he says, "I'm just being practical."

You are flamboyant and Taurus is quiet, but as solid and steady as the Rock of Gibraltar. There's a lot going against the two of you as a team, it's mainly your egos and unyielding natures that get in the way.

VIRGO/TAURUS

An excellent team, like two peas in a pod. Both of you are honest, reliable, and trust one another completely. You are workaholics. Efficiency is a must. Schedules are a delight. You are both punctual, love details, and work in an orderly fashion. The two of you are conscientious and want to give the job your all. What's more, you do!

You both have excellent ideas: common sense, logic, good reasoning, and practicality are used. You are anxious to avoid mistakes — therefore neither one of you will rush into anything. The two of you want to make doubly sure that losses are avoided and gains are attracted. Your seriousness shows by the way you work and stick by one another.

Both are methodical, complete tasks, and like neatness. Your partner won't complain about anything but you will. You are picky but won't have to exercise your critical eye on Taurus. He's as much of a perfectionist as you are. The Taurean enjoys your long explanations; you are more of a talker than he is. This man's silence is appreciated in the office because everyone's able to do his job without too many interruptions.

You are more adaptable than the Taurean. It's difficult for him to make changes and adjustments. As set as he is, you have a way with words that can influence him to budge. Perhaps it's your down-to-earth approach that finally wins him over. When the two of you join forces, you're bound to be successful.

LIBRA/TAURUS

Both of you are charmers although you are much more bubbly than Taurus. You have more to say while Taurus doesn't indulge in idle chitchat; she limits her conversation to things that are pertinent to the business.

Libra and Taurus are both cordial, polite, and obliging. Peace and harmony are sought and maintained. You are lovers of beauty. Taurus may decorate her office for show, whereas yours is decorated for good looks. The Taurean is able to help you find the balance you are always seeking. She won't like keeping the company in debt or the amount of money you spend. Taurus will restrain your spending habits. You may not like her frugality, but inwardly you know that you need to be controlled, so you'll usually give in and let Taurus be the boss. You respect her penchant for being better safe than sorry.

Both desire neatness. The two of you have a lazy streak although Taurus tends to work the hardest. She can't understand why you need to rest after putting in long hours of labor.

You are indecisive where Taurus is decisive. But if you ask her to solve a problem, don't expect a quick answer.

You admire the Taurean's profit-making plans. If you stick with her, you'll fare well. However, your sign rules the scales and if you dip back and forth constantly changing your mind, you may jeopardize your chances of being a winner.

Neither one of you is temperamental or likes to quarrel. However, Taurus wants a business that lasts forever whereas you want to make a killing and retire to a leisurely life-style. This could be a drawback to the relationship if you are partners. However, it's a dilemma that can easily be solved when success happens.

SCORPIO/TAURUS

Even though you are opposite signs you tend to complement one another and can be a great working team. There is a comfortable feeling when you two are together if you don't allow your differences to interfere. Both trust one another (that's difficult for you to do, Scorpio). Neither one of you laugh that much; it's all seriousness with no play, just hard work.

You compulsively buy machinery, mechanical gadgets and spend a bundle on objects you call your "research items." This is one of the biggest things you and Taurus disagree about. You are ready and willing, but not always able, to gamble on the new. Taurus is afraid to take a risk; he doesn't trust the new unless it's been proven to be superior to the old.

You say, "Taurus is cheap." He says, "Scorpio is a spendthrift." He can help curb your impulsiveness if you listen to him. And it would be to your benefit.

You are a whiz and breeze by as fast as the wind. Taurus can't and doesn't try to keep up with you because he wants to make sure that every step he takes leads to the top. Perhaps you should consider doing the same.

Once Taurus has committed himself he sticks, regardless of the dissensions in the relationship; he dislikes change. Because he is slow and set in his ways, you can't fathom how this man is on the way up to the pinnacle of success. But if you give him a chance, go along with him and stop arguing, then the two of you can wind up together in the winner's circle.

SAGITTARIUS/TAURUS

You are restless and don't have the patience to put up with the Taurean's slowness. You don't mince your words either and your tactlessness gets you into difficulty. But you don't care. Diplomacy is something you need to learn, especially if you want to be successful.

Both of you are loyal and honest. However, Taurus is much more dependable than you. And it bugs you that this woman is so frugal and old-fashioned. You are extravagant; you want the latest new equipment and hang the cost. So where can this lead to? Up the creek if you don't learn to save a few bucks, and Taurus doesn't learn to be more adaptable to modern times.

Neither of you is bossy; this is a plus for the both of you. You can follow orders joyfully or give them firmly. Taurus is obedient because it's her duty to be so; therefore, you won't clash in this area. However, if you want quick success, cast your net in a different direction: you tend to have opposite traits.

You do need the Taurus practicality and good business acumen used for buying, though, and Taurus needs your selling ability and courage to expand. So if you can weather out your differences, you'll eventually make it to the top!

CAPRICORN/TAURUS

Both of you have the same goal — the top of the mountain. It's a slow climb upward. You (not Taurus) use people, but both of you take advantage of situations and, if you fall a step back, neither of you will quit. Security is important. The two of you will sacrifice and put up with a lot of unpleasantness just to gain material rewards.

You admire Taurus because he, like you, is neat, orderly and well organized. Both of you stick with your carefully laid plans. A budget is important to the two of you and it's always adhered to like glue to paper. Both are frugal in all affairs; however, when it comes to wining and dining a client, you differ — Taurus picks up the customer's tab; you allow the client to treat you. Both associate only with prominent people; you may find a need for them, Taurus enjoys the company of those who have status; it's an ego trip for him and a money trip for you.

You two are strong, dependable and respect one another for using common sense. Both of you dislike wasting time; however, to outsiders it may seem you are, especially when you go over everything with a fine-tooth comb. The two of you will never skip over anything that seems unimportant. Mistakes are seldom made because both are thorough, methodical, and perfectionists.

You gripe and complain about your hard lot in life. You have a bit of a martyr complex. But Taurus doesn't pay attentions to your mutterings. Instead, he blocks out you and all other discord, while he steadily applies his energy to the task at hand. The two of you are the best astrological sign combination to make a billion dollars! So go do it!

AQUARIUS/TAURUS

Taurus makes you a nervous wreck because she doesn't resolve problems or make new commitments without thinking about them for days, and even weeks. You can't understand why she is unable to make quick judgments like you do. Her being so slow on the draw makes you lose those golden opportunities you think are awaiting you.

This woman holds you back from modernization. You want to move ahead with technology and can't wait to try the latest "in" device, gadget, or machine *before* it's well known. However, Taurus wants to use new equipment only after it's been successfully tried out. Thus conflicts result from your differences. Both are dogmatic and refuse to change your opinions, so no one wins.

You can't comprehend why Taurus has to be so sure of every step she takes. "Why," you ask, "can't she be game, jump in, and try something even a little progressive?" She will give you a detailed explanation, if questioned. However, I doubt that you'll ever have the patience to listen to her — it's the highlights that interest you.

Generally your operations are independent. You need space so you can do your own thing. If Taurus impinges on your right to be free, you may fight. You dislike anyone giving you orders or pinning you down and thus if you're in business together, this attitude may hinder success. In general this relationship has many drawbacks; there's more against it than for it.

PISCES/TAURUS

You admire Taurus; he works hard to achieve his aims. Idolization occurs when you see his resulting successes. His strength and solidity gives you a safe and secure feeling. You feel lucky to be associated with him. His actions make you believe with all of your heart that he'll never let you down. You depend upon him totally. He reassures you when you need to be uplifted. This man is just the disciplinarian you require; otherwise, you slip into the bad habit of procrastinating.

A quiet atmosphere is important to you. Therefore, you are relieved that Taurus is so quiet. His silence is peace to your ears. Both of you move and work slowly. If you lag behind, Taurus will not scold or rush you. Often he'll pitch in and do your job for you, or at least catch you up to where you should be. It's unlikely that you'll ever quarrel or disagree. Neither one of you is temperamental. Taurus is polite and respects your wishes and you in turn do the same with him.

You are delighted with the Taurean's detailed instructions. And his patience makes you believe that you will be able to fulfill the expectations he has for you. This man doesn't say anything that hurts your feelings, which makes you appreciative that you have this type of associate. You are glad that he doesn't ask many questions. When you have to be alert and ready to answer someone at an instant's notice, it jolts you out of your daydreaming. These moments of musing are necessary escape patterns that are used when the job is boring. If your work is creative or involves oral communication, you are not as inclined to doze off into never-never land.

You are impractical and Taurus is practical. However, instead of clashing, you'll give in because you believe that he's got excellent business knowledge. Taurus is more security-conscious than you are, although you like money. You are not tight with a buck, you'll spend it on new machinery and take chances. If Taurus says, "No, it's not the time to do it," you'll listen to him and obey his commands.

Actually the two of you work well together. Your dramatic flair gives just the right touch to the Taurean's seriousness. In your estimation, Taurus will guide you in the proper direction at all times; he'll protect you from making mistakes. Through his influence, you can avoid those sleepless nights that keep you awake worrying about every little thing.

Chapter Five

Gemini Compatibility In business

If you were born between May 21 and June 20, your Sun is in the sign Gemini. However, you may also express Gemini traits if Gemini is dominant in your horoscope (refer to the Introduction, Page 1) even if it is not your Sun sign. If this is the case, you should read and treat this chapter just as if your Sun sign is Gemini.

GEMINI PROFILE
Getting Acquainted With The Gemini Personality

The Gemini man is easy to get to know if you always remember that you are dealing with two people — the twins, sometimes known as Dr. Jekyll and Mr. Hyde. Once this is understood, it'll simplify dealing with him whether he's your partner, employer, employee, coworker, or client. You'll never know, from one moment to the next, which twin is going to emerge. His ideas and thoughts change as often as the wind and his conversation is just as erratic. Gemini can talk, talk, talk on a vast variety of topics. Sometimes he seems to know everything.

The Geminian can't bear to be confined to one spot. He stays in continual and physical motion. Try to make him stand still and his nerves will become so frayed that he gets the jitters. This man thrives on a merry-go-round work schedule and he's not one to jump off. In fact, the faster it goes, the happier he is. Gemini must use his mind constantly. He is so versatile that he can do almost any job he's confronted with and he *needs* new tasks to satisfy his curiosity and love of change.

Gemini keeps up with all of the latest inventions and timesaving methods. One of the twins likes to take risks on new ventures while the other prefers staying with the old and familiar. Unfortunately, the Geminian has the bad habit of getting his fingers in too many pies, of starting a project only to abandon it when he gets bored.

If the destructive twin emerges, you can expect confusion and disorder; however, if the constructive twin is around, you can expect some brilliant ideas and the work to be finished in a jiffy. Give Gemini freedom to communicate and you may enhance your profits as well as reach your goals with him in business.

IF YOU ARE A GEMINI

Because you're always so restless you may ask, "What can I do to get out of this position and into a better one?" Success can be achieved faster if, when you deal with others, you adhere to the following advice.

When dealing with an employer, you should avoid getting too familiar. Your usual first-name basis should be shunned unless your boss has okayed it. Any personal questions you have are best left unanswered. Try to realize that you are not equals on the job even though you may feel you are.

Try to concentrate on one project long enough to conclude it. Avoid trying to take over your employer's job because you've become tired of yours. Don't jump into conversations that don't concern you. You are not getting paid to meddle in the business of others.

Use your innate intelligence on the job. Don't overdo asking the "how" and "why" of every little thing that comes along. This action can displease a boss and make him think that you are not capable of performing your task. However, if you are working for someone who encourages questions, go right ahead. Guard against impatience — a downfall of yours. Give the job a chance of working rather than ditching it for some new venture. When you apply yourself, it's easy for you to get a raise and promotion.

When dealing with partners, employees and coworkers avoid being too critical. A sleepless night (you have many of these) makes you cross and crabby. Sharp, caustic words cause difficulties that are not always easily remedied. Losses occur when you throw logic out the window. Don't rush into quick decisions, stop and allow yourself a few moments to think. Use your brilliant mind to solve problems rather than make them.

Curb your desire to liven dull routine. Idle chitchat or bursting into song makes it difficult for others to concentrate. But the worst occurs when you can't resist playing loud rock music on the radio. Realize that you may be the only one there who can work in such an environment. If you're the boss, use earplugs; otherwise, your employees may not turn in their best work.

You are physically and mentally ahead of most people. Not everyone can work at your pace, so be patient with those who have difficulty keeping up with you. Realize that those who move and think slower than you may be accomplishing just as much as you in the long run. Perhaps fewer errors are made and their work is neater. However, if they are not productive that is an entirely different matter. Give others a chance and they may prove beneficial.

When dealing with clients your main problem is your unpredictability. They have to guess whether you'll be on time or late. Realize that being punctual impresses everyone. It shows that your are dependable and thus implies the same of the product or service you're offering.

You like to consummate a deal as quickly as possible, but you may lose a sale if you rush a customer. Bide your time and curb your impatience. Speak slowly so your client can grasp everything you are saying. It's difficult for you to realize that other people think carefully about something before acting upon it. Once you understand this, you'll be 100 percent ahead of the game.

Your curiosity can be a boon to business when you get others to talk about themselves. However, it may backfire if you do it to be nosy rather than gracious. Gossiping is one of your worst faults even though it's part of your nature. Learn to control this destructive urge, otherwise your client may not trust you and, consequently, you could lose his business. When you tell tales about your other customers, he thinks, "I wonder if he talks to them about me?"

To go one step further, once you as a Gemini know or can recognize the sign your partner, employer, employee, coworker, or client is, read his sign's chapter to learn how best to deal with him as well as to understand his compatibility with you. If you wish to know what he thinks about you, read the Sun-Sign Compatibility section starting on Page 59. The remainder of this Gemini section deals with how other relate to you, what they can expect of you and how they should handle you. Let's go on an interview with your sign, okay?

AN INTERVIEW WITH A GEMINI

A Gemini employer interviewing you: Your resumé will be scanned so briefly that you'll swear she didn't read it. But she did! Be ready for some quick questions that may or may not make any sense to you. Don't go into lengthy explanations; speak right up and get to the point immediately. Be alert! Be prepared to talk to her even if she's on the telephone or engaged in other conversations.

If she asks, "Do you have any questions?" feel free to question her. The more inquisitive you are, the better your chances of getting hired. You'll really be in with her if you tell her how she can improve her business; she's always open to suggestions.

If she wants you to work odd hours on an overtime basis, go along with her; otherwise, forget about this job. Gemini likes employees who are adaptable; it's a must because she is unpredictable. If she asks you to go to work for her immediately, do so if you want the job.

If you're interviewing a Gemini applicant: Interview this man the moment you see him, otherwise he may slip away. He's so restless and impatient that it's difficult for him to wait around unless he's found someone to chat with. Once the interview starts, you'll notice he's bright and alert with a gift of gab that bowls you over. His questions about your business come flowing out so fast that just as you answer one, he's asked another. And then to top it off, he gives you business ideas that are overwhelming. Gemini amazes you with his ability to grasp everything instantly and solve your problems just as fast.

It's best to hire him right then and there because he's so changeable. Also start him to work immediately; that's when you'll notice you've hired two people (he's twins). Keep in mind that if Gemini gets bored, he'll quit so fast that you'll be perplexed for quite a while afterward.

Now that the interview is over, first let's go to work for a Gemini and then see how Gemini is going to fare as your employee, okay?

YOUR GEMINI EMPLOYER
What Does Your Gemini Boss Expect Of You?

If you were transferred from one department to another, Gemini may, out of curiosity, ask you why. However, regardless of the reason, she will give you a chance to prove yourself. If you left another department because you were sloppy, this won't bother the Gemini. All she's interested in is that you are productive and finish a job quickly.

On a moment's notice, your Gemini employer expects you to stay late. Your going along with her changes is taken as a matter of fact. Don't be surprised if your work schedule is changed daily or that your time to come to work is changed weekly. You'll discover that working for a Gemini is similar to putting a jigsaw puzzle together.

Your Gemini boss expects you to make her job easier and to improve sales or working conditions. She will pick your brain for ideas. This woman wants to communicate with you on an intellectual basis. It's necessary for her to keep her mind constantly active because this leads to new deals and new profits. Gemini tires of conducting business in the same way so she's always looking for anything new.

Gemini anticipates that you are as adaptable and flexible as she is. She'll give you a chance to prove it when she says, "Drop what you're doing right now and start this new project." Your Geminian employer will be pleased if you're able to make quick decisions in the same style she makes them. This is one boss who doesn't like to waste valuable time. She expects you to work while she's talking. If you are able to do so, Gemini will be happy that you are on her payroll.

How To Handle Your Gemini Boss

You won't be bored with this employer. The office will be like a madhouse: fellow employees will be dashing about or you'll hear voices busily engaged in conversation on the phone or with a customer. When the atmosphere is electrically charged with noise and movement Gemini is able to accomplish her tasks with uncanny energy. So, be a part of it — move fast, make snap judgments, speak up, and do your job quickly.

If something has to be questioned, don't beat around the bush — get to the point. If Gemini suddenly darts off while talking to you, go back to work, and don't be surprised if she returns in a jiffy and resumes talking where you left off. Try to keep us with her when she switches from topic to topic — don't let it annoy you, just calmly lead her back to the one that interests you.

Your Gemini boss never knows what she's going to do from one moment to the next; so go along with her rather than try to predict her moves — especially if you are her secretary. Make believe you are on a picnic or being entertained and you won't get disturbed by her actions.

If the Grand Central Station environment is too hectic and noisy for you, look for another job. You won't get peace and quiet working for a Gemini. If you can't blend in with this hustle and bustle, you'll have an interesting job as well as one that is productive and pays well. A Geminian is not cheap; however, she may forget to give you a raise. Don't be afraid to ask for one. You may have to remind her more than once because usually she's preoccupied with numerous projects. Don't fume silently because she again forgot to give you the salary boost; just approach her another time when she seems less busy (if that day ever occurs). Gemini may surprise you by giving it to you right then and there.

Keep mum about dissatisfactions. Gemini is nosy and somehow is aware of the dirt and gossip going on in the office. When she dashes by, she strains to hear even the lowest whisper. Her facial expression may fool you into believing that she didn't hear a thing, but don't count on it. Her ears are tuned in to pick up every voice in the room and her eyes don't miss anything. There are two of her (she's twins, remember?). She isn't disturbed by personal chitchat as long as you can work at the same time. It's when production halts because you want to yak that she will fire you without explanation!

Don't get too exasperated when Gemini orders you to change tasks in midstream and then, an hour later, tells you to resume work on the unfinished project. Try to understand that she's keyed up, on edge and makes decisions without thinking them carefully through. Ask questions if you are in doubt about a procedure. She wants you to be inquisitive. Don't get emotional with her and cry about anything. She's a thinker, not a feeler. Tears will only get you thrown out the door because they are a waste of her time and energy and hold her — and you — back from accomplishing important tasks.

Your Gemini employer is always looking for ways to improve business. She may use you to experiment with a new fangled idea. Gemini will admire you for expounding any theories you may have to improve the business so talk about your innovative ideas with the boss. Keep up on the latest procedures and equipment. Help her stay streamlined and modern. It's music to her ears when sales are increased. If you are instrumental in bringing this about you can expect a promotion.

Be prepared to answer Gemini's questions. This is one employer who is interested in why you are performing a specific job in a particular manner. It's not meant as an insult, so don't take it that way. She does not want to give you a rough time intentionally. When Gemini makes inquiries it's because she wants to understand everything connected with your operation. She's constantly on the alert for ways to speed up your production. If you have any suggestions be sure and mention them. This will brighten her day because it gives her something new to think about. And Gemini loves to think.

If you are a sensitive person (Cancer and/or Pisces dominant), guard against getting your feelings hurt by your boss. Don't blame yourself, her probing and pressure has nothing to do with you. Try to understand that Gemini is so mentally carried away with those castles she builds in the sky that she lacks a true down-to-earth warmth.

Keep your Gemini employer in stitches by telling her a few quick jokes while you're working. She is able to keep up with your one-liners, discuss business in between each punch line, and continue to work all the while. She is extremely capable of jumping from one subject to another without being thrown for a loop. In fact she delights in this type of mental exercise, especially if she benefits from it financially or if the humorous jokes give her a lift.

If you notice that Gemini has abandoned a project, ask her if she'd like you to complete it. It may make you wind up working overtime because you haven't finished your own tasks. But to Gemini it's little things like this that make you an invaluable employee.

Gemini doesn't like to sit still for long; it makes her feel as if she's trapped like an animal in a cage. She's got to have a job that keeps her moving; if it doesn't she'll find a way to be on the go. If you are working in an outer office, be ready at all times for your Gemini employer to emerge.

If you see your employer's secretary entering her office to take dictation, don't relax thinking that your boss is going to stay in her office for a while. A few minutes later she may burst out and suddenly appear alongside you to ask if you finished the report you were working on. Almost before you answer, she may disappear back into her office to finish the dictation she started. This is still no time to relax — Gemini is likely to return to your desk minutes later to ask you about something else. With this employer you must be prepared for constant interruptions. If you are the type who likes routine without disruptions, look for employment elsewhere. At least with Gemini you won't have very many dull moments; in fact, you'll have a lot of laughs and can still be a success sign.

YOUR GEMINI EMPLOYEE
What Can You Expect From Your Gemini Employee?
You've probably got a member of MENSEH in your employ. (Most Geminis have high IQs, as well as creative minds that never seem to stop.) If you act on his large-scale dreams, be prepared for a flourishing business. Not only will your office take on a new look, but expansion can be expected on all fronts.

Gemini is known to be a jack-of-all-trades, so expect a multi-talented employee who will get the job done quickly. His desk may be a mess with everything scattered every which way and he may not be the neatest person you ever saw, but I'll bet he'll be the fastest.

Don't be surprised if you discover you've got an unpredictable employee on your payroll. Gemini, on his own initiative, may arrive early, skip coffee breaks, take short lunches and burn the midnight oil working overtime. This pace could continue for several weeks and then suddenly he'll go in the opposite direction: he arrives late to work, takes long coffee breaks and lunch periods and leaves early. But regardless of his hours of work input, the job will be completed in a jiffy. It's as if you have two employees working for you instead of one — and you do since Gemini is twins, remember?

Gemini can talk you into raises and promotions so fast that your head will spin. Later you'll be flabbergasted by your actions. It's not the money nor the title that interest this fellow, it's the challenge of talking you into it that makes him do it. Gemini feels he's playing a word game when he can put something over on you; it's good for his ego and breaks up monotony by giving him something new to do.

How To Handle Your Gemini Employee
Give Gemini any type of job to do and you'll be amazed at how well he performs. If it's something he's never done before, he'll attempt it and probably outdo those with experience. However, make sure there is plenty of variety involved with every task. If you bore him with routine, make him adhere to a schedule or punch a clock, he won't be a permanent fixture; he'll walk off the job without even giving notice.

Gemini is restless and can't stand being pinned down. Therefore don't confine this fellow by hiding him in a corner. Let him run errands and move about. Send him out of the office and let him handle the fieldwork. Send him in your place on business trips or take him with you. Gemini was born with a gift of gab. Allow him the opportunity to express himself. He excels as a publicist or in sales. Gemini can talk anybody into buying a product or doing business with the company he represents. His clever way of speaking makes him a natural when it comes to handling people. Use his greatest asset — the ability to communicate — to your advantage.

Never run out of projects for your Gemini employee. He must be kept occupied every second and with more than one thing at a time. It's a must for him to keep his hands, mind and tongue (all three ruled by his sign) wagging constantly and simultaneously. If he's busy with these three areas of his body you'll have no complaints from your Gemini employee.

His nerves (ruled by Gemini) can't take the quiet; it drives him stark, raving mad. Many a Gemini has yelled and screamed on the job for no other apparent reason than to make a bit of noise. Of course, when this occurs everyone thinks that the Gemini has cracked up and is having a nervous breakdown, and in many instances there is nothing closer to the truth. Usually those who experience this are Geminis, or have it dominant in their horoscopes and just can't take the silence that resembles a mortuary or monastical existence. So keep your place lively; even music will help or keep him out on the road where he really belongs. Or let him talk to customers on the phone or in person.

Send Gemini to conventions and workshop seminars. Let him sit in on business meetings. His mind clicks rapidly with innovative ideas while he listens to others talk. If there is a question-and-answer period followed by a lecture, you can bet that Gemini is the one asking the most questions. Hold a conference with him afterwards, and be open-minded to his ideas that may sound crazy to you; give them a chance because most likely they will prove profitable. If you have ideas but don't know how to bring them to fruition, tell them to your Gemini employee and be ready to take action.

If you have problems with other employees, Gemini is a great troubleshooter. He's an excellent peacemaker and can get people back on good speaking terms with one another again. Or if customers are angry and complaining, let Gemini talk to them; they'll go away laughing. He can charm the clients with his personality and tell them the words they want to hear.

Gemini will take time off from work to do the things he wants to do. He may use sickness as the excuse or he may tell you the truth, depending upon which twin emerges — the honest one that may risk losing his job for being frank or the dishonest one that saves his job for telling a fib. It's best to go along with him if he has been financially rewarding to your company because it isn't every day that you can get someone who is as productive as your Gemini employee. The same goes for those days when he comes in late. Don't get angry or say a word to him about it. He's well aware that he's tardy and will try to make up for it. However, if he doesn't and he maintains a routine of tardiness, then you will have to speak up and let him know who's the boss.

Your Gemini employee may want to take a vacation at an odd time of the year — a period that is not listed on the company's time slot. Or perhaps he's scheduled for a certain month, and decides to change it on the spur of the moment. It's difficult for Gemini to stick with plans. Perhaps he heard about a trip to the Casbah that a group of tennis buddies are going to take. So he wants to join them. Be adaptable and make changes if permissible and possible; otherwise, Gemini will quit, get his severance pay, and spend it on his overseas journey.

If Gemini is discontent he won't hesitate in telling you what's wrong. There's no fear in this fellow. He's confident and expects you to make changes in his behalf. If you don't he may quit. He's sure he can get a job elsewhere. Because he's changeable, and doesn't hold grudges, you can wheedle him back if you meet some of his terms. Weigh his value rather than getting angry and throwing him out. He may be an employee who can bring success to your company. And that's what it's all about, isn't it?

YOUR GEMINI COWORKER
What Can You Expect From Your Gemini Coworker?

There are just a few basic facts to keep in mind when working with this woman she's inconsistent, nervous, talkative and noncompetitive. Gemini works so fast that she accomplishes more in an hour than most people accomplish in a day. However, don't let that worry you so much that you do inferior work. Gemini can't stand doing nothing so don't be surprised if she pitches in and helps you out if you are lagging behind.

Your coworker may be a gossip like, the late Geminian Hedda Hopper. She wants to know all about you and everyone else on the job. Gemini may be the ringleader in the office and make suggestions. "Let's all chip in and buy a birthday gift for _____," or "Let's have an office party." Be ready for those Friday lunches that are really disguises for intellectual discussions.

Daily, you'll be amazed when Gemini tells you about a new method for modernization; it's something she's read or concocted on her own. Be prepared for her to talk you into experimenting with this newfangled idea. "It may speed up production," she'll exclaim. What's more, after proving it's value, don't be surprised if she wants you to go with her to the boss so you can verify everything she says. Gemini's dual nature sticks out like a sore thumb. She may dish out flowery compliments that are as sweet as perfume flowing from her lips, and a few seconds later she may nag, criticize and find fault with anything that doesn't meet her standards. Her sharp tongue may wound you; it keeps her in hot water continually. If you don't want to quit and you want to get ahead, you'll have to learn how to get along with Gemini so you are not affected by any of her actions.

How to Handle Your Gemini Coworker

If you are training your new Gemini coworker, you'll discover that she's bright and alert. She learns rapidly because she's curious about everything. When you are through instructing her, you may be stunned that she knows your job as well as hers, especially if she proves it to you by offering to help when you fall behind. Gemini thrives when she's learning something new, so teach her everything you know and she'll be right there to give aid when needed.

Gemini's hunger for ideas and interest in new concepts may lead her into pestering you with tons of questions. Also, she likes to probe to see what makes you tick. However, she resents anyone getting too close or familiar with her. If you ask her about why she thinks a certain way, she'll put up a facade or change the subject. So, to get along with this woman, leave the inquiries to her and tell her only what you want her to know.

Never tell her a secret because she will tell everything she knows (Scorpio dominant or Gemini on the harmonious side are the exceptions to this). Gemini is known as "the Messenger." She sticks her nose into other people's business and listens carefully for tidbits that might be useful for one of her schemes. This love of news makes her feel that she's a necessary part of all that is going on at that moment. Gemini joins in and interrupts conversations. It's easy for her to twist facts, take them out of context, jump to conclusions, and spread gossip about quickly. By the time her tattletales get back to you they have been maliciously blown out of proportion and she may deny she ever started them or gave away a confidence.

By now you should know that Gemini loves to chat. She's glib, but often too talkative. Be prepared for her to involve you in a conversation while you are working. Regardless of how much yakking she does, it doesn't interfere with her output. If you can handle this without getting fired, then engage in witty and intellectual conversations. Don't bore her with domestic issues or everyday trifles. Gemini has a good sense of humor, enjoys jokes and interesting stories.

If you're the type who needs to concentrate on the job, it will be necessary to mentally block out everything Gemini says. Furthermore, if you want to get to the top, it's best to avoid unnecessary conversations such as those that are not work-related. If you mention this to her, she may be temporarily offended and later forget about it and start babbling all over again. If you ignore her completely, tensions will mount. If you don't do something about it you could be fired. So get Gemini aside on the coffee break and explain to her that it's nothing personal because you like her but that you can't afford to lose your position. She will probably be cooperative; however, due to her changeable nature, it won't last long. Eventually you'll have to transfer or hope that she does. However, if Gemini finds you boring, she may quit. A paycheck isn't as important to her as an interesting job with some idle chitchat thrown in.

Once Gemini adopts an idea she will do everything in her power to put it into practice, even if she must hurt you to do so. She is a mental pickpocket. This woman may take your concepts and explain them to the boss as if she was the originator of them. It may appear that she behaves in this fashion because of an ego trip or that she wants to get "in" with her employer. However, it's because she enjoys imparting information to others and, from the time she received your notion to the time she relates it, she has forgotten where she heard it.

Be ready for Gemini to give you advice; she assumes that she's being kind and tireless in putting herself out to fulfill your needs. Also she believes that you really want her counsel. But you may view it as an interference from a busybody. When you work side by side with a Gemini you've got to be prepared for any and everything. Boredom is her biggest enemy and may lead to wild antics to relieve the monotony. If you join in, and are on the verge of losing your job, Gemini may go to bat for you. However, because of her inconsistencies you can't count on it and, after all, you didn't have to follow suit, did you? If you want to be successful don't be unduly influenced by Gemini's wildness.

YOUR GEMINI CLIENT
What Can You Expect from Your Gemini Client?

This woman will flit in and out of your establishment as quick as a bird in flight. She'll be talking a mile a minute, wanting to know the "how" and "why" of everything you have to offer. Don't be surprised if she tells you about the latest "in" product you should be carrying. She isn't being bossy or an egomaniac, she is just delighted whenever she has the opportunity to impart information to others.

Gemini might make you nervous because she doesn't stand in one spot while you are quoting her prices and explaining the use of each article she has inquired about. Either she paces the floor or peeks into every nook, cranny, window and open box that is in sight. You may think that she's not listening to you, but she hasn't missed one word you've spoken. Once you've stopped talking, you'll be well aware that Gemini heard everything you said — she'll either buy one object, or several, and say, "I'll take this and this and this; here's the money, wrap it up. I'm in a hurry." And out she goes, smiling, and telling you she'll be back on another day.

If you call Gemini on the phone to make a sale, expect quick questions, answers, and a "yes" or "no" response in between her conversing with other people. It may be difficult to hear if there is a lot of noise going on in Gemini's office (usually there is) or home (no difference, except try to catch her there).

If you go to Gemini's place of business, expect a real eager beaver, especially if you have a hot new item that has just been made available to industry. This woman is interested in modernizing and using the latest machinery and equipment. Cost is not considered; she will not hesitate to take a risk. In fact, Gemini says, "I'll take it," before you've finished explaining the pros and cons of its operation. By these actions it's easy to spot a Gemini — especially when she doesn't stop yakking.

How to Handle Your Gemini Client

One important item to keep in mind when you are dealing with Gemini is that you are dealing with two people — the twins — and you never know which one is going to emerge — the tightwad or the spendthrift.

Your Gemini client is known for her tardiness. It seems that she's always being held up somewhere. Most of the time her continual blabbing is what makes her run late. Besides, she abhors sticking to a schedule, so you should always allow for her late arrival.

Gemini is not consistent; therefore, if you received a large order from her last week, don't count on another big order this week. This woman is about as dependable as the weather report. One moment she's all for the product you are selling and the next, she's against it.

Most of the time you can count on Gemini making a fast decision. However, if you catch her in one of her indecisive moments, you may lose a sale. There are times when she has bitten off more than she can chew and just has too much on her mind. If you notice that she's weighing the pros and cons, that's your clue that Gemini is in one of her rattled periods. So, be patient, because maybe she'll purchase something. Or explain slowly the value of your product. If you tell her to come back after she's given it some thought, you may never see her again. Gemini forgets about what's in a store unless she passes by and sees it in the window or advertised. So, think twice about using this approach.

If you are slow by nature, you may lose Gemini as a customer. She demands fast action from the moment she walks in the door until she departs. This includes your moving and talking at a lively pace. Leave the details out; just give her the overall picture. The shorter your speech, the quicker your sale.

Don't be surprised if Gemini gossips about your competitors, neighbors, or customers (those she knows that frequent your establishment). Naturally, you know better than to join in and give her tidbits that she can spread around. Try to get her to concentrate on her reason for walking in your door. (Hopefully it wasn't just to tittle-tattle!) It may take some doing; however, if you can arouse her curiosity about something that is more exciting than the people the two of you are acquainted with, Gemini will switch her total attention toward that direction. If it's something that she can learn, she'll be all ears. Perhaps the discussion can lead into the "for sale" items in your store. And, without thinking, Gemini may purchase something. Thus, you don't hurt anyone's reputation, you maintain good customer relations and through continuing this mode of operation you make money and are headed in the right direction to becoming successful.

YOUR GEMINI PARTNER
What Can You Expect From Your Gemini Partner?

You may pat yourself on the back because you teamed up with this man — he's adaptable, intelligent, quick-minded and skillful in everything he does. He's got Bob Hope's sense of humor, the late Bennet Cerf's cleverness with words and the late President John F. Kennedy's progressiveness (all Geminians). So what do you do with a partner who has a gift of gab and innovative ideas? Either you go along with him and take the same risks he takes or you hold him back from fulfilling his grandiose dreams.

This fellow may make you a nervous wreck (he's one) as he dashes about doing five things at one time, talking on three telephones simultaneously and dictating to his secretary in-between all of this hullabaloo. Or he may surprise you the next morning when you walk in the door because the decor has been changed, furniture moved and the walls painted another color. Or the noisy atmosphere may be a bit much, especially when you can't think straight. And just as you thought you got him away on a field trip, he's running back in the door with a brainstorm that he believes can revolutionize the business and increase profits.

The office may be turned topsy-turvy most of the time. Don't expect Gemini to be organized, systematic or tidy; utter chaos rules the day. He is unpredictable, keeps his own hours — they may be odd — but he works so fast that lost time is more than made up for. Gemini fidgets at meetings or paces the floor — he must be kept moving constantly. If you handle him properly, success is almost guaranteed.

How To Handle Your Gemini Partner

You can avoid upsets and clashes if you don't pay any attention to Gemini's consistent changes. Also get used to his vacillation about whether he should sell out and go into another entirely different profession. Try to understand that it's in his nature to be contradictory and reverse his opinions from one moment to another as well as to seek new fields to conquer.

It's difficult for him to make decisions because his dual nature sees both sides to every question. This leads to dissatisfaction and frustration. However, let him handle all emergencies because he is able to make excellent split second decisions and take immediate action.

Don't stop Gemini from talking; it's important for him to communicate and get his ideas across. Often he's misunderstood because when his mind races ahead of his voice, something other than what he intended can pop out. Avoid slowing him down, because this will only confuse him. However, you can ask for explanations and he'll gladly give them.

Gemini is always on the lookout for something new to discuss. In a business debate he can argue on one side and halfway through switch over to the other side. This might make you a little berserk, but just take it in stride; it's typical for any man born under the sign of the twins. If you wait long enough (a few minutes or so) he'll be right back to the starting point. Sometimes it's best to just go ahead and do things without getting Gemini's opinion. The Twin is open-minded and tolerant. If he gets angry it won't last. He just goes about his duties merrily as if nothing ever happened. Gemini doesn't remember quarrels or hold any grudges. Generally he's easy-going and cooperative. However, if he's thwarted in an important project, he may turn on you, for he cannot endure defeat.

If a dilemma arises, don't cry or get emotional. Gemini doesn't have any sympathy for tears; they just don't move him. He respects those who use their brain and think, not those who feel, cry and whine. So avoid any scenes of this nature.

Gemini can't stand being bogged down with details. He will be grateful if you take care of this end of the business. When you need help with a task, this man will be right there; he's eager to please. No extra job is too much for the Twins. He will come in early and work late if necessary.

Gemini will always avoid repetitive chores for the novelty he demands. This means that they are pushed in your direction. You may be annoyed with this as well as with his penchant for dropping one project in favor of another. Anything that is too humdrum or easy, usually is abandoned by Gemini. Try to understand his restlessness and desire for a mental challenge and don't force him to finish a task. He rebels against being pressured, and his other talents more than make up for these little personality traits.

This man dislikes routine, following a schedule or making deadlines. Don't pin him down to any time commitment. He is extremely productive; if he knows a job has to be done, he will accomplish it quicker than you can blink an eyelash. Often it's completed before it's due date. That's the type of surprise your partner enjoys giving you. There are moments when you can justly call him unreliable; however they're few and far between. You'll forget any goofing off he did when the profits from a new venture he initiated comes rolling in.

Handle all finances. Keep Gemini on a tight budget otherwise losses may occur through his sudden whims. Make sure all checks are countersigned. This man thinks big and wants to expand every time the company's earnings are increased. With Gemini as a partner, success is easy to achieve.

Sun-Sign Compatibility

This section deals with each sign of the zodiac in relation to a Gemini Sun sign. Knowing how your sign blends with a Geminian takes you one step beyond understanding his personality and one step closer to understanding how to handle him. Greater insight is invaluable — it not only helps a business to prosper, it also encourages peace of mind on and off the job.

The following Sun-Sign compatibility summaries, with the exception of Gemini/Gemini, *are from the point of view of the person dealing with Gemini. Note:* For the Geminian's point of view, see the Sun-Sign chapter of the person Gemini is dealing with, i.e., Libra — refer to the Libra chapter which explains how Gemini thinks about Libra.

ARIES/ GEMINI

Just as you start to say "jump" the Gemini is already hopping about. You both dart in and out of the office at such speed it's a miracle you don't collide. Swift action such as this has always pleased you. Chores are performed quickly. You find the Gemini mentally challenging. Your competitive side is stimulated by Gemini's actions. It's a neck-and-neck race to see who finishes a project first. When you put your heads together even more is accomplished: ideas are readily and rapidly exchanged, and quick decisions are made.

You approve of Gemini's up-to-date business views because they match your own. In a conversation this woman's lack of continuity doesn't throw you at all. In fact, you are always able to bring her back to the initial topic when you feel the time is ripe. You have plenty of guts yourself; therefore, you admire Gemini's nerve in risky ventures. "Thank heaven she's adaptable," you exclaim as you order her about.

But when the Gemini fails to make a delivery on the date promised, you lose your temper. And her constantly changing plans rile you to no end. However, you manage to deal with these bad traits of hers. Your impatience shows when she keeps you waiting, but your anger disappears quickly because she makes a witty remark or quickly consummates a deal. It all happens fast, and you like the fact that Gemini keeps you on your toes. You are a fabulous twosome who can make a fortune for someone smart enough to employ you, and listen to your suggestions, or go along with your fantastic notions.

TAURUS/ GEMINI

Ever since Gemini's been employed here, the office has been disorganized. "It's frustrating when you're never able to find important documents and reports," you tell a fellow worker. But you find it amazing that there's always a slew of sharpened pencils in sight, that is, until Gemini grabs one so fast that he knocks the rest of them all over the desk and floor.

The Gemini chatter is extremely disturbing, especially when you are working on a task that requires an enormous amount of concentration. His skipping from one uncompleted project to another upsets your desire to finish what's been started. However, you're stunned when he suddenly goes back to a job and finishes it just as suddenly. But those chores he completely abandons for you to finalize, slowly arouse your anger. However, when you let off steam, Gemini just smiles. Nothing seems to faze him.

You are in awe of Gemini's ambidextrous nature and his ability to cleverly word everything he says to you and the customers. He constantly throws you off guard and you dislike not knowing what to expect from one moment to the next. These actions he pulls vary to such extremes that it may be more than your good solid nature can take. You are well aware that he has two distinct personalities, but in general it's one too many for you. If he would use his stable, practical, and reliable side you'd be happy. Most likely you will realize that he can be an asset to business with all his multitalents but, along the way, he may be more than you care to handle or put up with.

GEMINI/GEMINI

You are one team that will make people dizzy, regardless of whether they are just watching or listening to the two of you. There will be some who swear that both of you are insane, while others rave about your genius. It may ruin your nerves for the two of you to associate with each other; however, you'll love every jittery moment that transpires.

When the two of you work together, it will be like a carousel ride that never stops. Your legs are in constant locomotion, your arms and hands move as you talk and chain smoke. The telephone, meetings, and customers keep you busy yakking most of the day and far into the night. Anyone entering your business establishment for the first time, would think that he's in a mad house because of the noise. But the two of you are at your productive best in a busy, noisy environment.

You admire each other for the ideas that flow between you as rapidly as water from a gushing spring. When talking, you may finish each other's sentences. And when you put your two heads (it's really four heads — two for each Gemini twin) together, the brilliant results may be your shining hour.

CANCER/GEMINI

You think that Gemini is a little neurotic because he paces the floor, twitches when seated and jumps up and down from his chair every few minutes. And yet he manages to accomplish a lot — sometimes even more than you. It disturbs you that he seldom stays put long enough for you to corner him to ask him about your current project. When you are able to stop him, he dashes his views off so hurriedly that you can't write down his complete instructions. And, then when you look up to ask him to repeat his words, he's disappeared. His haphazardness and constant rushing about, invariably puts you behind schedule and makes you as helter-skelter as he is.

You do like his good sense of humor, though and highly respect his ideas and find him interesting and fascinating to be around; he breaks up the monotony you dread.

You admire his cleverness, but not when it's at your expense. And at times he hurts your feelings.

It's an ordeal for the two of you to complete tasks and this is a disadvantage in business. Gemini's lack of common sense disturbs you. Both of you need balance, and someone to stabilize you. Hopefully others in your working environment can fit the bill.

LEO/GEMINI

You are spry, with lots of vitality, and find it easy and challenging to keep up with Gemini. Her sparkling personality brightens up the day. The office isn't in the doldrums when she's around. You admire her wit and those fabulous ideas she springs on you daily. However, you wish she could be more stable.

Gemini's good for your ego because she lets you boss her. You can persuade her to do most jobs easily. She follows your commands regardless of how overbearing you become. Gemini doesn't seem to resent your being in charge. And when you tell her off, she actually seems to be enjoying the attention you give her. Her uncanny ability to adapt and adjust quickly to changes and the plans you make meets with your wholehearted approval.

If you are stuck with a dilemma that needs solving instantly, you know you can rely upon Gemini's brilliant answers. Generally, she comes up with the right solutions. She's not very organized, but she surprises you with bright ideas for revamping the company's needs which may lead to expansion. Gemini's willingness to take a risk in business ventures makes her just the type of woman you need to have in your corporation.

Her vivid dreams, schemes, and propositions, appeal to your desire to be rich and successful with all your undertakings. Often her notions sound too unreal and unattainable, but with your determination, solidity, and hard work, they can become a reality. She's an intellectual who, if given the opportunity, can increase sales and make the profits roll in.

VIRGO/GEMINI

Gemini doesn't use logical reasoning or sound practical judgment, and that irritates you so much that you wind up criticizing her endlessly. If you are looking for an important report on her desk, it's almost impossible to wade through the papers, books, and personal effects that are piled seemingly a mile high. Stress is really felt if you need that report before you can finish a certain project. It may be a long wait for Gemini because you're aware that she's usually late. You feel further tension because you are now thrown off of the schedule you pride yourself in maintaining.

Yet you are in awe of her intellectuality and her knowledge in a wide variety of subjects. But you can't understand why she doesn't use common sense in everyday trifles. With this excellent mind she has, you just wish that she'd settle down and tend to business methodically.

Gemini cancels appointments on the spur of the moment; you find this annoying. Or just as you approach her to sign an important document, she darts out the door. Her tendency to start a half-dozen projects, then dump them because she's bored, drives you up the wall. If she'd only stick to things, you'd be happy. Because you can't stand to leave things undone, you wind up completing them for her.

Neither you nor Gemini will ever know which one of the twins will emerge. It's a constant guessing game. There will be moments when you swear you're losing your mind; however, you may wind up with more material gain than you had bargained for — it's purely a gamble.

LIBRA/GEMINI

Gemini is a boon to you because he promptly solves your problems. If it wasn't for him, you'd spend days just weighing the pros and cons of a matter. You appreciate his interest in helping you, not only with your indecisiveness, but with the tasks you lag behind in. There are times when you just don't have that much energy to work. This fellow is constantly surprising you. You are fascinated by Gemini's unusual mind. You never tire of listening to his stories, theories, or latest bright ideas. He seems to know everything. You enjoy learning from him; it makes your job all that much more enjoyable. And you are not disturbed when he's late, cancels an appointment, or is unreliable.

Both of you are dreamers, and build castles in the sky. Gemini is good for you because he will put action behind his airy hopes so they'll become a reality. Your belief in him spurs him on to fulfill his and your, ambitions. Your dual nature (Libra's scales, indicate a duality) and his blend harmoniously, and can bring financial security to the two of you.

SCORPIO/GEMINI

Gemini's Dr. Jekyll-and-Mr. Hyde routine makes you see red. She makes commitments and then breaks them. Her flaky and flighty actions are more than you can endure. You dislike the way she flits back and forth across, or in and out, of a room. And when she leaves things undone and walks out for the day, you are ready to battle.

It bothers you to work with, or for, anyone who is not dependable. Her live-for-today, *not* plan-for-tomorrow attitude makes you doubt that she's good for you as an associate. Although she doesn't tend to business the way you think she should, at least she somehow manages to get a job done ahead of schedule. So you can't complain about that.

Gemini's constant yakking and her nosiness when she inquires about personal affairs goes against your grain. You dislike anyone prying into your secret and private life. She gossips too much for you, too. But you must admit that when you are nasty and sarcastic, she takes it like a trooper. You do admire her for that , if not much else.

One of the Gemini twins pleases you: the one who is sensible, dutiful, serious, dedicated, and truthful. But that twin who lies, makes errors, omits the details, and only writes down the highlights, and gives instructions the same way, makes you so angry that you scream at her. You try to understand Gemini with your probing and investigative methods. However, she's wise and resents anyone getting to know the real inner her. So if you are going to be associated with Gemini, don't even try to understand her — you never will. She doesn't, so how can you?

SAGITTARIUS/GEMINI

The two of you will never be bored working together. It will be a laugh a minute while you yak, labor on your tasks and talk on the phone to customers simultaneously. You both run so fast that a few collisions will occur. Gemini will make a witty remark, you'll chuckle and the two of you will be off and running again.

You both have many projects brewing. Constant motion is a must; without it you feel stifled. Stagnation is something you both try to avoid, even if it means getting into mischief. Both are known pranksters and like to have fun on the job, even at your own, or someone else's expense.

Gemini doesn't always finish his chores. Often you'll jump in and help him. You, too, can get lax, but generally, it's short-lived. Of the two, you are the most stable. Gemini is a vacillator but that doesn't faze you in the least, nor does it interfere with business. In fact, you are intrigued by him; mainly because you see so much of yourself in him. You are opposite signs in the zodiac, but your traits are similar; thus, you understand each other thoroughly.

The two of you are in the winner's circle. Both are adaptable and can make quick adjustments and changes. The versatility between the two of you is mind-boggling. Accomplishments are easy to attain. Activity seems to be the key word that describes this relationship.

Neither one of you can handle money frugally; both are extremely extravagant. However, if Gemini's conservative twin emerges, you'll be in tip-top shape. It's best to hire an accountant who can put you both on a budget. If you're just coworkers on a job, then finances won't be a problem.

CAPRICORN/GEMINI

Gemini exasperates you. She's inconsistent when you're consistent. You like order, she seems to like disorder. She wants to chit-chat, you prefer silence. You dislike change, she is changeable. Your attempt to stabilize Gemini appears fruitless; just as you think you've done the impossible, she reverts back to her old habits. And that's when you are almost ready to throw the towel in but your stubborn nature won't let you — not yet, that is.

You really get vexed when she doesn't stay put long enough for you to give her the proper instructions. But later, you forgive her because she heard and remembered every word you said. How she can dash about and tend to chores while you are talking is beyond your wildest imagination.

Somehow you have an inner sense that Gemini is not a permanent associate. You dislike not being able to fully trust or rely upon her. She comes in at all hours and, yet, you can't really complain (although you do), because she still manages to wind up all projects ahead of schedule.

Gemini doesn't seem to be interested in the same material goals that you are. You want to get to the top and don't mind working hard to get there, whereas Gemini starts out with the same goals, but along the way she changes. Just when you think you understand what she's all about, and how to handle her, your theories are blown away.

You admire Gemini's intellect and find her notions stimulating and excellent for the business. But if you mind taking chances (you do) and living from day to day in constant fear of what she'll do next, you should look for another partner.

AQUARIUS/GEMINI

Gemini's brilliant ideas for modernization have you dumbfounded; they sound like the theories you've bandied about for years but until now you didn't have anyone who would be gutsy enough to put them into practice. The time passes quickly while you two indulge in conversations that most people can't comprehend (both your IQs are high and you both talk fast). Both of you enjoy experimenting with new techniques that may speed up production. You don't count the cost; it's the notion of actually doing it that intrigues you both the most.

It doesn't disturb you that you are more tenacious than Gemini. He may be a bit flighty but you can understand that, after all, you also are moved by sudden and irrational whims. Most people think that you both are erratic and crazy for entering into enterprises that deal with products that are untried, ahead of the times and off-the-beaten track. But you are happy that Gemini has jumped on the merry-go-round with you.

You find it a welcome relief that Gemini doesn't waste precious time making lengthy explanations. He dislikes getting bogged down by detail just as much as you do. You like his lively mind; sluggish thinkers bore you. Gemini has just the right disposition — friendly and outgoing — that peps you up and makes you want to achieve your ambitions. His way with words has you mesmerized most of the time.

The two of you are a whiz together. It's a relationship that is full of surprises every time you turn a corner. As a team you work well together. If you are employed it should be for someone who is as progressive as the two of you.

PISCES/GEMINI

Half of the time you can't understand what Gemini is babbling about. She talks too fast for you. It's not your fault you make so many mistakes, it's hers. How can she expect you to listen to her and work and what about those instructions she blurts out on the run?

Gemini certainly knows how to hurt your feelings when she criticizes your errors. And when she shoves you to work faster, you just do everything all wrong and that leaves you so embarrassed. You can't help it if you're sensitive and she makes you cry in front of everyone. You'd think she would get the message that she's upset you. "But no, she's heartless and doesn't care whether I'm suffering or not," you wail through your tears.

With the passage of time you've learned that if you want to escape from a Gemini ordeal all you have to do is go into the world of fantasy where everything is peachy keen. In this type of existence, you don't hear the noise or what she's talking about. Your work gets done automatically. That may suit you fine if you are working just for the paycheck. However, if you're partners the entire business could end up in hot water. Your dreams could turn into nightmares that would make you worry even more than you already do.

Chapter Six

Cancer Compatibility In Business

If you were born between June 21 and July 22, your Sun is in the sign Cancer. However, you may also express Cancer traits if Cancer is dominant in your horoscope (refer to the Introduction, Page 1), and even if it isn't your Sun sign. If this is the case, you should read this chapter just as if your Sun sign is Cancer.

CANCER PROFILE
Getting Acquainted With The Cancer Personality

This woman is not easy to get to know. Once you understand what motivates her, it'll be a cinch to deal with her whether she's your partner, employer, employee, coworker, or client. When you first meet her she disguises her timidity with a cool and unapproachable appearance. But once you get to know her, she's friendly, and warm-hearted. Cancer, like the crab (her sign's animal symbol) retreats within so she can't get hurt.

There won't be much ruckus or excitement going on with her in the office. She's quiet, and tends to business seriously. This woman moves slowly, and speaks carefully, lest she say something that will cause offense. Her actions are more deliberate than fortuitous. If she has to rush to finish a job, she'll panic and get emotional because she's fearful of making a mistake.

Because Cancer gets bored easily, she needs a variety of tasks to do. Risky ventures frighten her. She shies away from new equipment and modern methods; it's the tried and true that appeals to her. She does her job the same way every day.

The Cancerian is unswervingly devoted to whomever she works with, employs, or deals with in business. She may remind you of a mother hen taking care of her chicks. When you treat her gently and understand her desire to be needed, you'll have a head start on attaining success with her.

IF YOU ARE A CANCER

Because you desire security you may ask, "What can I do to get ahead?" Success can be achieved faster if, when you deal with others, you adhere to the following advice:

When dealing with an employer don't be a shy mouse. Speak up, let the boss know that you have ideas of your own. If you hold back from expressing yourself because you are afraid of getting fired, having your views rejected or your employer yelling at you, then your fears are standing in the way of your promotion.

Prior to entering your superior's office, try to realize that you're not going to lose your job just because you gave him a suggestion. If the boss doesn't go along with your views, he's entitled to his opinion. At least by speaking to him you have shown an interest in your work and his company. That alone gives you a big fat plus mark in his book. Tell yourself that if he screams, it's nothing personal.

Perhaps he's just busy and uptight because he has a lot of unsettled problems on his mind. Let his words go in one ear and out the other, and you'll skip a tearful scene. Continue to work hard, let yourself be seen and heard (but smile more often), attend workshops and take classes, apply the knowledge gained — and you'll improve your chances of getting a better position.

When dealing with partners, employees and coworkers guard against feeling frustrated if circumstances are continually adverse. If an atmosphere is disharmonious it will affect you tremendously because you are extremely sensitive to your environment. Also, you have to avoid being too sympathetic, and spending most of your working hours with someone else's personal problems that are taken on as if they were your own.

Clinging to the past — and streamlining operations — could cause financial losses. You are stubborn and manage to retreat into a shell when circumstances are not to your liking, such as when modernization is proposed. Don't hide. Study the facts, see how others have benefited, rent or lease rather than buy and, then, make your decision about its value. Don't close your eyes, ears, and mind to something that may be extremely profitable.

You get upset and confused when others rush by, perform tasks hurriedly or speak so fast that you get lost or confused. Realize that others get nervous and feel unproductive if they slow down. Try to understand their character; after all, the traits that disturb you can be responsible for the company's success (and yours).

When dealing with clients your problem is that you move and speak too slowly. The impatient type of customer may go out the door by the time you either get around to waiting on him or understanding what he is inquiring about. But you'd rather lose a client than hasten your pace; money and a job aren't that important to you. If you can't comprehend what he's saying, don't ask him to repeat himself more than once. You feel what a person needs, wants and dislikes. So don't be afraid to follow your instincts (usually your gut feeling is 100 percent accurate), and chances are, you'll ring up a sale.

You do your best when working in an establishment that caters to the public and has a rapid turnover, such as a store or restaurant. In such an environment you meet all types of people. You respond to those who are kind and you are turned off by impolite people. Your fear of ridicule or embarrassment may hold you back from asserting yourself; so guard against it. Watch your emotions; don't take anyone's bad manners personally. Tell yourself that a person's behavior has nothing to do with anything you've done. Keeping this attitude is helpful to you and your pocketbook. You enjoy catering to others, so keep it up and success will be yours.

To go one step further, once you, as a Cancer know or can recognize the sign your partner, employer, employee, coworker, or client is, read that sign's chapter to know how best to deal with him as well as to understand his compatibility with you. If you wish to know what he thinks about you, read the Sun-Sign Compatibility section starting on Page 78. The remainder of this Cancer section deals with how others relate to you, what they can expect of you and how they should handle you. So let's go on an interview with your sign, okay?

AN INTERVIEW WITH A CANCER

A Cancer employer interviewing you: Your resumé will be carefully looked over. If he starts to get personal, don't be alarmed. It means that you've passed his test for ability and past job references. Now he wants to get his feeling or impression of what you are really like. He may lead you into a conversation innocently and proudly boasting, "Oh, these pictures here are of my family. Do you have any children?" Or, if your application stated single, "Are you interested in getting married and having children?" These are clues that you are talking to a man who has Cancer dominant in his horoscope.

Speak slowly so he can digest your words. Respond with warmth and sincerity (he can sense coldness and falseness). Having family ties puts you "in" with him. He may hire you right away, depending upon his moods — they vary from moment to moment. Once you are part of the company, you may become a permanent fixture.

If you're interviewing a Cancer applicant: She may get apprehensive and worry that you don't like her if you keep her waiting. She won't run away, though, it took all of the courage she could muster just to get to your office. Cancer will sit still with an immovable facial expression that tells you nothing. But inwardly her stomach is tied in knots because she's afraid you won't hire her. (She lacks confidence in her abilities.)

She's shy as the late Princess Diana (a Cancerian) but once you start interviewing her, she'll relax a little — because that lets her know that you are interested in her. She will answer all questions in a very businesslike fashion, but don't expect her to say much (she's afraid of goofing up). Cancer may inquire about the company's benefits because she wants to be well-provided for. She's security conscious, although not money hungry so she'll want a reasonably good salary. Don't ask her to start work right away because she has to adjust to the idea of it first.

Now that the interview is over, let's first go to work for a Cancerian and thus see how Cancer is going to fare as your employee, okay?

YOUR CANCER EMPLOYER
What Does Your Cancer Boss Expect of You?

If you were transferred from one department to another, regardless of the reason, Cancer will try to be helpful and will not make any demands, other than you do your job. He'll put himself in your shoes and feel that you're going through a trying period and need understanding.

Cancer expects you to work as hard as he does. He doesn't care if you are a slow learner; he's patient. This fellow wants you to be productive, honest, and dependable. He is strict about rules and regulations. Cancer expects you to walk the straight and narrow pathway, to his methods of operating a business. He's not bossy; usually he leaves the order-giving to others.

This man doesn't go for any goofing off on the job. He wants you to tend to your responsibilities and be as serious as he is. The office may have a somber tone and yet it may be cozy, homey, and warm. It's important for the Cancerian to be a success. He expects you to help make him one. Don't be surprised if he asks you to complete the tasks he leaves in midstream because he's not in the mood to finish them.

Cancer's strong need to express his paternal instincts might embrace taking you under his wing. He believes his fatherly advice is in your best interest. After he has nurtured you, and you have achieved the goals desired, Cancer glows like a proud parent, especially if you've been instrumental in making his business boom.

How To Handle Your Cancer Boss

Be neatly groomed. Cancer doesn't care whether you wear jeans or finery as long as you are clean. However, there are exceptions — it depends upon the nature of the business and the position you are in. If he's in a business that has an opulent front and caters to politicians, the society crowd or wealthy customers, he'll want you to look chic.

Cancer won't be disturbed if your working area is cluttered — usually his is! If you need to make room on his desk to lay down some samples of a new product, don't remove any family pictures. Leave them intact on his desk. Avoid ever criticizing a member of his household or even joking about a relative of his (even though he may do it). Don't you agree or join in. If you do, you'll be out of a job.

If you have family problems that take you temporarily away from the job, he's sympathetic. Generally he puts domestic needs before business. But if you make a habit of it, and can't solve your difficulties, then he may want to discuss it with you. Cancer wants to be needed; if he thinks he can help you, he'll glow. Once you work for this fellow you'll be aware of his protectiveness. Don't let his interference in your personal matters upset you; he means well and feels that he's a member of your household.

Cancer doesn't like to change employees. He likes to keep the same help. It's as if everyone is a part of his business family (he thinks of it secretly in this way). Because you are all part of his clique, he is going to see that everyone gets medical and financial benefits justly due them.

Now and then Cancer won't mind that you're late. But he really demands punctuality of his employees. This fellow may avoid mentioning it to you on a few occasions, but if it becomes a habit, he'll start to pout and give you a cold icy stare. That's the warning that something is wrong. If you haven't surmised that it's your tardiness that's causing this indifferent treatment then you'd better approach him about it. It'll come pouring out (he's held it in for a long time) so quickly that you may be flabbergasted that Cancer can talk that fast and excitedly.

If you make errors, Cancer may disregard them as being part of human nature to err. However, if it continues over a prolonged period of time, he will believe that something must be mentally disturbing you. If there is something bugging you, let him know about it. Cancer can lighten your load with a few sympathetic words. He's amiable and earnest about trying to help you. This appeals to his desire to be needed.

Just because he's taken you under his wing don't think he'll tolerate laziness. He's paying you for working and that's exactly what he expects out of you. If you don't measure up to par, either he'll let you go or he won't give you a raise. However, when he thinks you're deserving of a larger paycheck, it'll be a generous sum.

Cancer is sensitive but covers up with a cool exterior. Inwardly he's afraid he might fail, so outwardly he compensates by running a business sternly. He is tenacious and doesn't mind if it takes years for him to be in a lucrative position. If you can help him achieve his desires to be in top spot, he'll be forever grateful. Cancer will never forget how you made his way up the ladder easier and how you stood by him in his darkest moments. So pitch in and you'll not only be his friend for life, but may equally be in his employ for the same duration of time.

If you've got any bright ideas for modernization, appeal to his vivid imagination. Draw him a picture or visually create it with your words. Don't expect to get immediate results from him. He's got to digest and absorb the entire plan. Once it's been assimilated, he still may not rush into it. It's got to be discussed repeatedly. This man is really an old-fashioned type of boss; a real fuddy-duddy who dislikes getting into new areas mainly because he's so unsure of himself. He is barely secure with the regular operations of a business, so to try anything different taxes his assurance and makes him wonder if he can do it successfully.

If you want to get in good with your boss, sympathize with all of the work he has to do. Say, "I think it's fantastic how you can accomplish so much. I don't know how you can labor so hard and still be nice to all of us. Especially when you take a personal interest in our problems. No wonder you're tired at the end of the day." This praise is just what your Cancerian employer needs. It's important for him to feel that you care about him. He's readily and acutely affected by his environment, therefore, compliments make him happy and give him the affection he craves.

Cancer is known for his good memory. He never forgets what you said, or didn't say, or how you helped, or didn't help, his business. This man is aware of everything going on although you may think otherwise. Don't do anything you shouldn't even though you think he's not paying any attention to you. This man can get rubbed the wrong way and instead of telling you about it, he'll retreat into a shell and cry silently over his wounds — "How I had such faith in her and she let me down."

You now have to work on getting him out of the shell. It'll take a lot of coaxing to get him out. He may not speak with more than a grunt for "hello" and "good-bye" for a few days. Promise him all kinds of goodies like better job performance and kindlier relationships. If he's still cranky he can be moved with emotions. Make him feel sorry for you. Remember he bruises easily. Avoid criticism. Be gentle. The crab won't bite; instead he'll slowly crawl out of his shell and be elated that the two of you have settled your differences.

Cancer often appears weak and easily managed because he is quiet and modest. But don't try playing jokes on him. He doesn't like to be considered unintelligent or made to feel like a fool. So, leave the pranks at home. He responds to encouragement even though he's your employer. Occasionally Cancer may appear domineering, but it's a brash front. He actually wants someone to boss him; it makes him feel protected and cared for. If you take the reins, don't overdo it; just a light touch is all that is needed — he's still the one who's paying you a salary, remember? Treat him right and you'll be successful all the way around.

YOUR CANCER EMPLOYEE
What Can You Expect From Your Cancer Employee?
When you first hire your Cancer employee her uncertainty shows in the snail-like pace she maintains. Little by little Cancer picks up the pace as she becomes convinced that she's proceeding correctly. When she's sure that she knows her job thoroughly, then she feels she's merited a raise (this could be months later). However, she may not ask for it. If she gets it without asking, then she'll *really* work for you.

You've got a hard, sometimes slack, worker who shows no pretense. She's genuine, aboveboard, and trustworthy. You can depend upon Cancer because she doesn't swerve from her steady intent. This woman won't let you down. She may go out of her way to help you, especially if you've acted benignly and been lenient.

Cancer will try, to the best of her abilities, to do everything expected of her. She doesn't have her eye on your position because she can be content staying where she is as long as she gets her weekly salary. Cancer's not the type to be self-employed (unless she's got other signs that are more dominant than her Sun in Cancer), and go out on her own, unless she's inherited money or has an income she can rely upon. And even then she bides her time and must be certain that she's making the right move. This woman doesn't want to spend her cash reserve on anything that's unprofitable.

Cancer likes to spend time with her family, so don't expect her to work overtime, on weekends, holidays or to take projects home with her to labor over. Generally, her home and domestic ties come before a business. And yet, she's an earnest, dedicated and zealous employee who not only works for steady wages, but is devoted to you if you treat her humanely.

How To Handle Your Cancer Employee
Cancer is obedient and will try her best to please you. However, don't let her complaisance goad you into rushing her. She is one woman who doesn't bear up well under pressures and deadlines. When a time limit is set, she makes mistakes, which lead to a few trickling tears running down her face. If you want the job to be performed accurately, then don't prod her.

Cancer doesn't tell you how to run your business. Don't expect any ideas from her. It's not that she doesn't entertain them, it's just that she isn't confident that you'd listen or that they are really that great. So, if you are the type of boss who is open to suggestion, be sure to ask her if she's ever thought of ways you could improve your business. The very fact that you are taking your valuable time to ask for her opinions and notions raises her ego, makes her feel important, needed, and liked. Even if she doesn't have any thoughts toward your company's betterment, you've done her a world of good by asking — and in turn you've got yourself an employee for life who will try even harder to be more efficient.

Cancer is liable to change as quickly as you can flick the ash of a cigarette. However, don't let that worry you. She isn't about to let her moodiness make her quit a job or completely abandon a project. Routine does bore her and she is known to start tasks and leave them unfinished while working on another; eventually, she returns to the original chore and perfects it. This procedure to break up the monotony does her, and ultimately the business, a world of good — it's comparable to getting a breath of fresh air when you've been shut up indoors all day. So, unless there's an emergency brewing, leave her to her methods and you'll have a contented employee.

If Cancer's home life is peaceful, she is pleasant and friendly; otherwise, this woman may call in sick because she wants to take time off from work to weep. However, if she thinks you'll dock her paycheck, she'll show up with a long face and lip protruding. When she sulks that's a sign that something is wrong. If you leave her alone, you can depend upon her to do her duties. She'll work persistently, regardless of what's going on inside of her because she delights in depositing money in the bank on payday. However, rather than having her mope around, you may send her home. But then, after a while, you'll begin to realize that his could be a habit of hers and you'll tire of pampering her like a baby. The best solution to your problem is to get her to open up and explain what's bugging her. Once Cancer feels that she has your empathy, she finds her difficulties are more bearable.

You won't discover Cancer goofing off, telling jokes or being nonproductive. She tends to business regardless of how dissatisfied she is with her lot in life. If you get too bossy, Cancer may take it to heart and think you don't approve of her work. She is extremely touchy and even gets her sensitive feelings hurt if your tone of voice hits her the wrong way. If you want her to do a fantastic job, use your authority in a kindly manner and say, "I know I can rely on you to put your all into this project and come up with something stupendous." With those words, you've torn away self-doubts and inspired her to do her utmost to live up to your expectations.

Cancer can't wait until it's time for her coffee break because it lets her unwind and at the same time snack on something tasty. Lunch is never missed; it's a necessity. She gets cranky if she skips a meal. There is nothing more important to a Cancerian than food. She must be nourished regardless of how depressed or elated she is. If you want to have her skip lunch or a coffee break because she'll be tied up with you on some enormous project that needs to get out immediately, order some food in or let her nibble out of her lunch bag. By the way, if you give an office party, make sure there are plenty of victuals and your Cancerian employee will think you're tops.

Cancer is not interested in running the company so you won't have to feel threatened by this. She's not against a promotion; however, it's the money that goes with the position that intrigues her. Cancer is not title-happy. Her job is part of her security; however, it's her earnings that she manages to save that are her real future nest egg — security.

This woman will hang on to the job forever if the pay is right and the two of you get along without any bad emotional scenes. Cancer is patient and is not in a hurry to advance to a higher position. However, she does expect to be compensated fairly with a wage increase every now and then, especially when she believes it's merited. If she doesn't have a salary hike, she'll quit. That will take some courage on her part because she's not a quitter. So give her those raises she deserves. You'll be amply rewarded by a loyal and devoted employee who will try her best to make your business successful.

YOUR CANCER COWORKER
What Can You Expect From Your Cancer Coworker?

There's just a few basic facts to keep in mind when working with this fellow: he's moody, unhurried, and isn't about to vie with you. Cancer doesn't strive for superiority because he feels inferior, especially if you are a whiz on the job. So don't expect him to try to equal your output. Cancer has to slowly build up his confidence; as each plateau is reached he becomes more sure of himself. This fellow knows that the day will come when he's in a top position. Don't be surprised if he winds up being another John D. or Nelson Rockefeller (both Cancerians).

This man is extremely curious but his shyness, and fear of being given a cold shoulder, holds him back from asking personal questions. Once he feels relaxed with you, he may engage in some friendly chitchat. However, most of the time he tends to his duties because he's afraid to risk losing his job.

Cancer won't tell you how to do your work or interfere with your schedule. However, be prepared for him to observe your every movement — he watches you out of the corner of his eye. If he believes you've got real know-how and are headed quickly to the top, he'll mimic your actions. Once he's perfected them he's pleased with himself and hopes that the boss is too.

This fellow is mild of temper although if he's forced into a corner, he'll speak up. If he thinks he's right, there's no reasoning with him; it's his emotions you're talking to, not his mind. Cancer enjoys being useful; therefore, if he believes he can help you achieve your goals, he'll do his best to make your dreams come true.

How To Handle Your Cancer Coworker

Cancer is mediumistic and, on or off the job, he's continually receiving sense impressions. Once he feels that you are an okay person in his books, he'll have the courage to divulge those hunches he receives. They may be about you or someone close to you. Don't hurt his feelings and good intentions of wanting to help you by balking or making fun of him.

If you are skeptical of his premonitions, or a nonbeliever in general, humor him and you'll avoid seeing a distressed Cancerian crawl into a shell of silence. When this occurs he'll pout and nod when spoken to — and that's about it! If in the future he receives another psychic flash concerning you, he'll never tell you. Not even after you admitted his instincts were accurate. According to his outlook, you put him through a mental anguish he doesn't wish to repeat, therefore he's not about to chance another hurt.

Cancer's moods vary so much that you may have difficulty trying to keep up with them. Often he may chip in toward buying someone a gift; it may be a lavish donation. At other times, he may not want to part with a dime. Don't try to convince him that he should contribute to the supervisor's retirement present. He may feel embarrassed if you make an issue of it. This fellow will stick to his guns. However, if he does put a buck in, don't try to con him into giving more. You should feel lucky you got him to part with his dough in the first place.

Cancer enjoys food more than anything else, and will gladly spend what he has on it. If you have a clique in the office that goes out to Dutch-treat lunch once a week, or month, invite Cancer to join you. This fellow is shy and fears rejection; therefore he doesn't approach anyone to ask, "Can I tag along?" Cancer enjoys being part of a group — it gives him the feeling that it's a family; something dear to his heart. Expect a no answer at first because Cancer believes that you don't really want him to come with you. He thinks you are just being polite. Coax him into going by telling him that he's needed to make up an even number — six instead of five; or any other excuse you can think of should suffice. He just wants to hear that you really want him.

This man isn't nosy but he loves to gossip about trivialities that may range from cleaning his house to planting a garden. You may be annoyed wasting your time in conversations of little importance. However, if you turn a deaf ear toward him, he'll think you aren't interested in him. To keep the peace you can tell him that you'd rather not talk while working because you don't want to get fired. Add in that you need the security of steady employment — that should do it! Cancer's afraid of missing a paycheck — so you've hit home with that one!

Cancer absorbs his environment like a sponge. His system is so sensitive that he picks up the feelings and thoughts of everyone present. When he's with jovial people he blossoms like an early spring flower. When he's with gloomy people, he droops like a wilted flower. He does his best work when there's laughter ringing in the air. That's when Cancer will bend over backward to help you out if you're behind. Therefore try to keep happy vibrations within the confines of your office, and not only will you be happy and more productive but so will everyone else. And that is what pleases the boss, and helps you get that promotion you want.

This fellow likes to hang on to his office possessions. Never take anything off of his desk without permission. If you want to use his stapler, ask him and he'll graciously offer it (he likes to be needed, remember?). After you've used it, put it back in the same place it was when you removed it. Don't change chairs with Cancer; if you do, you'll see a cranky crab. Once he is comfortable and feels homey in something, he feels it belongs to him. Furthermore, due to his strong sensitivity, he will tune in to your vibrations the moment a part of his body touches that chair. This could disturb him and interfere with his work. It also makes him send out negative thoughts in your direction. And that you don't need, especially if you want to get a raise and advance to a better job.

YOUR CANCER CLIENT
What Can You Expect From Your Cancer Client?

This man may waddle like a duck, especially if he's heavy-set. He notices everything as he passes by each counter. Occasionally, he'll stop, pick up an object, fondle it and look for a price. Cancer is known as "the feeler of the zodiac." He needs to touch something or someone; it's as if he's making sure that it, or the individual, is tangible. This stems from his insecurity complex.

If the item isn't too expensive, he may consider purchasing it. However, don't expect this fellow to buy it the first time he looks at it. Cancer is a comparison shopper, so, if you've got the cheapest price in town, he'll be back. He may engage you in conversation if he's in his outgoing mood. If Cancer feels sorry for you because the store is empty and you've told him that business is slow (after he's asked you, of course), he might buy an inexpensive object to help you out.

If you're a waitress in a restaurant, you can expect Cancer to be as slow as molasses when reading the menu. He has difficulty deciding what to order. Once you start to serve him, watch him eat: he lingers over each piece of food and bite that is swallowed. It's as if he really relishes every morsel eaten. If you bring him the next course too soon, he'll tell you to keep it warm in the kitchen until he's finished the victuals on his plate. (I once had dinner with a Cancerian who took one hour to eat a shrimp cocktail.) Because his sign rules the stomach, he must take his time eating so his food will digest properly.

How To Handle Your Cancer Client

Don't expect to make an immediate sale on any product, system, or machine that has recently been developed. This man isn't about to chance anything novel. He wants a sure thing that will reap in the profits; something he's used to. These traits, plus his seriousness and warmth, are keys to let you know that you're dealing with a Cancerian.

Just how do you win Cancer over to your side? First take an interest in him personally. Ask him if he's married and has a family. Talk to him about his children and watch him beam. If you have a member of your household that's giving you a problem, get Cancer to lend his sympathetic ear. He loves to be needed and may help you solve your dilemma.

Second, satisfy his strong urge toward self-indulgence. Take him to a restaurant that is known for its cuisine. He's gullible in this type of atmosphere. Appeal to his desire for security. Tell him how much money he can make from your products. If they have been around for a while, and have been proven by tests to be useful, ninety-nine percent of the time, divulge this bit of news to him.

Leave the jokes at home and be serious. Don't push. If you made the mistake of rushing him, his downcast eyes, protruding lips and silence means that you had better clam up and change the subject because you've gone too far, too fast. Start discussing wines, gourmet food, gardening and anything pertaining to the home. Ask him if he's got any hobbies. Continue to chitchat on an informal and friendly level. Don't discuss business anymore; leave it for another day — Cancer needs time to let what you've already said sink in.

Wait for about a month and call him on the telephone. Don't mention your merchandise. Tell him that you've been thinking about him and was wondering how he's been. It's important to establish a friendship basis with this man and then you can proceed from there to sell him your goods. (Cancer is a very humble person who yearns to be needed by others and to know that someone cares about him.)

Let a little time pass, a week or so, and ask him if you can drop by his office, or better yet — take him out to lunch again. Get the usual domestic conversation out of the way and then relate all the latest data you've collected on your wares. Because you are now friends, he's going to be more open-minded than before. Show him letters from satisfied customers. At the rate you're now going, it won't be long until he's joined the ranks of your other clients. When you negotiate or sell to a Cancer, patience is needed and it can pay off substantially.

The Cancer gait is immediately recognizable as he totters through the door. Let him look around without disturbing him. After a few minutes engage him in conversation. If he's got his eye on an antique salt and pepper shaker set, pick them up and let him hold them. You might say, "Oh, aren't these charming? And so well made. Isn't it a shame they don't make things this well anymore?" You have probably hooked him with those words. Cancer is quick to buy old goods that can't be found elsewhere. He knows what is valuable, so do you — using the right approach on him helps you to become that much closer to success.

YOUR CANCER PARTNER
What Can You Expect From Your Cancer Partner?
You've got an honorable associate who is receptive to your kindness and needs. She has faith in you; if she didn't, she would never have gone into partnership with you. Once she's found her niche, she doesn't stray — she likes to stay put. Often her slow and deliberate actions are mistaken for laziness. It's her perseverance that makes her successful, therefore, this should rub off on you too!

How To Handle Your Cancer Partner
When you get a money-making idea, explain it slowly to Cancer so she can grasp every word you're saying. Give her time to think about it. She needs to absorb, assimilate and feel something before she can make a decision. This woman's

interested in cashing in on anything that's lucrative. Show her all the pros of why a particular machine will speed up production, it's savings for the corporation and what the company stands to gain financially from it.

Just because the profits are rolling in, Cancer does not wish to expand overnight. She prefers taking the earnings and investing them in solid assets (real estate, bonds, treasury notes). Once she sees a continual flow of money coming in, then she will consider an expansion program. If the two of you don't see eye-to-eye, it will be difficult to achieve your goals. If you want to get along with this woman, you've got to listen to reason, be adaptable and practical. Once Cancer has decided upon a course of action, she seldom swerves. If you're a Taurus, Leo, Scorpio or Aquarius then you are just as stubborn as she is; thus a stalemate is likely to occur. And that's not the way to run a business successfully, is it?

Cancer tends to be overly imaginative so be prepared for occasions when she will feel you've slighted her. You may believe that you are innocent of any such action. Once you notice that her face is like a marble statue when speaking to you, or that she's avoiding looking in your direction when you are talking to her, that's the give-away that you've done or said something that has offended her.

Start questioning her and if she was wrong you are going to have a difficult time convincing her that you're guiltless. However, if she was right, be big enough to admit your fault and apologize. Don't expect her to start smiling right away; it takes her a while to recover from a wound. Cancer is too sensitive to the words and actions of others. She can't seem to help it that she's a bundle of emotions ready to burst at the seams at any given opportunity. You have to treat her with kid gloves, be understanding of her nature and, in the long run, it will pay off. This woman is a staunch partner who will go to bat for you and try her best to please you.

This woman is secretive so you may not know what's going on inside her mind. She covers up her suspicions and feelings. Cancer does not think of you as a rival but more as someone she looks up to. If she suspects you only went into business because you needed her money until you made enough to buy her out, you'll really have some explaining to do. If it's true then expect your partner to go about with a sullen face, give you the silent treatment and never again trust you with anything. If this occurs you're better off dissolving the corporation.

Cancer wears her heart on her sleeve, although she hides it with her aloofness. Her tears flow, silently, in front of you, but outwardly when alone. If you are aware that she's in a bad frame of mind because she just doesn't seem up to par, ask her, "What's wrong?" Most likely she'll tell you about her personal problems because you were concerned enough to inquire. Cancer takes great delight in relating her upsets because she wants sympathy. If you cater to her whims, she'll never forget it. But take notice: just as "Rome wasn't built in a day," neither will Cancer bounce back that fast. She is changeable and follows her gut feelings. Give her a chance, and be patient — success can be just around the corner.

Sun-Sign Compatibility

This section deals with each sign of the zodiac in relation to a Cancer Sun sign. Knowing how your sign blends with a Cancerian, you go one step beyond understanding his personality and one step closer to knowing how to handle him in any business situation. Greater insight is invaluable because it not only helps a business prosper, it encourages peace of mind on and off the job.

The following Sun-Sign compatibility summaries, with the exception of Cancer/Cancer, *are from the point of view of the person dealing with Cancer. Note:* For the Cancerian's point of view, see the Sun-Sign chapter of the person Cancer is dealing with, i.e., Scorpio — refer to the Scorpio chapter explaining how Cancer thinks about Scorpio.

ARIES/CANCER

When you give an order you expect the Cancerian to respond immediately. However, with him, nothing gets done very fast. His slow-moving ways infuriate you and you blurt out things that only make matters worse, especially when Cancer runs out of the room crying. That annoys you all the more because you don't like to waste time catering to his childish emotions, moods, or fears.

You disagree on both transactions and how to handle the business. The Cancerian's outdated methods oppose your updated methods of operating. You dislike Cancer holding you back from expanding, spending money or moving ahead. Furthermore, his personal problems don't interest you. And you can't endure his whining about them anymore.

Cancer's indecisiveness bugs you. Your impatience shows every time there's a rush job. Your refusal to sympathize with him deepens the gap between the two of you. He is just too sensitive for you. If you're the boss you'll either fire him or push him to the brink of quitting. In business you hinder one another and make it difficult to achieve success. Therefore you are better off if you are not associated with one another.

TAURUS/CANCER

This woman's changeability baffles you, but don't let it interfere with her job performance. In fact, you admire the steady, diligent pace Cancer maintains. You are glad that you can rely upon her. She may lean on you but you don't mind giving her your support when she needs it.

You appreciate Cancer being protective of you on the job, especially when she doesn't let the boss know that you are the one, not she, who is responsible for holding up production. She shows her loyalty when she defends you against others.

Cancer is one associate who has the same conservative outlook you do. She shares your interest in setting money aside for business investments rather than spending it on high salaries for the two of you. With this partner you can make plans to gradually expand. She's not in any more of a hurry than you. In fact, like you, she believes in the slow but sure approach. Cancer agrees on your decisions, the bills are paid promptly and unnecessary debts are not attracted. The two of you work extremely well together.

GEMINI/CANCER

You can't stand losing precious time answering Cancer's questions; especially since he wants you to repeat everything over and over again just so he can understand it. His lack of intellect disturbs you. The first time you rattle off instructions should be enough for anyone to catch on. This fellow holds you back from accomplishing your tasks. If he keeps it up, you may give them to him to finish.

Cancer puts a damper on the office gaiety. He's too sullen to be around. Why can't he sparkle and laugh or just tell a few jokes? His quietness makes your nerves jump.

You tire of babying Cancer every time you say something that causes offense. He's just too thin-skinned for your money. If you have to stop and think about every sentence before you speak, you'll go crazy. He just doesn't have a good sense of humor.

Often you can see why he's penny-pinching, but you are annoyed with his cutting down the expense account allowance. He is so fearful of taking a risk that he holds you back from making a fortune with your newfangled ideas. Cancer's just not modern enough for you. The main problem with this relationship is that you are a *thinker* and Cancer is a *feeler;* these opposite tendencies just don't jell properly for business success.

CANCER/CANCER

Often you are compared to being like two peas in a pod. However, you'll notice some — not many — differences. Both of you are capricious — you never know when the urge will strike you to quit working on a job halfway through it. When you do, lo and behold, there's Cancer stopping her project and finishing yours.

Material gains are important to the two of you. Conservative trends are indicated. Both of you are sensible and security conscious. Practicality is used in all business transactions. The bills are paid on time. There's money in the bank for outside investments and toward an eventual expansion program. Both have seen to it that there are adequate benefits and insurance plans for your employees. You treat your help like they are members of your household.

Both of you like to eat; lunch may be a delightful feast. You may bring in homemade baked cookies and the other Cancerian may give you a taste of the family-recipe apple pie. The two of you are courteous to one another. You'll treat each other fair and square in business as partners, on the job as coworkers and in a boss-employee relationship.

Both of you tend to look into something before leaping in. You play everything on the safe side. The two of you are able to soothe each other when upset and encourage one another when a lack of confidence sets in. You'll root for each other, too, which makes working together a pleasant experience.

80

LEO/CANCER

You're a firm believer that success comes from large-scale operations. Cancer is too tight with the budget and doesn't allow for big, quick expansion. He holds you back from attaining your dream of running an empire. Money disagreements are a daily occurrence. Cancer just doesn't think big enough for you; he's afraid to go after enormous wealth. And, regardless of how much you talk to him, he clings to his beliefs. You are just as stubborn and stick to yours. So, neither one of you are going anywhere fast and that causes your temper to fly. Usually you wind up hurting his feelings.

You are thankful that Cancer is loyal and sticks by you even when you make a bad investment, decision, or can't pay him on time because of other indebtedness that has to be taken care of first. He's given you some helpful advice that probably you should have heeded.

When Cancer tells you that you are an inspiration to him, your ego swells and you think, "Maybe he's not so bad after all. He's slower than my other employees, but he manages to get the work done. I guess I should keep him on the job."

But this relationship is similar to mixing oil and water together; you're stable, Cancer's changeable; you're extravagant, Cancer's a tightwad. You are in a hurry to get to the top whereas Cancer doesn't want to rush. He waits too long for deals to culminate (in your estimation) and you go leaping in.

You two could make a go of it if you tried to compromise; however, both of you are too unyielding to give in. As partners it tends to be a no-go association because your differences are too great — you'd feel held back and Cancer would be in a constant emotional upheaval.

VIRGO/CANCER

Your desire for security matches Cancer's. It's a relief to have a partner who is so practical and who can keep you out of the red. You don't have to argue to keep her conservative. She manages to save on just about everything — just like you do, when you use the backs of old envelopes for scratch paper.

It doesn't disturb you that your coworker is crabby; you have your bad days too. Cancer doesn't seem to mind, but you have noticed there are bounds you can't overstep. If you do, her facial expression is a giveaway — as cold as a day in January. Underneath her mask of indifference is a kind, warm, and caring person who brings you mixed vegetable juices when you don't have time to go out to lunch.

You are glad that Cancer's so stable, it's just what you need in an employee. She never steps out of line. You are happy to have someone who leaves you alone to tend to your chores. However, when she's in doubt about something, you are elated that she wants you to give a lengthy detailed explanation.

Cancer labors arduously. However, she's not a workaholic like you are. If she was you'd be a lot happier. But you really can't complain because she is competent — and tries her best to be thorough. When her work is error-free, you're pleased, although you may not show it.

LIBRA/CANCER

Clutter you can do without; however, it seems Cancer can't. You are neat and like everything arranged so it looks pretty. You'll spend money on an elegant office and can't understand why Cancer can't see that it pays off to have a front. His furnishings look like they might have been his grandfather's, they seem so worn. However, you won't say anything because it might hurt his feelings.

Besides Cancer is so nice to be working with. He's one coworker who is courteous. You are so glad that he's slow, that way the boss won't say anything about *your* leisurely pace. When he switches from one job to another, you're amazed he finally manages to finish them all.

Cancer's ups and downs parallel yours. However, his are whimsical while yours result from your seeking balance. You're both indecisive. Cancer uses emotion, not reason, when making a decision. You use logic, weigh the pros and cons and seldom err. Because Cancer tends to hold things within, your discussions are limited. You're not a mind reader even though Cancer can sense psychically what you are thinking. This may prove frustrating to you in the long run because communication is very important to you. You like a fair exchange of ideas bandied about, even though you admit they may be farfetched at times.

SCORPIO/CANCER

Cancer always keeps busy but somehow she manages to lag behind. You guess it's because she's not as fast as you are. But you admire her, she is persistent and is determined to finish something even after she's left it hanging in midair a few days ago.

As a partner she is as dedicated as you are and does turn out to be one hundred percent in your corner at all times. You are distrustful of most people; however, Cancer has won your confidence from every angle of the business. Although she's not as gutsy as you when it comes to taking a risk on a new machine, you do think highly of her opinions.

Your Cancer coworker doesn't try to outdo you. Her noncompetitiveness makes it easier for you to shine in the supervisor's eyes. Cancer is as secretive as you and minds her own business, which raises her value even higher in your estimation. Once you've accomplished your goals, you wouldn't mind having Cancer work directly beneath you.

The two of you are a very compatible team. You can rely upon each other; something you both need to know. She doesn't make you angry; thus, less tension is caused when in her company. She dislikes the deadlines you thrive on and can't stand the pressure you dish out, but nevertheless these differences don't surface that much. When they do, they are not that noticeable by either party.

Cancer's lack of confidence is handled by your domination. She enjoys letting you be the boss and making all of the decisions. What more can you ask for? And she — for that matter?

82

SAGITTARIUS/CANCER

Your ultraprogressive ideas to plan far ahead in the future meet with Cancer's disapproval. He lives for the moment and can't see beyond his nose. This infuriates you and when you tell him how old-fashioned he is and that he'll never be a success, he suffers silently. His narrow-mindedness is too much for you to handle. You absolutely refuse to put up with it and his whining. You tire of catering to this childish man who should learn that he shouldn't take his emotions to work with him. And you continually remind him of this.

This is one relationship that generally is a disaster right from the start. You are an extrovert. Cancer is an introvert. You are a squanderer, he's a scrooge. You are a prankster and are a good sport if others play jokes on you. Cancer is the opposite. You make Cancer's eyes well with tears every time you unintentionally open your big mouth.

Your partnership doesn't have a chance of lasting very long. The moment Cancer opposes your modernization plans, you are likely to dump him and go out on your own. The two of you just don't see eye to eye.

CAPRICORN/CANCER

Unlike your Cancer partner, you keep abreast of new developments in your field. New techniques are applied to the business when you deem necessary; Cancer lets you have complete control. In the beginning she balks, but once she realizes that you are not going to rush into them, she relaxes. Your step-by-step procedure to modernize operations is easy for Cancer to follow, especially when you explain the details in a logical manner. When you are ready to make the final and big change-over, you are pleased that Cancer is excited as a child with a new toy.

Your Cancer employee may not be a slave to the job the way you are but you can count on her to be there when you need her. Her conscientiousness makes up for her lack of drive. There are very few people whom you can trust; Cancer is one of them. She's loyal and you know that she'll continue to work for you long after others have come and gone.

The two of you are opposite signs in the zodiac and yet somehow manage to complement one another. You are a user, Cancer's a helper. You're unemotional, she's emotional. You can stick to a schedule, Cancer has to break away from it. However, you can con her (with ease) into returning to the treadmill again. Both have a cool countenance. You are tactful, diplomatic and have a knack of handling her so her feelings don't get hurt.

Security is a must with the both of you. However, you are more driven toward gain and profit than Cancer. But she won't hinder your ambition to be rich and successful.

AQUARIUS/CANCER

Cancer is such a slowpoke that you're always giving him a helpful hand. Your work is done in half the time he does his. He's continually holding you up, making you late with production. Why he will perfect a job just to get a pay check is beyond you. Also, you can't understand why he sulks over your abruptness. You can't waste your valuable time pampering him.

As a partner you are thankful that Cancer pays attention to the details you are continually missing. You have an open mind to suggestion, search for new techniques and are gung-ho about experimentation. Cancer and you clash; he's afraid to reach up and grab a star; you're not. You are exasperated with Cancer's fuddy-duddy views and actions.

Money gives you the independence and freedom to do whatever you choose. But Cancer hangs on too tight to every dime. The two of you disagree about where the profits should go; he wants them in tangibles, whereas you want to donate them to a crusade to help the Indians. You can't understand why Cancer wants to have money if it's not to spend on humanitarian endeavors. In business you are a bad combination; Cancer is behind the times, clinging to the past; you are ahead of the times, paving the way to the future. There's no compromise — you're obstinate, Cancer is tenacious of his opinions.

PISCES/CANCER

You get good vibes from your Cancer coworker. She doesn't upset your sensitive system by saying anything offensive. Her quiet makes it easy for you to concentrate on your work. When there's a lot of noise your mind wanders. However, if the project absorbs your imagination you fare well.

Cancer is so wonderful, giving aid and sympathy (just like you do) when you long for it. It's easy for you to dismiss your worries after talking to Cancer. Her knowledge of how you should handle your finances for your retirement years lifts your spirits.

Since Cancer has been in your employ, your frustrations and conflicts have lessened. You don't find yourself at loose ends like you did with your former employee. You are pleased with her job performance as well as her kindly manner. And you are delighted that she wholeheartedly approves of your plans. Her admiration makes you try harder to bring them to realization.

You are fascinated by your partner's ESP. You, too, are psychic but only with other people, not yourself. Cancer's predictions came true and you're glad she was against investing the company's money in that oil stock that turned out to be a fraud.

Cancer brings out your flair for the dramatic and inspires you to promote everything on a grandiose scale — the ballyhoo you love — and that can bring the two of you affluence.

Chapter Seven

Leo Compatibility In Business

If you were born between July 23 and August 22, your Sun is in the sign Leo. However, you may also express Leo traits if Leo is dominant in your horoscope (refer to the Introduction, Page 1) even if it is not your Sun sign. If this is the case, you should read this chapter just as if your Sun sign is Leo.

LEO PROFILE
Getting Acquainted with the Leo Personality

The Leo man is easy to get to know if he's approached properly. Once you understand what motivates him, it'll be a cinch to deal with him whether he's your partner, employer, employee, coworker, or client. He's fearless in his pursuit of power. Like the Sun (center of our solar system), he is ruled by, he's got to be the center of attention. This man's a brightly burning Fire sign who shines in everything he does. And like the Sun, he can't help but be noticed. He lights up a room when he walks in with dignity.

Leo has enough vitality for several people. He has high goals and his strong constitution and determination give him the strength to achieve them. Often he overreaches his mark. He's daring and takes risks that others dread. This man is a dynamic leader who isn't afraid of anything. All you have to do is look at him, and you'll get the message.

His non-stop schedule spurs him to venture into realms that can make him wealthy and powerful. He's an entrepreneur who is into half a dozen projects and he's usually the president of many corporations. He is demanding to those who labor under his dominion. He lives for deadline pressures.

Like the Sun, Leo is self-sufficient. He's generous and loyal to those who serve him well, but his pompous, overbearing manner are difficult for many to handle. When this side of his nature shows he may lose partners, employees, or clients. But with all his faults, and his good points, he's forever seeking to find his "place in the Sun." Help him and you'll go to the top too.

IF YOU ARE A LEO

Because you thirst for glory and affluence you will wonder to yourself, "How can I achieve my aims quickly?" Success can be attained faster if, when you deal with others, you adhere to the following advice.

When dealing with your employer you should guard against appearing superior. You strive to rule everyone because you feel equipped to handle everything. Sometimes you forget that you are talking to the man who pays your salary. If you do have ideas for improvement, suggest them kindly — not in a way that deflates your boss. In other words, say, "What do you think of _____ idea?" Instead of, "Your method isn't right. You should do _____."

If your employer follows your advice, you've got to watch the way you brag about it. You can take the credit for it by mentioning it briefly. However, this may be difficult for you to do, because your desire to be important may make you disparage your boss and aggrandize yourself. Your ego could cost you your job if you're not careful.

If you haven't received the raise or promotion you think you deserve, mention it to your boss. Don't approach him angrily. Be calm, assured, concerned — *ask* him why your raise hasn't come through. If it's due to your job performance or personality, correct it. If it's due to lack of experience on the job, be patient and work hard to prove you're worthy of an advancement.

When dealing with partners, employees and coworkers, be on guard against lording it over them. Your domineering attitude makes them resent you. No one, including you, wants to be ruled by a tyrant. Your desire to lead makes you behave in this manner, but it attracts the enmity of those around you. You can still be authoritative without creating hostility. Be kind but firm and say, "Would you please do _____ for me?" The response you will receive from this approach will make your ego blow up twice as high as when you dictate.

Your competitiveness may cause others to feel inferior and rancorous toward you. When you act like you are better than they are, you attack their ego and deprive them of their desire to gain esteem. So, compete without being boastful.

Give compliments to others when they merit them and, in return, you'll get the praises you crave. Have faith in those you deal with. Trust them to make sound decisions and realize that you aren't the only one who knows what to do. When you believe in others — and you tell them so, they will go out of their way to live up to your expectations. And, this may be instrumental in helping you realize your goals that much quicker.

When dealing with clients don't be too forceful pushing your wares. Give others time to make a decision; not everyone is as impulsive as you. Also, you need to realize that your preconceived opinions about what your customers need and want to buy, are not *always* accurate. Your main problem is that you can't take anyone turning you down. If you are not careful, your egotism may be your ruin.

If you don't want to face rejection, give your indecisive client some samples and brochures to look over in his spare time. If you want to avoid calling him, and possibly being embarrassed by a no answer, say, "Call me if you are interested." The problem with this is that he may forget all about your product. The more attention you give it, and him, the better your chance to sell your item.

Try this — tell your prospective customer, "I'll call you in a week to see if you have any questions about it." This approach does not demand a yes or no answer (although he may give you one,, and it keeps you in contact with him. It makes him feel you are being attentive. Thus you can save your ego from being damaged and possibly ring up a sale.

To go one step further, once you know the sign of your partner, employer, employee, coworker, or client, read that sign's chapter to know how best to deal with him as well as to understand his compatibility with you. If you wish to know what he thinks about you, read the Sun-Sign Compatibility section starting on Page 95. The remainder of this section deals with how others relate to you, what they can expect of you and how they should handle you. So let's go on an interview with your sign, okay?

AN INTERVIEW WITH A LEO

A Leo employer interviewing you: Your resumé will be briefly scanned (the overall picture is all she needs). This woman looks for high academic credentials and is interested in your former positions, why you left and whether these are prestige companies. Leo uses a direct approach. Be honest. If you're not she'll fire you when she discovers the truth.

This employer wants to know (although she won't ask you) how you are going to benefit her. If she gets an inkling that you're the type who will learn the business, take her contacts and open your own establishment — she won't hire you. Also, you will not be considered if she thinks you are going to outdo her.

In her smug manner she may order you to report to a supervisor and start to work immediately. It's her way of testing you to see if you are going to be easy or difficult to handle. If your excuse is sound and logical as to why you can't begin at that very moment, it'll be accepted.

If you're interviewing a Leo applicant: He is punctual and wants to be interviewed as scheduled. If you dilly-dally too long, he'll leave. If you get a chance to talk to this man, you'll discover he's friendly and has a good command of words. He may sound almost rehearsed. He looks good, although he may be stiffly courteous.

Leo will try to impress you with his know-how. You'll notice his high opinion of himself the moment he starts boasting about his past performances. He is frank and delights in telling you how hard he works and how much he enjoys putting in long hours.

This man may boast that he can improve your business. Don't be surprised if he gives you some pointers right then and there. Not only do his ideas command attention — so does his very presence. Hire him right away or another corporation will.

Now that the interview is over, first let's go to work for a Leo, and then see how Leo is going to fare as your employee, okay?

YOUR LEO EMPLOYER

What Does Your Leo Boss Expect of You?

If you were transferred from one department to another because you had difficulty with a former boss, Leo will be constantly on guard to see if you are going to cause her any difficulties. However, as far as your job performance goes, this woman will expect you to toe the mark and turn out excellent work.

Your loyalty is fifty percent of the job. Leo wants you to have abiding faith in her. Never criticize her or the corporation. If she hears about it, you'll be fired. She expects you to be proud that you are working for her company; she wants you to be as devoted to it as she is.

This woman expects you to keep your desk neat and tidy. Most likely the office is a showplace, and she wants to keep it that way. If you don't, she'll embarrass you in front of everyone by putting you down for being a slob.

Leo's wrath will show if you get a bright idea for an up-and-coming project and then, without her permission, initiate it on your own. She expects you to tell her about it so she can add her own views. Expect your plans to be altered when you tell her about your notion. And don't be shocked if she takes credit for the entire undertaking!

This woman expects you to get a job done quickly. If you are lax, she'll goad you into picking up speed. Leo wants you to welcome her novel ideas with praise and enthusiasm. If you do, a raise might just be forthcoming.

How To Handle Your Leo Boss

Leo demands that you conduct yourself in an orderly fashion at all times. She forbids you to gossip, tell jokes, sit with your legs propped up on the desk and any other unbusinesslike action. To her this is undignified, uncalled for, and a waste of the time she is paying you for.

Don't be lackadaisical when performing a job. Lethargy will not be tolerated. Leo will let you go rather than have a listless employee on her staff. Give the job your all. Tend to your chores. Don't meddle in areas that don't concern you.

Take as much of her work load from her as possible. But don't bruise her ego when you do it. Tell her that you know she has more important tasks pending and that you'd be glad to finish this unimportant job. She may be appreciative but you won't *hear* it from her. It will show in your next pay check — she's generous, sometimes overly so, but it's her only way of letting you know how she feels. It's difficult for Leo to compliment someone because in her eyes, no one is greater than she. But she is grateful for all the favors you've done.

If you are late once in a while, Leo may not say anything to you. But if it looks like your tardiness is developing into a habit, she'll be quite candid when she warns you that, as a result of your actions, your job is in jeopardy. Agree with her. Tell her you won't do it again. Change the subject by complementing her with, "Oh, I like your suit..." (whatever else you can think of)... "I've been meaning to tell you how much I admire it and your taste in clothes." With those words, Leo will forget she's angry with you. Unfortunately for her, but fortunately for you, flattery is her downfall.

This woman won't mind your taking time off if it doesn't interfere with her plans. If there are deadlines to be met, you should not mention that you have something to attend to that will take you away from your work. If you call in sick at a time when she's got all of this pressure, and needs you for a specific duty, you'll hear a sound similar to a lion's (her sign's animal symbol) roar emitting from her mouth. Leo can be rather lenient, but don't take advantage of her kindness. Be considerate and don't ask for favors at the wrong time.

If Leo wants a report on a particular day at a set hour, make sure it's on her desk at the scheduled time. Keep all detailed accounts, letters, statistics, and statements out of sight — she can't stand to be bogged down by them — just give her a brief synopsis of what they contain. This woman is difficult to please, but she'll be appreciative that you've spared her the ordeal of wading through a lot of trivia.

If you think your typewriter is slowing down your work, and would like a word processor to make your job less tiresome as well as faster, mention it to Leo. This woman is all for the latest equipment available. However, sometimes she is so preoccupied running the large-scale part of the business that she overlooks minor areas. Once you've brought it to her attention, she may redo the entire office with the latest equipment available. Leo doesn't count the cost, she likes the finest and most expensive. She wants things streamlined, not only for expediency, but so she can show it off to the customers. This woman will beam with pride when remarks are made as to how intelligent she is to be progressive. In fact, she may be told she's got the most ultramodern office they've seen — that comment will make her glow as bright as the Sun.

Leo's craving for center stage is satisfied when she presides over meetings. With the spotlight on her, she demands your respect (so give it to her full blast) and knows that she's a true leader. Leo can command an army (Napoleon Bonaparte, emperor of France, did and so does Fidel Castro — both Leos) or an entire corporation. She takes great pride in the way she runs an organization. And she wants to be proud of you, too; therefore, don't let her down. But remember her gratitude won't be shown in flowery speeches; it'll be in the form of a bonus, substantial raise, or promotion.

If you don't agree with her ideas, it's best to keep it to yourself. Usually she is stubborn and won't change her opinion regardless of how brilliant you are. But if you must oppose her notions and risky ventures, be tactful. Never belittle her. Praise her and all the wonderful accomplishments she's made in the past. Then, go into: "I don't think that this new idea is going to be comparable to your other achievements, or as profitable. But, I have admiration for your judgment and modernization techniques; after all, you're in a better position than I to know all the inns and outs of your proposals."

Your Leo boss may take an interest in your private life, especially if it's interfering with your job performance. She enjoys giving advice because it makes her feel superior to you. If you have a personal problem and tell it to her, expect her to lord it over you by telling you what to do. This woman is bossy, enjoys running your life inside and outside of the office. Leo wants *total power* at all times and with everyone (Leo-born Benito Mussolini is an example) and may enter politics as did the late, Bella Abzug (another Leo). Once you've followed her counsel, be sure to thank her for it again. Tell her that you are grateful she took her precious time just to aid you in your hour of need.

This woman is not cheap. She'll see that you are well paid for your labor. She won't purposely hold back a wage increase. (Such low acts are beneath Leo's dignity.) This employer will give you a raise if it's merited; or she'll get reports from your supervisor. She understands that money can buy her the best employees available and you're one of the best or you wouldn't be working for her. Therefore, think twice about asking for an increase in your earnings (it makes her look like she's not aware of what's going on).

If she gets wind that the competition is interested in you, you'll get first-class treatment — wined and dined — if she still thinks you're tops. All you have to do is prove to her that you are successful.

YOUR LEO EMPLOYEE

What Can You Expect From Your Leo Employee?

This fellow takes pride in his appearance and abilities. You can expect to see a sharp dresser with a brain to match strutting across the room with a smile on his face. Leo is not shy. He'll boast that he can solve your problems — that he has the answer to everything.

When business pressures arise that need immediate handling, you can expect Leo to take command of the situation. This fellow is so conscientious and diligent that he'll burn the midnight oil just to accomplish a job. He's interested in anything that taxes his strength and lets him attract attention to himself. Leo's waiting for the applause. If it doesn't come right away he may appear arrogant and pretentious.

This fellow will put forth a great effort to show you that he's better than anyone else. Most of his laborious activities are so impressive that he can't help but stand out. If you pat him on the back, he'll put in even longer hours of toil. He's confident that everything he does is going to pay off.

Leo's a climber, and in a hurry to get to the top. He won't wait around for a post he already believes is his. If you don't give him a raise or promotion, you can expect him to notify you that he's quitting. It's more important for him to have a title than a salary increase. If you put his name and position on the door, he'll be devoted to your corporation. It makes him look influential and gives him the dignity and respect he craves. Then he can brag about his status, flaunt his importance and lord it over others.

How to Handle Your Leo Employee

Don't be too bossy or he'll quit. This fellow doesn't like to take orders because he considers himself equal to you. When you become over authoritative, Leo takes it as an insult. He is sure he can do a job without your taking a "mightier than thou" attitude toward him.

This man has to lead and, in his charming way, he may insist that you allow him to take over some of your duties. Because of his kind manner and apparent sincerity, you may believe that his motive for taking some of the burden off of your shoulders is that he wants to be helpful. Don't let that fool you. He probably wants to get your job, or if you're the owner of the firm, he may want to be on the board of directors. Anything to satisfy his desire for importance. Or Leo may want to learn everything he can about your business operations so he can later start up a competing corporation. He may even take your contacts and use them for his own advantage. Keep this in mind. If you're the type of boss who isn't disturbed by the

Leo taking over, then you don't have anything to worry about. Otherwise, when Leo starts throwing his weight around, the two of you will clash.

If you want to see your Leo employee beam, give him his own office, nameplate and all the trimmings. Because he needs to impress others, he'll pay money out of his own pocket to furnish it. Price is no object. His tastes are impeccable, although he may lean toward the ostentatious — gold (ruled by his sign) items — a letter opener, pencil holder, clock, pen set; trophies on the tabletops will be shining brightly. All of his awards, certificates and achievement records will be hanging on the wall. While in his presence, read them and make comments about how incredible it is that one so young could accomplish so much. Then admire his trophies, asking him about how he won them. And top it off by telling him how proud you are to have a man with so many honors on your staff. That's all Leo needs to hear — from that moment on he'll do everything within his power to make your company grow from a small concern to a gigantic corporation.

He's a doer who doesn't waste time fulfilling what's expected of him. A Leo never goofs off (if he did he wouldn't get the compliments he so eagerly waits for). Give him a title (even if it's something you concocted just for him), a big fat salary and treat him royally; as a result, you'll realize that he's an asset and can increase your business tenfold.

Leo's courageous, gutsy and will take chances regardless of who is on the paying end. Give him a liberal expense account. He's a generous tipper and can charm any customer over a few cocktails or a meal. If he takes a long lunch, don't fret; he'll make up for it by working late. His luncheons may wind up a deal faster than anything else.

Give him an important function so he can shine like the true star he thinks he is. This fellow is a braggart that can put the company's name up in lights. He gets around a lot: most likely you'll run into him at the country club, theater, opera, ballet, or in a nightclub or restaurant. Leo also attends many social events that may be politically oriented. While out, he makes it a point to talk to wealthy and powerful people. He will mention the name of your corporation and distort the truth a little by upping his status. Leo has to feed his ego and besides, he believes wholeheartedly that he's qualified to be in said rank.

This fellow suffers from an inferiority complex that is covered up by a superiority complex. By putting on the big front, and boasting he's on the top level of management, he assures himself outwardly that he's really that great. Inwardly, he's insecure. When he accomplishes phenomenal deeds he may gain surety and stop bragging because others are busy praising him. However, you can't count on this; it could make him even more of an egomaniac than he is. Usually the older Leo gets, the more mature and settled he becomes — however, only if he's fulfilled his extraordinary ambitions. Therefore, if you encourage him, feed his ego and help him realize his greatness, he'll prove it to you with the fine job he'll perform for you, which will be for the betterment of your business.

If you make rules, expect him to break them. Leo dislikes being told that he has to obey regulations. He believes he's the king of his jungle. This is one Lion who can't be caged in, so don't confine or hide him away. Let him be out in the limelight where he can be seen, do his best work, and bask in the applause received from it. Never criticize him in front of anyone; if you do, you'll never see him again. And that's not the way for you to be successful, is it?

YOUR LEO COWORKER
What Can You Expect From Your Leo Coworker?

There are just a few basic facts to keep in mind when working with this woman: she's competitive, dominating, and has a swelled head. Leo prides herself on being smarter than most people. She moves and thinks fast. Don't expect her to help you out if you lag behind, but she'll gladly give you instructions on how you can improve your job performance. If the boss comes around and asks, "Who is responsible for holding up production?" Leo will point an accusing finger at you. Then she may vauntingly show her completed tasks. Be prepared for her to further embarrass you by telling your employer that she gave you a briefing on how you can perfect your chores and keep up with everyone else.

This woman is as fashionable as the late, Leo born couturiére, Coco Chanel. Be prepared for your face to turn red if she doesn't like the way you are dressed; she may tell you about it when others are within listening range. Or she may criticize you for not wearing makeup and being glamorous. Or she may brag that she doesn't make as many blunders as you do. If you are sensitive (Cancer, Pisces) you may feel like hiding under a table when she pulls these scenes. However, if you are also an egotist, there will be a clash for supremacy. If Leo's actions are upsetting, perhaps you'd be better off if you transfer to another department. If that can't be done, then you'll have to learn how to handle your Leo coworker.

When she's not busy tooting her own horn, she can be the milk of human kindness. Leo will share her lunch with you, bring you sweets from home, and be quite delightful with her winning ways. However, when she's polite, it is in a condescending manner.

How To Handle Your Leo Coworker

Accept the fact that she's vain, a braggart, and is going to put herself above you, continually. Clashes and upsets can be avoided if you give her attention. Praise her for her abilities. Tell her that you just know that someday she will be a supervisor and that you can envision her leaving that for a job in top management; perhaps as a chief executive officer of the corporation. Pay Leo compliments whenever you have the opportunity to do so. Tell her that you like her dress, shoes, jewelry, lipstick, hairdo or whatever. Watch her light up the skies with her sunny smile.

Leo appears to believe that you are beneath her. It's her own insecurity that maybe you *are* above her that makes her try to knock you down a peg or two. Thus when you build her up, she hasn't any need to tear you down. You'll be able to get along with her if you understand this craving for adulation that is similar to a starved child's ravenous hunger. If you ignore her, she'll find a way to demean you. And this will only bring about strife on the job and that is not the way to get ahead.

This woman may assume the role of boss even though your employer has hired both of you to work in the same capacity. Leo wants to be the big cheese. Often her ego and desire to command takes over without her even being aware of it consciously. Don't be too startled if she even gives orders to your immediate supervisor. She just can't seem to help herself even though it could result in her being fired. It's best to go along with her if she's right. If she's wrong, then just do your job in your usual routine way. Give her a compliment and she'll forget about throwing her weight around. Now that you understand why she wants to dominate, you will be less upset and inclined to argue, cause a scene or get yourself into trouble. If you decide to rebel against her actions, think twice. Is it really worth risking your job just to satisfy *your ego?*

If you discover accidentally a new method of processing your work and it's superior to the old way, don't divulge any information to Leo. Tell your boss about it first because otherwise Leo will beat you to the punch and claim it was her idea. Of course, along the way, she probably would have added in an improvement.

This woman says what she means even if she runs the danger of being blunt and offensive. Don't get upset by her straightforwardness. She dislikes lies and thinks that candidness is the best policy. If you are mannerly and respect her honesty and openness, you'll fare rather well. She's got a hot temper, so try to avoid making her angry. However, she quickly forgets quarrels and doesn't hold any grudges.

Don't question her authority on a new procedure. If you do, be ready for an argument. You've attacked her ego and now she has to defend it the best way she knows how — and that's to belittle you. She has fierce pride and has to protect it. Leo is stubborn and will uphold her views throughout the stormy encounter. One thing you won't forget about the scene is the majestic manner in which she behaves; it seems to say, "You see I am the ruler of the jungle."

If you are a sneering faultfinder, Leo will not pay any attention to your cynicism. She can't bear to waste her valuable time listening to your remarks. So avoid getting yourself in a dither and tend to your own job. If you are suspicious that she's questioning you so she can go tattle to the boss, immediately dismiss this negative thought from your mind. She is extremely ambitious to succeed, but she's not the type to stoop to such a mean trick. This woman is too busy pushing her talents to bother with you. She has her mind on success and that's where yours should be too.

YOUR LEO CLIENT
What Can You Expect From Your Leo Client?

This woman walks in the door proud as a peacock. She's just as vain as a peacock too. You'll notice that when she passes by a glass counter, she looks at herself first, the merchandise second. Leo knows what she wants. She manages to pick the most expensive item, without looking at the price tag. She doesn't care about the price, it's quality she wants.

If Leo's not in too big a hurry, she may ask for the store owner. She prefers dealing with the top brass rather than an underling. If you are the proprietor and you are not giving her the attention she demands, she'll walk out the door haughtily.

If you are a salesman who calls on your customers, expect to see Leo sitting erect in her elegant chair like a queen on a throne. She will approve or disapprove of you immediately. This woman won't hesitate to tell you what she thinks of your product. She expects you to be as honest as she is. If she feels that you are being dishonest in any way, she may dismiss you contemptuously. However, if you have gained her confidence, Leo will purchase your goods quickly.

You'll notice that Leo is only interested in hearing about the highlights of your product. And, watch her eyes sparkle when you tell her the financial benefits that can be gained if she uses your goods. She is friendly, appears to be stiffly courteous in an arrogant way and makes you feel like you are beneath her. However, her delectability may compensate for this superior attitude she takes. There are little give away clues that let you in on the fact that she's a Leo.

How To Handle Your Leo Client

How do you deal with someone so pompous? It's best to ignore this facet of her personality and realize that beneath this facade lies a kind and warmhearted person. If you want to impress her, try any one of these lines — or use them all. "It's an honor meeting you. Your office is so prestigious; you have impeccable taste. I've heard so many wonderful remarks about your company and, especially, about how you've managed to build it up to such a large business. You must be proud of your many accomplishments."

Take Leo out to the most expensive restaurant you can find. She's a connoisseur and loves to be seen in a fashionable eating establishment. Suggest one of the flaming deserts. She enjoys the theatrics of it from start to finish. Speak as eloquently as you can and discuss how you intend to help her increase sales and speed up production. If this woman tells you about an idea, give her your undivided attention. Throw some flattering commentary in every now and then. Don't let her smugness throw you for a loop. Cater to her ego and it's a cinch you'll consummate a deal.

Make your sales spiel so entwined with her goal (success) that she becomes enthusiastic about your product right from the start. If Leo gets enthusiastic about your goals because it will enable her to get the recognition she craves that much faster, she'll rush you into a delivery. Once you see her smile, you've got the sale wrapped up.

There are certain give away signs that let you know you are not making a hit with her. If Leo's getting bored with your conversation, she'll inform you that she's extremely busy and could you please tell her as briefly as possible about your wares. Once you start talking, if she starts to pick up some papers on her desk you'll know that you have overstayed your welcome. So, make it short, sweet, and snappy. Give her a nice compliment, thank her for being so generous with her valuable time and make a quick exit.

If you want her to be a regular customer, skip the details, get to the point, write the order up fast and deliver the products either ahead of schedule or as promised. If you're in a store and wait on Leo, dispatch her order immediately —

94

including the special gift wrap she insists upon. If you're a waitress in a restaurant and your customer has an affected air of importance and a warm, dignified smile, you can bet she's a Leo. Give her service befitting a queen and you'll be over-tipped. Furthermore, she'll probably ask for you the next time she comes in. And isn't that one step toward your goal of becoming successful?

YOUR LEO PARTNER
What Can You Expect From Your Leo Partner?
You may think that you made a wise decision when you chose to go into a partnership with this fellow because he's stable, progressive, oozes power and is a man of principle. You may think you've got the late Henry Ford (the industrialist), Bernard Baruch (the financier) and Cecil B. DeMille (the motion picture producer) all wrapped up in one individual— they were Leo's too!

So how do you cope with one who can revolutionize the business world, make a fortune one year, lose it the next, and produce everything on such a grand scale that he's soon back on top?

Leo has so many outstanding traits if you can just put up with his egomania. Perhaps that's the main ingredient for his greatness and success. He's got the Midas touch and is never down for long. This man enjoys offering favors but doesn't want to be asked to do them. More than likely, he has contact with people in very high places. If he doesn't today, he will tomorrow.

The elegant and prestigious offices are kept in tip-top shape at all times. Leo is capable of assuming heavy financial obligations and laborious responsibilities. Enormous operations and holdings are attracted when you team up with this man. So, if you want to hitch your wagon to a star that shines brightly, but who needs to be handled properly, Leo may be just the one for you!

How To Handle Your Leo Partner
This man's a gambler who is willing to risk just about everything he owns on making the business a success. He's not afraid to go into debt for the most modern machinery and equipment available or to spend enormous sums of money on a large advertising campaign. If you are the conservative type you are going to clash with this extravagant Leo.

Go over the books with Leo and explain the financial situation the two of you are likely to encounter if he goes ahead with his plans. Don't be surprised if he convinces you that he's right. Leo can be charming and when he smiles like the Sun is shining on him, you may feel like moving skies for him. But if he fails to talk you into going ahead with his schemes, expect his temper to come to the fore. Of course, the Lion's roar is never as bad as it sounds. If you've upset him, just "yes" him or leave the room. Don't argue because that will make matters worse. Leo thinks he's the only one who knows what to do. If he's wrong and later is told so by you, he won't admit it. He just can't take blame. So be ready to hear excuses and alibis and blaming you or someone else for the loss or problem attracted.

Be creative. Don't shy away from telling your Leo partner about your conceptions that can make millions for the company. Or if you have a tax-cut proposal or a project that can cut down on costs, thereby saving your corporation enormous expenses, speak up. Leo can take an idea and turn it into a thriving enterprise. Let him use his flamboyant personality to promote it. If you knock down his views or the way he goes about handling a project, you'll attack his ego. You can tell him something, but do it pleasantly, complimentary and diplomatically. Once he's praised, he'll purr like the pussycat he can be.

This man can't stand to waste his valuable time with details. He dislikes tending to things in bits and pieces. Any item that is essential to the total effect bores him; it's the final outcome that he enjoys dealing with. His mind is not trained to see the minute parts but to look at the all-inclusive panoramic view. It's not the smallness that perks his senses, it's the grandness. Therefore be prepared for him to be quick and to the point with a few simple words, leaving the fillings to you. If you want to really be "in" with your partner, tend to the trivia and leave the momentous areas for him.

Leo wants to climb to the top of the mountain and stay perched there basking in his glory; he also wants an enormous bank account. Don't hold him back by being lazy; pitch in and work as hard as he does — early mornings, late evenings, weekends, holidays. Don't fret at the first class treatment he gives a potential client. Avoid disparaging him for having lines of open credit. He needs it so he can splurge when taking a customer to a restaurant, country club dance or to the golf course. This fellow does everything in a big way; he expects the results to be the same, and, usually they are.

Leo thrives on adulation; he can't exist without it. The more you compliment him, the harder he'll work. Let him know how much you appreciate him. Tell him that you are happy and proud to be in a joint venture with him. If you don't, he may ask you, "Don't you think I made a wonderful deal with _____?" Or he may say, "How do you like all that money I saved the company?" He wants respect, so give it to him. Leo isn't the type to praise you. In fact, he may belittle you if he thinks you're overshadowing him. However, if you bestow all those words of greatness on him, he'll have no need to put you down. In all relationships there's some giving; you give to him when you build his ego and let him be the boss; he gives to you when he's honest, loyal and uses his talents to make you both wealthy.

Sun-Sign Compatibility

This section deals with each sign of the zodiac in relation to a Leo Sun sign. By knowing how your sign blends with a Leonine, you are going one step beyond understanding his personality and a step closer to knowing how to handle him in any business situation. Greater insight is invaluable — it not only helps a business prosper, it encourages peace of mind on and off the job.

The following Sun-Sign compatibility summaries, with the exception of Leo/Leo, are *from the point of view of the person dealing with Leo. Note:* For the Leonine's point of view, see the Sun-Sign chapter of the person Leo is dealing with, i.e., for Sagittarius — refer to the Sagittarius chapter explaining how Leo thinks about Sagittarius.

ARIES/LEO

You find Leo exciting to work with because he, like you, gets involved zealously in executing a task. You admire him for undertaking enormous projects that are risky in their very nature. Leo's such a time-saver, not getting you involved in details. His ability to see the overall picture of how everything should be accomplished seems to match your own talents in that direction.

The Leonine is a stabilizing influence that you prize more each passing day. You appreciate the way he encourages you to complete one job before starting another one. His bossiness you find challenging. It's like a game for you when the two of you try to outdo one another but, amazingly, this doesn't seem to create any problems.

Leo, like you, is strong, direct, forward, and outspoken; thus, there isn't any evading of issues or wasting of time haggling about something. You are delighted that he performs his job as quick as you can. When Leo beams and makes a favorable comment about your ingenuity, you are inspired to surpass yourself. You glow when he's able to bring those ideas of yours to perfection. You admire his intellect and business know-how. You don't mind going along with Leo when he changes from one mode of operating to another. He has your respect in all past, present, and future undertakings. You know that he's executive material, just like you are. Both of you are good workers and are an asset to one another.

TAURUS/LEO

Your Leo partner and you disagree over the disbursement of salaries paid to employees. He's generous to a fault and you are sensible and practical. Leo wants them to start with high wages because he thinks they'll work harder while you think they'll be more productive if they have a raise as their incentive. Leo wants to increase an employee's earnings every time he thinks the person has done something spectacular while you think the individual was just doing his job.

You are glad to have a friendly coworker like Leo. However. When he becomes authoritative and tries to lord it over you, you become angry. When you ignore him, he tends to brag more, but his boastfulness doesn't disturb you.

Leo is in too much of a hurry to reach the top, whereas you are too slow and prodding to get there. Thus, you'll take your time and Leo will rush to reach this higher position. You should both compromise and follow the path between these two extremes. However, both of you are stubborn; neither one of you is about to budge.

You need security in a partnership and don't feel it with Leo, whereas he needs someone who will believe in his future plans and who is willing to take a risk to attain them. Your personalities clash but if the two of you can be a little more flexible it would be easier to be a winning combination.

GEMINI/LEO

You admire your Leo coworker for her zeal and enthusiasm. It doesn't upset you when she gets authoritative and tells you to do something for her. But she gets angry sometimes when you are gabbing — it seems to disturb her concentration. However, you know just what to say to calm her down — "A little flattery never hurt anyone," you say to yourself.

You are relieved to be working for a boss who doesn't look over your shoulder to make sure you're doing the job just right. Leo is great because she just gives you an order, expects (and knows) you will obey while she tends to her own duties.

Your Leo partner has the same progressive concerns as you. It tickles you pink when she spends large sums of money on a new concept, especially if she gives you a chance to experiment with it. Her cash disbursements are sometimes unwise. But she takes wild chances and you find it exciting — it breaks up the routine.

Your Leo employee is a blessing. You are glad you hired someone who is so helpful. She does well when you give her some of your chores to finish. This is one woman you can count on. Her enthusiastic approach on the job is delightful. She beams when you ask her to supervise the other employees while you go out to see a client. Later, when you return you are positive that you chose the right person to be in charge — everyone finished their work ahead of schedule.

The two of you are a great pair in any type of business arrangement: owners of a company, coworkers, or boss/employee. Sales should ring up fast into the millions.

CANCER/LEO

Your Leo partner makes you fear for your financial security because she throws away money recklessly. Her extravagance is something you can't understand. Why she spends so much to wine and dine a client is beyond you. You think it's just showing off and not good business sense. If your products are in demand, and your services are excellent, shouldn't that speak for itself? Why waste time and a lot of greenbacks to entertain someone? When you tell her about your views, she doesn't agree and even belittles you for being stupid.

Working with a Leo is a delight. She's open and trustworthy. It doesn't disturb you that she finishes a job quicker than you or that she gives the supervisor ideas that puts her in good with the president of the company.

When your employer gets a little domineering, it's understandable because after all she's the boss and pays your salary. She's so generous with those raises that you want to stay here forever. You are sure that she respects your opinion because on more than one occasion you saved her money by telling her about a hunch you had.

Your Leo employee is indispensable. She is conscientious and able to take your place when you are called away on urgent family matters as well as when you take a vacation. While you are away, it's amazing how she handles the organization perfectly and makes a few deals to boot.

LEO/LEO

You compete with your Leo partner. You're not about to let him outdo you. You know that you are superior to him and will prove it when you consummate that big deal you're working on. Luckily you both agree on modernization and giving your clients the VIP treatment regardless of the cost involved. You are elated that your Leo partner wants to make a fortune and is willing to take the same risks as you.

Your Leo coworker keeps you on your toes as you struggle to beat him to the top. Neither of you like second place and will go out of your way to reach first place. Your coworker sure does brag as much as you do. But you can boast about the boss accepting and using one of your ideas. However, later, you are dismayed when your Leo coworker had given him the same idea.

Your Leo employee reminds you of yourself when you were trying to get a higher position. You are aware that he's trying everything to land your job as supervisor. However, you'll let him vie with you until you will give him the job when you consummate a deal to open up your own business.

Your Leo employer and you clash because he's cheap when it comes to passing out compliments. All he does is boast about *his* achievements. You dislike getting subordinate treatment from him when you know you are just as clever as he is. You enjoy discussing issues and having a hand in making policies and your boss allows, even encourages, that. However, he takes the credit for everything. It doesn't matter, though, someday you'll be his competitor across the street.

There will be a definite clash of egos regardless of whether you are partners, coworkers, or in a boss/employee relationship. Both strive to rule and both are leaders. So who is going to outdo whom? You are just too authoritative and unyielding to attract a harmonious relationship.

VIRGO/LEO

You value your Leo partner because she has so many wonderful traits that you lack. This woman sparkles with enthusiasm when dealing with the customers and huge projects. She's not afraid to tackle anything; you admire her adventurous soul. However, the money she spends goes against your conservative nature. But what the heck, you do feel secure with her, so why not take a chance?

Your Leo coworker is quiet so you can concentrate. She finds shortcuts to speed up the work so you don't lag behind. You enjoy doing the precision jobs she finds distasteful. The two of you work well together because you can handle the details for her and she answers the phone and talks to the customers — something you prefer not to do.

It doesn't annoy you to take orders from your Leo boss. She is superior to you, that's why she's in the top position. And, besides, that's what you are getting paid for anyway. You are glad that she's appreciative of your perfectionism. Her raise lets you know; you'd be embarrassed if she complemented you in front of everyone.

You are proud of your Leo employee and all that she accomplishes. Her ideas for streamlining your business are invaluable. You appreciate her desire to produce the best and make your company the finest. Perhaps you should promote her and make her your assistant.

LIBRA/LEO

What a relief to have an associate who makes all of the final judgments; his decisive actions seem to be beneficial. He inspires you with all of his various undertakings. You just hope that you'll have time to recuperate in between all of this mind-blowing activity. You're glad that Leo doesn't get upset when you take it easy. He's a perfect leader; you're thankful that he enjoys having the power you so readily grant him. You are confident that his expansion plans will make the two of you rich.

Your Leo boss glows when you tell him that you know his new "baby" is going to top all of his other projects. He has been persevering with it day and night for the last few months and has been generously giving you a substantial increase on your paycheck. It's a pleasure to be working in an office that is plush and clean; you abhor filth, disorder, and ugliness.

Your Leo employee is a welcome addition to your concern. He is brilliant and has given you some valuable tips on the stock market. "This fellow is easy to handle. All I have to do is bolster his confidence and he'll bend over backward getting a job out," you tell your wife.

Peace and harmony are requisites for you at all times. Luckily your Leo coworker is quiet and congenial. Together the two of you could make it to the top.

SCORPIO/LEO

You are impressed (but you'll keep it a secret) with your Leo partner's optimism. She makes some moves that would frighten others, but not you. You will show her that you can be just as daring —and even more so — than she. You hinder her desire to rule the association. She's not superior to you and you tell her so every time she puts on her "better than thou" air. The best arrangement you two have is that you're behind the scenes working and she's out front talking to the customers.

Your Leo partner has your same persistent drive to get to the top. Both of you hang on to the bitter end — and that's just what it may be when you two get together. Both of you want the presidency so will have to settle for an equal partnership rather than a corporation.

Both of you will challenge one another; however, you are more of an outward fighter than she is — Leo won't stoop to doing anything sneaky or dirty but she'll try to win in her own way. Your egos will oppose one another for supremacy and both are unyielding so it's a real problem relationship. However, the combination of talents, minus ego and other difficulties, could make for a fantastic team that could go far — all the way up to the multimillionaire level.

SAGITTARIUS/LEO

Others have told you that your Leo partner is an egomaniac but you haven't noticed it. You think he's fabulous and enjoy telling him every chance you get.

This man is important so why shouldn't you treat him like a king? You don't mind his dominating ways: it's easy to just go along with him. You believe if you listen to his advice, let him rule and combine your abilities with his, it'll all pay off some day when the two of you are wealthy

Your Leo employee is loyal and dependable; he's as honest as you and you are known to lose money because you can't lie or deceive a customer. This is one person who has some unbelievable ideas for your business. You've listened to him a few times and as a result your profits increased and so have his wages

You are both full of fire and take immediate action on all undertakings. The two of you think big and are always ready to make changes and improvements. The faith and confidence you have, not only with yourselves, but with each other, can make you perform gigantic tasks.

Both of you take an optimistic approach in all of your endeavors. You are seldom down, thus there aren't any negative vibes to attract discord. It's a big fat plus all the way. The two of you can do everything you've dreamed of doing with your corporation.

CAPRICORN/LEO

Your Leo partner is as concerned about her reputation as you are about yours. She wants recognition too and will go out of her way to get it. You value this woman because you know she's as money-hungry and driven as you. It doesn't disturb you that she will give you a few orders — the end result's what counts.

You are impressed by your Leo employer's generosity. To have a big bank account so you can later go into your own business is a must. Therefore, working for this woman who is giving you raises every time you do something stupendous just spurs you on to do more. You've got the energy of three people and don't mind working day and night to get ahead — and this boss doesn't interfere, she encourages it.

A Leo for a coworker is easy for you to handle. After all, you are known for your diplomacy. She works as hard as you and is just as reliable. Her long-range plans to get to the top seem almost identical to yours. You've noticed that she doesn't falter along the way. This is one person you'd consider going into partnership with.

AQUARIUS/LEO

Your Leo coworker frowns about the haphazard way you go about your duties. He puts on an air that he's better than you. But you believe that everyone's an individual so if he wants to act that way it's all up to him and no one else. As long as you get your job done, that's all you care about.

You are delighted that you work for such a progressive man as Leo. Your attention span is easily broken if you find a job dull and boring. Routine chores are not your cup of tea. However, with your Leo boss you seem to perk up. He's always giving you unusual tasks that let you work on your own. This gives you the freedom and independence you so desperately need.

Your ideas are ahead of the times but your Leo partner approves of them wholeheartedly and takes action to bring them to fruition. With this man you are sure that your hopes will be realized. His energy and enthusiasm are similar to your own.

You are opposite signs in the zodiac and have differing traits: Leo's motives are to make money, receive recognition and status; you want to satisfy your creative urges, to experiment with the new and to help mankind. The two of you meet head on when you refuse to be ordered around by Leo. Both of you are so fixed and opinionated that nothing will make you change your minds. There are some drawbacks to working professionally together.

PISCES/LEO

You enjoy the company of your Leo coworker and you are always interested in listening to her talk about her future plans. She thinks big just like you. However, she's got more stamina and courage than you. But with her beside you, perhaps you can get ahead after all.

Your Leo employer is demanding and bossy. She expects you to get the work finished on time. When you surprise her by cutting your work load in half, she behaves as if you were supposed to do just that. You'd like a compliment once in a while but with her it never seems to be forthcoming. You are ready to quit when she embarrasses you in front of everyone. However, she leaves the room when she sees the tears well up in your eyes.

The material gains that you both seek may be attained in this association. However, if you procrastinate and get lackadaisical, you'll hold Leo back somewhat. Money is important to you as a means of security and to give away to those in need. But Leo wants it for power and status.

You are excellent in promotion, therefore, you can do some wheeling and dealing that will make Leo look as grand as she feels. Together this is not a bad combination because you follow orders as readily as Leo gives them. But you are adaptable, she's inflexible; thus, you'll be the one who gives in constantly.

Chapter Eight

Virgo Compatibility In Business

If you were born between August 23 and September 22, your Sun is in the sign Virgo. However, you may also express Virgo traits if Virgo is dominant in your horoscope (refer to the Introduction, Page 1), even if it is not your Sun sign. If this is the case, you should read this chapter just as if your Sun sign is Virgo.

VIRGO PROFILE
Getting Acquainted With The Virgo Personality

This Virgo woman isn't easy to get to know. Once you understand what motivates her, it will facilitate dealing with her in business, regardless of whether she's your partner, employer, employee, coworker, or client. Virgo may appear mousy but don't let her looks fool you. She's intensely active mentally and is a walking encyclopedia of knowledge. This woman is industrious as any workaholic. However, nothing about her is obvious because she sits quietly in the background while she slowly and carefully performs each task.

Virgo is even-tempered. She will not allow herself to become angry easily. This woman can be swayed by logic, reason, and finesse. She won't allow you to hurry her into making a decision. She has to mull everything over first. A Virgo can find flaws that others overlook. She's apt to judge severely other people's imperfections as well as their plans.

This woman is not a speculator, dislikes hazards, and sticks with a sure thing. She's always practical. Virgo thinks of success as a job well done. She doesn't strive for top spot. She labors mainly because she loves to work. This female can't stand being idle for one second. Her motto is "give service to others." Thus she is productive and accomplishes her set goals. Money is not her god — but she likes to be paid for her efforts. However, she's never truly compensated for the labor expended. She's an asset to anyone in business.

IF YOU ARE A VIRGO

Because you want to be helpful to others, you may ask, "What can I do to achieve my goals?" Success can be attained faster if, when you deal with others, you adhere to the following advice:

When dealing with an employer perk up and smile more often. Your cheerless appearance makes the boss think that you don't enjoy your work. And the customers may assume incorrectly that you don't like your boss or even that he's a Simon Legree, especially when they see you slaving away at your desk.

You need to work in a neat and orderly environment, otherwise it affects you mentally and physically. When you are unhappy in messy surroundings, you have a crawly feeling, can't think, become confused and make mistakes more easily. That's when the nit-picking starts.

Indubitably, your job performance is excellent. Just get some sparkle into your personality and perhaps a raise and promotion will be forthcoming.

When dealing with partners, employees and coworkers be on guard. You expect others to be perfect and you must realize that *your* idea of flawlessness and the other person's may differ. It's true that you are seldom wrong when you point out the faults of others. However, it's the way you go about it that causes offense — you are too sharp in making criticisms. If you must speak out, be considerate of another's feelings and use tact. If you create hostility with those you deal with it's harder to be successful.

You've got to realize that it takes all types of people to run an organization. Due to the nature of their Sun or dominant sign not everyone pays close attention to detail the way you do. Thus, don't have a fit and start picking at those who failed to notice whether their i's were dotted and their t's were crossed. Instead, appreciate that different individuals are needed to handle the type of work that is not your calling. By understanding others and not getting upset over their errors you'll create a peaceful atmosphere. When everyone feels harmonious they work better together. In the end, they'll accomplish their goals that much faster and you will prosper in the process.

When dealing with clients your main problem is your personality. You should liven up, be less impersonal, avoid coolness and formal politeness. People like to do business with you when you are friendly, helpful (you are), casual and personal, but if someone walks in with a haughty air, be yourself and you'll hear the cash register ring. If your customer is smiling and appears happy-go-lucky, though, you'll lose a sale if you don't brighten up.

If a client throws down some papers on the top of your desk don't be a fussbudget and scold him for this action. This may embarrass and anger him, causing resentment and a possible loss of business for you. Also avoid emptying the ashtrays or cleaning up after him while he's sitting there. Give him your *undivided attention* if you want to keep his account. If you must be orderly, remove the empty paper coffee cup or soft drink can without being too verbally fastidious.

When you take a customer out to lunch don't talk just about business. Ask him about his hobbies, get him to converse about those matters that interest him. This will make him more keen to deal with you. And when transactions occur your bank account increases.

To go one step further, once you as a Virgo know or can recognize the sign your partner, employer, employee, coworker, or client is, read that sign's chapter to know how best to deal with him as well as to understand his compatibility with you. If you wish to know what he thinks about you, read the Sun-Sign Compatibility section starting on page 113. The remainder of this Virgo section deals with how others relate to you, what they can expect of you, and how they should handle you. So now let's go on an interview with your sign, okay?

AN INTERVIEW WITH A VIRGO

A Virgo employer interviewing you: The first thing she will notice about you is your appearance. She wants you to be immaculate and well-groomed. Good manners are a necessity as well. Your resume will have been carefully scrutinized and analyzed beforehand. She will test you with some questions that will let her know the type of mind you really have. Virgo will ask for answers which require logic, good reasoning powers, clarity of thought, proper pronunciation, and lengthy explanations. She'll be paying strict attention to every word said — this woman is trying to ascertain if love of detail is part of your makeup and whether you use sound judgment. Therefore, explain your conclusions sensibly and thoroughly. She's in no hurry so don't leave anything out.

This woman won't hire you right away. She has to weigh everything about you against everything about all of the other applicants. This mulling over procedure will take days or weeks. Once you're on her payroll if you don't live up to her expectations, you'll be fired.

If you're interviewing a Virgo applicant: He won't be disturbed if you keep him waiting. Virgo wants a job and understands that you are a busy person. Meanwhile, he'll read a nonfiction book that will further his knowledge in the business world. When you get around to interviewing this man you'll discover that he's informative. Be ready for him to ask questions about the company and write down the answers very neatly on a piece of lined paper. He will inquire about the corporation's health plan (he's conscious about having a sound body and staying in good shape). Also he will want to know if the company is set up to pay for it's employees to go to college, night school or special seminars (he's education happy). You may think it's odd that he doesn't have much to say about the salary or raise periods. It's because he knows that he's a good worker and that as a result, he'll be compensated fairly — if he's not, he'll quit. If you want him to start in right away, he will — if he hasn't made other plans.

Now that the interview is over, let's first go to work for a Virgo and thus see how Virgo is going to fare as your employee, okay?

YOUR VIRGO EMPLOYER
What Does Your Virgo Boss Expect of You?

If you're being transferred from one department to another, regardless of the reason, Virgo will give you a chance to prove yourself. The first mistake you make she'll be right there to point out your errors, inaccuracies, and what you're doing wrong. Then she'll tell you that it can be done much better if you follow her advice. This woman loves to impart knowledge to others — she's a natural teacher. She expects you to take her lessons seriously and apply them with the same dedication she has. Virgo wants you to be as competent as she is. Once she's trained you, she doesn't want you to fail or falter along the way.

This female is not forceful nor a leader in the sense of the word. But she does have certain rules that she expects you to pay attention to. One important rule is to be punctual; she's the type who may have a clock to punch when you arrive and leave — and don't think she's too busy to look at it. Later, she'll scrutinize it carefully. Virgo likes living and working on a schedule and she wants you to follow suit. She imposes regulations: No eating or drinking at your desk; no smoking in the office. This woman expects you to understand English and obey these rules. She'll see that they're strictly enforced and if you don't, she'll fire you.

Virgo expects you to know your duties and to go about them accordingly. There is to be no gossip on the job or talking on the telephone to friends or loved ones — personal calls are not allowed. You are getting paid to work and that is what this woman expects you to do — and not lethargically, but arduously.

How to Handle Your Virgo Boss

Don't wear flashy clothes or makeup that make you look like a cheap prostitute. Jeans don't upset Virgo too much — depending upon the nature of your work and the business. Virgo prefers a tailored, clean, look. Don't show up on the job dressed differently in a cocktail dress regardless of the reason. If you have to meet a beau for dinner or a party, change after work.

When you are messy Virgo gets in a dither even if it's only rumpled papers on your desk. She is annoyed when she sees smudges of ink, type, makeup or lipstick on reports, etc.

This female requires you to keep everything neat, tidy and businesslike. She gets bugged if you knock over pictures or anything else from your desk — the noise of it falling disturbs her concentration. If it contains glass and breaks, she'll help you clean it up (her sign rules maintenance work and being a servant) and all the while she will criticize you repetitiously. Also Virgo gets irritated if you drop boxes, reports or files on the floor. She may even help you put them back in order. If you spill ink on your desk or clothes, be ready for her to be cranky and fuss at you for being so sloppy. So to please her, don't be a litterbug, avoid disorder, move slower, and pay attention to your actions; it's when you're rushed that you mess up.

Regardless of your working capacity — secretary or mail — do not move the furniture, the plants or mislay any reports, files or important documents. Virgo likes sameness with everything in its proper place. She can't stand anything out of alphabetical order, so have files in correct order and don't misplace them. Keep your boss happy by having all working utensils in the right pigeonholes. Virgo wants everything to be at her fingertips; she must know where every article is in case it's needed at any given moment. If it's not, she doesn't feel efficient — and that's something that can disturb her deeply.

If you book her appointments, keep in mind that she will not go overtime with anyone; if a client is late, and his time is up — it's up! If you schedule her to be at a customer's office, or luncheon, give her ample time to get there and also from one client's to another. If Virgo doesn't have enough leeway, and thus is tardy, she'll be embarrassed and apologize several times before the meeting, during it and at the end of it. And when she gets back to the office, you'll never hear the end of it. In fact, she'll remind you of what you did every time she tells you to make her an appointment someplace.

Your Virgo employer is health conscious and believes that you should get checkups, see the doctor if you are ill and take care of yourself by eating properly so you don't get sick. (The large firms run by Virgoan's employ doctors on their staffs.) If you have an accident on the job, expect Virgo to be there with the first aid kit. She'll be understanding if you call in sick, but she's suspicious if you call in on the fourth day, after you've been off on a three-day holiday. This female will surmise that you went out of town — and are still there because you're having too much fun to return to work. So, if you ever pull a stunt like that, and she discovers it, you'll have lots of free time to go out of the city.

When this woman gives orders, write them down (that makes her think that you care about following them to the letter). Pay attention to everything she has to say, Virgo never wastes her time (she believes) in idle conversation (but she does get lost in details). Therefore in her opinion every word she utters is important. She wants you to abide by her instructions to the nth degree.

Virgo likes men and women who use their brains. She expects and admires intelligence in others. She would not have hired you if she didn't think you could cut the mustard. This is one female who is not creative, and if you are, let her know it. She won't get angry or offended if you suggest ideas that could improve the company — like speeding up production — or increasing its earning power.

This woman is practical; she does everything the cheapest way she can to save money. Both she and the company are on a budget that she strictly adheres to. Seldom does she give a bonus, so don't implore her to give you one. If you did something spectacular (perhaps it saved the corporation some money), don't expect her to give you a raise. Virgo considers everything job-related as nothing more than a duty to be performed. However, if she believes that you are a valuable employee, you will be compensated by the earnings you receive; the amount will be what she really thinks your talents are worth. So if you are the type who needs salary boosts during the year, look for a job elsewhere. However, Virgo will make an exception for someone who works as hard as she does, is free from errors, and a perfectionist like herself.

This female tends to her job methodically and diligently, but don't let that fool you. She still notices everything going on (her eyes are on your every little action). It's as if she's waiting for you to slip up. Make sure that the words are spelled correctly on all papers that are typed and presented to her. Expect to be torn apart every time you make a boo-boo. She won't let you get by with anything. Virgo believes that if you'll realize your mistakes, you'll correct them. She will continue to criticize you, perhaps twenty times in one day, until you don't goof. This woman thinks that by treating you in this manner you'll learn by it, and thus be faultless. If you can't take this nit-picking, look for another job.

If you're the impatient type Virgo may not be the boss for you, especially when she has to analyze everything to the minute detail, or she makes sure that all the i's are dotted before she can go beyond a particular point. This female takes time to make a decision because she has to mull over everything. If she is rushed she may tell a client that her employees can accomplish more in a given time than

107

can be actually done. Therefore, accept her slowness, her desire to be sure of every action and efficiency. If you don't, you'll turn gray before your time. Meanwhile, tend to your duties, be on time to work, don't spend too long on your coffee or lunch breaks (not even two minutes late). If Virgo thinks you deserve it, you'll get a promotion; this action may lead to your becoming successful

YOUR VIRGO EMPLOYEE
What Can You Expect from Your Virgo Employee?

He may get confused if he works in an office with busy looking rugs such as abstract or geometric design. So if you change the decor, don't be surprised if Virgo quits. This fellow prefers quiet colors that remind him of the orderly sanitary hospital look. He dislikes working in a noisy, busy atmosphere. Peaceful surroundings are a must. If your office is too hectic, topsy-turvy or talkative, it distracts him from giving his best — that disturbs him more than anything else.

Virgo is not original but can follow through with everything as ordered for him to do or as planned by another individual. This fellow is not dishonest; he can be trusted with secrets and money. He's not gutsy or pushy, but expects you to be. Virgo is a great organizer and excels in research. You may be in awe with the statistics, facts, and figures that he rattles off.

This fellow adapts readily to changes of plans. He enjoys his job so much that he may forget to take a coffee break. Virgo doesn't believe in taking time off for fun (he'll never call in sick unless he's really ill), and usually he dislikes vacations. If he works without one he may be just as happy, especially if he gets paid extra for overtime.

Virgo never shirks his duties, he's worth every penny paid him. He wants to do everything that is supposed to be done. This fellow loves to serve and be at your beck and call. He doesn't dilly-dally, gossip, or take company time for personal calls. If an urgent call comes from a family member, he gets nervous even though he may talk for only two seconds.

How to Handle Your Virgo Employee

This man is not motivated by power; all he wants is to do a good job (and that's exactly what he does). Virgo likes to work behind the scenes rather than out front. Keep him hidden away and he'll be elated (although you won't be able to tell it by his facial expression — he seldom cracks a smile).

He is an efficiency expert. This fellow knows just how long it takes in minutes or hours to do a job. Virgo likes to systematize everything. So let him handle your files and reorganize your office. By the time he's through everything will be running smoothly.

When this man arrives early and stays late or works weekends, don't be alarmed that you are going to have to pay him overtime wages. It isn't the extra money that interests him (although he won't turn it down, if it is offered) — it's the actual labor that has to be finished that is uppermost in his mind. So just let him be, give him a key to the office if he wants to come in before anyone else.

When Virgo goes to work for your company, or if you've transferred him to a new department, in the beginning he prefers to have someone look over his shoulder while he toils. He wants that individual to point out his errors and give him tips on how to perfect his tasks. But after he has learned his job thoroughly, and is confident with himself, then he doesn't like it when someone is watching his every move. So if you want to keep Virgo content, let him be once he tells you that he is sure of himself. This is one employee who will admit his own mistakes and try to learn from experience.

Virgo dislikes quick solutions unless it can be proven that they're the best and most accurate way to do a job. He just is too skeptical of things that are finished quickly and feels that he can't rely upon them. Therefore, most of the time this fellow does things the long and hard way. He has faith in the old method, believing that it's faultless. So don't goad or rush him into changing. However, if he's holding up production because he won't streamline his operations, then discuss it with him — that will push his panic button and get him to learn the new method by studying and practicing it outside of working hours as well as during the normal span of business.

Don't give orders, or anything else, too fast, because he can't cope with it. He's bright and smart and once he catches on, he'll be speedy. But prior to that, Virgo is going to ask you tons of questions. This fellow is interested in how everything is run and why you follow certain procedures. (He'll want to know what occurs before he gets a job and what happens after he's finished it — who gets it next and what does that person do, etc.) It's important for him to understand every phase of the operation. Once this knowledge sinks in, he is able to perform much better and quicker than he would without it.

Virgo likes to advance one step at a time. He has to be sure of each step; if he skips them along the way, he'll be a nervous wreck. So don't promote him too fast. This fellow is content to stay where he is until he knows his job thoroughly. You can compliment him, if he justly deserves it — and he'll know if you are feeding him the bull. He'll wonder what your ulterior motive is behind all those flowery words.

This man doesn't have an ego problem, nor does he strive for top spot. He doesn't like to be responsible for other people's actions, that's why he shies away from being supervisor. He refuses to be advanced to a higher post when he believes that he's unqualified for that better position. But once he's had the experience of working each job, in each department, then he is sure that he can guide others. However, Virgo is not the type to view them all as one big unit because he sees each department separately. So keep this in mind if you have thoughts of promoting him. And if he tells you that he is not ready for an advancement, don't try to talk him into changing his mind — go along with him.

Virgo likes everything the same. He plans his personal life around his office hours. If you shift his work schedule constantly, he becomes utterly confused and has to get his mind in order for the new hours. If this fellow runs out of work to do, he can't stand to sit still and read. Idleness makes him nervous, so find him a job to do in another department. If you don't, you may see your employee sweeping the floor and cleaning up as if he was the janitor.

He likes a steady paycheck and seldom goes out on his own, so you don't have to worry about him stealing your customers, and opening up his own business. Pay him well — what he's worth; if he asks for a raise, give him one — he's not unreasonable — if he's underpaid by his standards, you may lose a valuable employee and that's not the way to be a success, is it?

YOUR VIRGO COWORKER
What Can You Expect from Your Virgo Coworker?
There are just a few basic facts to keep in mind when working with this woman: she's aboveboard, ethical, exacting, a square shooter and censurer. Virgo is trying hard to do a good job, but she's not interested in battling you for a promotion. This female knows that her good, hard, and continuous work will pay off some day in the future. Virgo likes to accomplish her goals slowly with good work. Because she labors arduously, she may wind up with the same success as the late Grace Metalious, the famed Virgo Peyton Place author who wrote her manuscript tediously in longhand.

This is one person who isn't interested in your personal affairs and, furthermore, she doesn't want you to waste her valuable time in getting nosey with her. Virgo is going to spend every single moment engaged in severe and continuous work and will not disturb you unless she has to — and then it will be in connection with the job.

This female actually prefers to be alone; she welcomes confinement. However, she will stop and help you, especially if your work is dependent upon hers. If her job consists of serving — such as a waitress, she has her mind only on her customers and the job — everyone else is blocked out — that includes you and the public that she's not waiting on.

Be prepared when this demure and bashful appearing coworker suddenly tells you that you goofed. Her criticism will be harsh and may sound as if you had committed a big crime. It isn't that she doesn't respect you, it's that she feels you should know you made an error so you won't make the same mistake twice. Perhaps, if you heed her advice, you'll move up the corporate ladder that much faster.

How To Handle Your Virgo Coworker
If you're new on the job, don't expect Virgo to be very talkative. However, if you want something explained to you, ask her — she enjoys teaching. However, be prepared for a lengthy explanation and her repeating herself with the same words that might sound like a broken record. This female gets so bogged down by the detail of one thing that she can't go beyond that point — you'll get used to it now that the two of you are working side by side.

She's not the bossy type. If you have a serious problem that needs solving, she won't treat you in an inferior manner when helping you with it. Virgo will want you to be thorough and make everything clear and understandable. Don't rush her into making a decision. She has to analyze and carefully weigh all the pros and cons before giving you an answer. This deliberation process may take a few days because she wants to be sure of everything she tells you.

Try not to disrupt her work too often. If you finish a job and then are supposed to give it to her so she can do her part, place it on her desk — but not on top of anything. If there isn't any room, wait until she returns. Otherwise, Miss Finicky will come back and gripe and complain about how inconsiderate and messy you are. This female likes orderliness.

If it's part of your job to give instructions to Virgo, don't expect her to grasp anything right away. Talk slowly and circumstantiate everything you say. Be prepared to repeat yourself over and over again. Don't be alarmed if she fails to catch on immediately. This woman is cautious and won't budge until she's confident that she knows exactly why and what she's doing. She's got to have time to assimilate it mentally, practice and perfect it — she works for accuracy first, speed second. If she errs, don't criticize her too loudly because she's bashful and easily embarrassed. Once she's sure she's got it down pat, she'll go so fast that it'll make your head swim.

Virgo knows how to take the bitter with the sweet but she doesn't realize when she's handing it out. When she informs you of your weaknesses her sharp mind penetrates deftly. This woman doesn't react emotionally to anything — she's cool and uncomplicated. Thus she isn't aware that she's hurt your feelings. Her strong urge is to be of use to you — which she believes she is because she's told you the truth about yourself. But in so doing she wounds with her words like a man with a knife.

Keep in mind that this female is working on a schedule — either the company's or her own; it's the only way she can be truly happy. So if you aren't on one, don't waste time by gossiping with her. If you take up too much of her time, it will throw her helter-skelter — something she detests. You'll know it by her crankiness.

If you are lagging behind Virgo will help you out if you ask her to and if it doesn't interfere with her job performance. However, most of the time she may find a way to fit it into her timetable. This female is loyal and is not looking for compliments. So don't worry, she'll never take the credit for helping you.

Be pleasant to her even though she is so solemn you'd swear she was attending a mass. Believe it or not, she takes her work just as seriously and devotedly — it's almost like a religion to her. And she thoroughly enjoys every laborious moment she puts in on the job. So don't make fun of her — just let her be. She won't harm you. Virgo will not do anything against you to interfere with your getting a raise or promotion. She's not sneaky, envious, or resentful of your bettering yourself. If she is instrumental in your becoming successful she won't brag about it — she'll just be as pleased as she can be.

YOUR VIRGO CLIENT
What Can You Expect from Your Virgo Client?
You can spot a Virgo as soon as she walks in the door. She's meticulously dressed, looks shy, her head may be bowed and she's outwardly sedate — inwardly she may be a bundle of nerves. She stops at each counter and studies every-

thing carefully. She notices the price. If the price isn't there and she's interested in the object, she'll ask — otherwise she's not about to waste your time nor hers.

Virgo may ask you lots of questions about something she's interested in purchasing. She wants to know where it was made, what it consists of, how long it has been on the shelf, its history, if you happen to know it, and if it's been selling well. She will use this information when she goes to another store and does her comparison shopping. Although this woman is looking for a bargain she wants value in what she purchases.

When Virgo leaves this shop and, later, goes to another, she'll repeat these same questions. She's testy and wants to get everyone's opinion. It also lets her know who is truthful and knowledgeable. Once she's heard each clerk's side of the story, she'll put everything in its proper perspective. When she does go back and buy the object, it's done in a matter-of-fact manner, like a duty.

If you're calling on Virgo and expect to make a sale, be ready for her criticism if she finds fault with your product. Her tone of voice may sound sarcastic, but she doesn't mean it to be. She won't take a risk on anything newfangled unless you've given her all the facts and statistics of how others have done and every phase of the progress that has been made since your product has been on the market. If she is interested, she'll take her time studying it, and just may surprise you by placing an order.

How to Handle Your Virgo Client

Don't invite her to lunch. Visit her in her office so she can be working and talking to you simultaneously — it may be just cleaning up rather than actual mental labor She has to be kept busy utilizing all of her nervous energy in constructive endeavors. If she doesn't, you may see her bite her nails, pick at the skin on her elbow, pull out a few hairs from her arm and fiddle with her wristwatch. So it's advisable that you don't ask her to sit still and relax. But tell her it's okay for her to do her job while you're talking.

Avoid greeting her with a hail-fellow-well-met attitude. She's suspicious of the happy-go-lucky type. In her opinion they are big talkers out to make a fast buck. If you are optimistic and compliment her too often, she won't trust you at all. Don t blow anything out of proportion or exaggerate. Avoid making false claims; Virgo will have it checked out thoroughly before she buys anything. This woman doesn't put up with any distortions or beating around the bush. She wants you to get right to the point, but don't leave the details out in the process. If you have any ideas for Virgo they have to be logical and sound, or she won't spend any money or waste her time on them.

Guard against being personal or familiar. Be business-like, efficient and serious. You won't be able to tell how Virgo is responding because she is shy and covers up her feelings. She's precise and crisp, but she's a gentle person and really doesn't want to offend, although her words are often awfully sharp. Don't let her pickiness bother you. Also ignore her harping on a particular subject. Try to change the topic. If you are realistic and leave her with folders, brochures, and samples to read, you just might make yourself a sale. This is one woman who really likes to study everything on her own rather than just hear what you've got to say.

Be punctual. Avoid rushing her. Don't ask her to make any commitment right away. Give her plenty of time to think. Be patient. Make sure all contracts, leases, and other documents are faultless — she catches misspelled words quickly and is very outspoken about it. Try to be perfect and not only will Virgo be happy but you'll be on your way to becoming successful.

YOUR VIRGO PARTNER
What Can You Expect From Your Virgo Partner?

This is one man that you may be glad you teamed up with because he has excellent reasoning power, and is practical, materialistic and a toiler. He's got the analytical and research abilities, of Edgar Dean Mitchell (former astronaut), the precision and timing of the late Leonard Bernstein (the conductor) and the stamina of Gunther Gebel-Williams (star of the Ringling Bros. Barnum and Bailey Circus) — all Virgoans, So you've got a lot of talent wrapped up in this partner.

When Virgo invests in a business it's because he knows it's going to be a success; otherwise, this man doesn't shell out a dime. Before the two of you signed the papers, he carefully considered every angle. This man is patient and doesn't mind waiting for the profits to come rolling in. His advice on finances makes you believe that he's a real wizard — he is, and it's all hidden behind his somber and introverted personality.

This man can be conservative with small expenditures while he may spend plenty for big ones. If he has studied a modernization program thoroughly and came to the conclusion that large earnings could be derived from it, he will not mind investing in it. Virgo must have value for the money he spends.

This man expects you to put your all into the business — just like he does. He wants security for his old age. If you don't do right by him, he'll get out while he's still — ahead. Virgo will do his utmost to make the business a success, so why don't you do the same?

How To Handle Your Virgo Partner

Virgo wants to be in a position where he can do his work without having to be disturbed by anyone. Frivolous things — as he calls them are wining and dining clients. This is not his cup of tea. If he has to go to lunch with them, and trivial chitchat is the main topic of conversation, he gets bored, nervous and thinks he's wasting his precious time because he's not being productive. However, if business is discussed and deals agreed upon, Virgo is elated because he gained something from the luncheon (he killed two birds with one stone) he ate and tied up a contract. But he really prefers to be minding the store while you attend to these tête-à-tête.

Don't expect him to be a wheeler dealer or to sell anything. Virgo isn't interested, or qualified, for that type of work. He knows his weak points and that is one area where he rates high. This man is realistic so don't expect him to be creative or imaginative. If you ask him to visualize a project, he'll dummy up on you because he just can't see things in his mind's eye.

If you, or others who work for you, have fantastic notions (it won't be Virgo thinking them up), tell them to your partner: Virgo can pick anything apart (an idea, ad, contract, painting, etc.). He sees the flaws in plans and campaigns This man can spot the weaknesses in others as well as schemes — he can see through anything that is not right, views that are wrong, often with split-second timing; however, normally he requires time to deliberate. He has to get the statistics, check the facts and weigh everything to the most minute detail.

If you are involved with advertising your company's product, remember he can't mentally picture it. Therefore, appeal to his practical side. Then he can give you his down-to-earth approach as to why the public should buy it, what it's needed for and how it can be used. He applies logic and feasibility. He's sincere and honest in voicing his opinions. This is not any "yes" man. By listening to him you have a better chance of being successful.

Don't expect Virgo to get carried away with anything that has turned you on. He's just not the enthusiastic type. "I'm too pragmatic for that kid stuff," he'll tell you. This man likes precision and to investigate everything thoroughly before embarking on the wrong path. Give him privacy and don't disturb him with tons of questions. Let him work quietly without any disturbance — phones ringing, voices chirping or the noise of office machinery.

Virgo is versatile and as a rule can do more than one thing well. However, he doesn't like to drop one project suddenly for another. He must finish (it's almost a fetish) what he has begun. This man doesn't neglect or shirk duties, regardless of how unpleasant they may be, and he can't understand how or why others aren't more reliable. So don't be his target for the day or he'll nag you until you can't take it anymore.

Let your Virgo partner make charts, schedules and graphs. Leave the paper work to him and he'll be in good spirits (although his facial expression won't let you know that). His main problem is that he gets too bogged down by detail and doesn't view the overall picture thereby he misses important things. So, you will have to clue him in on the panoramic all-inclusive view. He uses good clear-cut objective thinking; he leaves himself out and just never thinks of anything from a personal standpoint. Generally his judgments are correct. This man means what he says and does; he doesn't treat anyone unfairly. So be right by him and you can't go wrong with him Then success will be just around the corner.

Sun-Sign Compatibility

This section deals with each sign of the zodiac in relation to a Virgo Sun sign. By knowing how your sign blends with a Virgoan, you go one step beyond understanding his personality and a step closer to knowing how to handle him in any business situation. Greater insight is invaluable — it not only helps a business prosper, it encourages peace of mind on and off the job.

The following Sun-Sign compatibility summaries, with the exception of Virgo/Virgo, *are from the point of view of the person dealing with Virgo. Note:* For the Virgoan's point of view, see the Sun-Sign chapter of the person Virgo is dealing with, i.e., Capricorn — refer to the Capricorn chapter explaining how Virgo thinks about Capricorn.

ARIES/VIRGO

Virgo's analytical approach bugs you. She's just too picky and fussy for you. Her desire for perfection irritates you so much that sometimes you just can't help yelling at her.

You really hit the ceiling when Virgo pleads with you not to spend so much money. Her practicality holds you back from making the fortune you know you're capable of earning. Because she's not competitive, you lack your usual get-up-and-go. Seemingly, you move mountains when you inspire your partner, but with Virgo's lack of enthusiasm you lose interest in your projects overnight. Her fear of taking a chance and leaping in just makes you think about dissolving your partnership agreement with her.

You appreciate Virgo's handling of details, which she seems so delighted with. And since you can't stand being bogged down by little things, this allows you to tend to the overall supervision of the job just what you enjoy doing, You are enthused by Virgo's ability to develop your idea and bring it to the attention of others; however, you're a nervous wreck waiting for it to happen.

Your natures are opposite: Virgo thinks and acts slow and methodical whereas you are fast and careless, you are a spender, Virgo's not. You need Virgo's explanation of the facts, love of detail and sense of order; otherwise you'd be in hot water. Despite the flaws, this partnership or working relationship could be a success!

TAURUS/VIRGO

You respect your Virgo partner. His conservative outlook and appearance blends with yours, so you two don't clash in this department. He doesn't oppose your expenditure programs — in fact he encourages the purchasing of used an overhauled machinery and equipment. You're pleased that he has a head on his shoulders and both of his feet on the ground. And it's a blessing to have an associate who is tidy and keeps everything in perfect order, just like you do.

You are delighted that your Virgo boss keeps you busy. He's never criticized you like he does the others The two or you work hard and don't waste time in idle conversation or nonsense. Both are stable, industrious, efficient, and patient. When you economize for the business, it is mutually agreed upon. Steady work in a quiet and peaceful office appeals to both of your natures; the two of you do your best under these conditions.

Both are dedicated to your duties and the success of the company; everything is taken earnestly. You admire and understand one another's drive. Success is achieved because you work well together — you're a perfect team!.

GEMINI/VIRGO

Your Virgo coworker sure doesn't have any sense of humor; she never laughs at your jokes. She just gives you one of her sour-puss looks and bobs her head back down to those papers on her desk.

You can't stand the tedious routine that your Virgo boss has imposed upon you. It makes you feel like a prisoner. She seems to be breathing down your neck, watching your every move. She's too critical about your not working in an orderly fashion; it's the only way to break up monotony, but she just doesn't seem to understand anything you do.

You and your Virgo partner are in continual disagreement over the way funds should be disbursed. She isn't interested in modern and progressive concerns, but you are. You are afraid that your competitor will corner the market before Virgo gets around to making a decision.

The two of you are not a good combination. You confuse Virgo with your flightiness and lack of continuity. She makes you a nervous wreck with her stability and continuity. You are always late and she's always punctual. She loves details and you can't stand being bogged down by them.

Your impulsiveness and Virgo's cautiousness don't mix well together. You are inclined to think that she's responsible for holding you back from attaining your goals. And she believes that you're keeping the company in debt. These factors make it difficult for the two of you to be successful.

CANCER/VIRGO

You feel comfortable with Virgo as a coworker. He doesn't rush you to hand in reports. Instead, he finds something else to do until you're ready to hand them over to him.

Your Virgo boss gives you an enormous amount of work to do. It's a miracle you have the energy to do it all. You look like you're strong but there are times when you think you'll go down under. However, Virgo doesn't know this and leaves you alone until you have enough time to finish a job.

Risks frighten you. However, your Virgo partner has reassured you that he's too prudent to do anything foolish. His practicality in business affairs matches yours. You thank your lucky stars for having someone as honest as Virgo as an associate. The two of you not only can receive an immeasurable amount of success together, but you also have an amiable relationship. You may be sensitive when Virgo gets picky; however, it makes you think that he does it because he's looking out for your best interest.

Both of you are shy and have retiring dispositions. But rather than causing a problem between the two of you, it builds a bridge of understanding. There's a strong trust that neither of you would do the other harm. It's not said in words, but it's felt by the both of you.

116

LEO/VIRGO

It's really great that your Virgo partner lets you run the company your way while she's busy taking care of the menial tasks you abhor doing. Her knowledge of facts sure does come in handy when you're ready to swing a deal.

You think highly of your Virgo employee. She's an asset to your corporation because with her analytical mind and practical ideas she manages to save the company from going bankrupt. You'll always find a place for this hard-working woman who doesn't mind coming in at odd hours to get a job out.

Leo and Virgo are not a bad combination as long as you ignore Virgo's criticism. There may be occasions when she tightens the purse strings too much and dampens your high-living and high-rolling style. But with your strong personality, you may have her in such awe that she doesn't squawk much.

Because Virgo doesn't strive for first place, and you do, there isn't any power struggle here. You know how to handle this woman so she will leave you alone to wheel and deal; however, on major decisions you will consult her and have found it valuable to do so.

VIRGO/VIRGO

If your job performance depends upon one another, it will be accomplished like clockwork. Neither one is disturbed by the other's slowness. You won't rush each other because both are concerned with doing a perfect job. You are delighted to have a partner who is as industrious as you are. His well-groomed appearance matches your own. You are impressed with his intelligence which he, like you, so modestly hides. It's comforting to know that you can depend upon him to handle the business when you are out of the office tending to affairs connected with the company.

This is a good team. Neither one of you is afraid to undertake a task that involves hard labor. Both are desirous of being constructive at all times. You may take on more than you should, but neither one will have it any other way. Both live, breathe, and plan your life around your careers — you are workaholics.

Your practicality leads you into considering the pros and cons before decisions are made. Both may get so bogged down by detail that the entire concept of an operation is missed. This disadvantage can be remedied by hiring employees who can visualize the overall picture.

LIBRA/VIRGO

A filthy and disorderly environment turns you off. It's so pleasant being around your neat and orderly Virgo coworker. This woman's output inspires you to be productive also.

The two of you could be financially successful. Your talents are opposite: Virgo needs to labor behind the scenes and Libra in front, talking and charming the customers. Virgo is industrious; Libra tends to be lackadaisical. Both of you tend to weigh the pros and cons of all propositions. Neither will leap into anything impulsively.

Since most of the work will be done by Virgo, you can expect her to pick you apart. So if you can put up with her calling you lazy, then you've got it made. If you feel she's unjust, you will angrily tell her off, quoting all that you've accomplished.

SCORPIO/VIRGO

Ordinarily you dislike sharing tasks with other people however, your Virgo coworker is the exception. Like you he's a perfectionist, pays attention to detail, sticks to a job until it's completed and doesn't seem to be afraid of hard work. This fellow doesn't talk or interfere with your concentration. Furthermore, he obeys your every command.

You admire your Virgo employer because he's got the patience of Jove — something you need. He keeps you busy with the type of projects you enjoy doing and doesn't interfere. This man lets you tackle a project your own way. He's not bossy; in fact, that's what's so great — you can tell him what to do and he listens to your advice.

You hold your Virgo partner in high esteem. He is consistent and dependable — two traits extremely important to your operations. However, he's afraid to take risks and you're not.

Despite this the two of you are a winning team. Success is practically guaranteed. Both of you are diligent, enjoy keeping busy and working around-the-clock. Neither one of you turns out slipshod work. Both of you are serious about the business and give it your all. You are a constructive and positive twosome. Every movement, mental or physical, counts. Both are organized. There aren't any flaws in the way you do or handle anything. The know-how you both possess can lead to the top of the summit.

SAGITTARIUS/VIRGO

All your Virgo boss does is pile up work on your desk. You don't mind doing it because you are anxious to please your superior and get that paycheck. You just wish that she'd smile once in a while to show that she's appreciative.

You get impatient with your Virgo employee who takes so long to complete even the simplest task. But you really shouldn't complain because her excellent work speaks for itself. You are amazed at her being so dedicated to a job. She has integrity, which you value highly. Her intelligence shows when she speaks. It's a shame she's not more outgoing — if she was, you could learn plenty from her.

This relationship has its pros and cons. As long as the two of you do your work separately, there isn't too much difficulty. However, you have opposite personalities; you are merry, she's sullen; you talk a lot, she's quiet; you are extravagant, she's practical.

Virgo's nagging brings out your candor — and you don't beat around the bush. You aim that arrow and hit your mark whether she likes it or not. She'll argue when criticized and so will you, so the storm rages. You're probably better off not being in business together.

CAPRICORN/VIRGO

Your Virgo boss is easy to handle. It's a cinch that he'll give you a raise and promotion. He is slow with decisions and tight with a buck, but you'll patiently wait it out. You know that he's a fair person and won't hold you back on purpose. When he thinks you're worthy, he'll advance you. You are sure that he holds you in high esteem because he almost grins when you ask for extra work on your day off.

You're lucky to have a partner who also abhors waste. Virgo, like you, puts all of his money back into the business. You keep abreast of new developments in your field and Virgo picks them apart for flaws. What a savings that has been! You are satisfied with the arrangement you have — he stays in the background while you're in the foreground being the front man for your corporation.

The two of you are well organized. Plans are made and strictly adhered to. Both are indefatigable and assiduous.

This is a sound relationship. Prosperity can be achieved through your combined efforts with more ease than if you both loned it. Your personalities blend well together, though both lack a sense of humor, you appear cool and detached and take the job earnestly.

AQUARIUS/VIRGO

You enjoy being kept busy; however, not when it's boring routine chores. You can only do those uninteresting tasks in spurts. Indubitably, your Virgo boss starts to fuss at you to get on the ball. You dislike taking orders from anyone, but Virgo isn't too demanding. It's just her meticulousness over insignificant things that bugs you. If this keeps up, you may dump the job for a better one.

You are intrigued by anything that is new, different and can save hours of labor, fatten your pocketbook and give you more free time outside of the office. However, your Virgo partner turns a deaf ear toward shortcut methods. There are moments when you wish you were not in business together.

The two of you are not suited for one another. However, you both have traits that are favorable for business success. If you put them together, learn to live with your differences and try to understand where each of you is coming from — perhaps then it could be a going relationship.

Your dislike for details is complemented by Virgo's efficient handling of them. Virgo is more practical than you and may frown upon some of your wild money-spending notions.

PISCES/VIRGO

You are weary from your Virgo boss's nagging, though you will be favorably impressed with your Virgo employee because he takes a load of responsibilities off your shoulders. Small details don't interest you, but you do realize that they are necessary. Therefore, you're thankful that Virgo enjoys working with them — he's so competent.

However you are upset because your Virgo partner is too frugal to take a chance on a big deal that is proposed to the company.

Basically the two of you are opposite signs in the zodiac and thus have traits that are dissimilar. You are too sensitive to the coldness and sarcasm of Virgo when he gets picky. His love of order gets completely shaken up when you get sloppy and make a mess.

His practicality does not blend with your impracticality. You are both on opposite sides of the fence — his small thinking opposes your larger-than-life schemes. Yet you are both adaptable and perhaps with this flexibility can adjust to each other's needs — but it's rough going.

Chapter Nine

Libra Compatibility In Business

If you were born between September 23 and October 22, your Sun is in the sign Libra. However, you may also express Libra traits if Libra is dominant in your horoscope (refer to the Introduction, Page 1) even if it is not your Sun sign. If this is the case, you should read this chapter just as if your Sun sign is Libra.

LIBRA PROFILE
Getting Acquainted With The Libra Personality

This Libra woman is rather easy to get to know. Once you understand what motivates her, it will facilitate dealing with her in business, regardless of whether she's your partner, employer, employee, coworker, or client. Libra may appear so chic and attractive that you don't think she has any brains. Don't let that fool you this is an intellectual female. It may take you a while to discover this because she devotes most of her time listening to you talk. She's extremely interested in what you have to say. It's easier for Libra to learn knowledge through a conversation than it is for her to read a book.

This woman is even-tempered until the scales (the symbol representing her sign) are tipped — then watch out! Libra can go from sugary sweet one moment to sarcastic the next. Then when she realizes she's off balance, she swings back to gentleness.

She is inconsistent due to her dual nature — the scales dipping to two extremes. She'll work, work, work for a while and then come to a sudden halt. Then she goes the opposite direction and rests, rests, rests. This female has to recuperate the energy expended. She doesn't have the strength to continue a strenuous schedule. Thus, when you see her taking it easy you may call her lazy.

If rushed Libra can make a quick decision. But an hour later she'll think it over and change her mind. Her indecisiveness frustrates her as much as everyone else. She wants to be fair and square and do the right thing so she has to weigh all the pros and cons on those Libra scales. Give her a chance and you will see that she can be an asset in your business.

IF YOU ARE A LIBRA

Because you are mercenary you may ask, "What can I do to get a better position and make more money?" Success can be achieved faster if, when you deal with others, you adhere to the following advice:

When dealing with an employer speak up and give him any suggestions you may have that could improve business. You look like you don't have any ideas, but in reality you are overflowing with them. Because you are so afraid of hearing a no answer and causing a scene, you take the line of least resistance. The problem with this is that your boss may think that you are just there to do your duties and collect your paycheck.

Because you have difficulty in sticking with one line of endeavor, you may use your charm to get your coworkers to finish a project. Try to complete the tasks that have been assigned to you. If you don't, the boss is eventually going to get wise — and then you won't get the raise or promotion desired. Luckily your personality is so pleasing that seldom does anyone have the heart to fire you.

Avoid taking the easy way out just because you dislike hard work. Not all employers are going to let your affability mesmerize them into keeping you on the payroll. Volunteer to stay late or come in on weekends. If you sacrifice your pleasures once in a while, you will have a better chance of reaping the benefits desired and becoming a success.

When dealing with partners, employees and coworkers avoid relying too much upon others. This is one of your main weaknesses. It's likely to occur when you ask someone to make the decision for you and take the burden of indecisiveness off your shoulders. Then if things go wrong, no one is harping at you. However, did you ever stop to think that the fireworks might start because you weren't interested enough to take the lead and make a commitment?

You are easily influenced and have to be careful that your judgment isn't swayed by others. Your hunger for praise and adulation can make you help those who use you to gain their own advantage. Because you have an intense need to be liked and accepted by others, you will go to any lengths to avoid discord. Often people walk over you just as if you were a doormat. But that doesn't last for long because when you realize it, your words cut them to pieces; you cool off rapidly and are willing to forget what transpired.

Avoid telling fibs just so you can maintain peace and harmony in your working environment. Sooner or later you'll be found out, and you won't like the opinions others have of you. Be truthful, but use tact and diplomacy.

When dealing with clients you may lose a sale because you are too lackadaisical. Get up from that chair you've been lounging in the moment a potential customer walks in the door. Avoid your usual saunter — walk to the counter quickly. Open the showcase instead of engaging in pleasantries. You can be amiable *while* you are taking the items out. If you waste time, it not only might make your client too impatient to stay and purchase an object, but it may hinder another possible sale coming from the person who just entered the store.

If a customer asks you, "Which one of these lockets would you buy if you were me?" A typical Libra answer would be, "The one on the left is more beautiful because of the encrusted stones. However, the one on the right is better made because it's an antique. The one on the left, though, is newer and more with the times. However, the one on the right is more valuable and the one on the . . ." Back and forth you'd go, unable to help your client make a decision.

Avoid being indecisive. When asked to make a choice between two items say, "Do you like old things? If so, I'd take this locket. However, if you prefer beauty to plainness, I'd purchase this one." This procedure lets your customer decide. Later, if she returns with it because she doesn't like it you won't be blamed. Also, this method speeds up a sale and that is what a successful shopkeeper wants.

To go one step further, once you as a Libra know or can recognize the sign your partner, employer, employee, coworker, or client is, read that sign's chapter to know how best to deal with him as well as to understand his compatibility with you. If you wish to know what he thinks about you, read the Sun-Sign Compatibility section starting on page 132 The remainder of this Libra section deals with how others relate to you, what they can expect of you and how they should handle you. So let's go on an interview with your sign, okay?

AN INTERVIEW WITH A LIBRA

A Libra employer interviewing you: Your resumé will be gone over carefully. Neatness in writing and appearance will be considered. He may test you with a few questions to see whether you are aggressive, adaptable, and a logical thinker. Be polite (it's a must with this man), speak softly and pleasantly. Tell him that you need a job that will keep you busy. Let him know that you don't mind working overtime, if needed. Ask him about the opportunities for advancement that his company offers. If Libra thinks that you are career driven and energetic, he'll hire you that much faster, mainly because these are traits that he lacks but needs for balance in his business operations.

Don't expect to be hired immediately. Libra has to be fair and give the other job seekers a chance, too. It may take days or weeks for him to weigh the good points you have against that of the other applicants. In the process he's likely to change his mind many times before he comes to any conclusion. He is fearful that he'll make a wrong decision that could affect his job. In the meantime, look for employment elsewhere.

If you're interviewing a Libra applicant: If you keep her waiting, she'll sit calmly and may converse quietly with the other job seekers. You'll notice that she's beautifully attired from head to toe and smells nice. She's so graceful and poised that she stands out in the crowded room.

When you interview this woman you may be surprised that she's also got a good brain. You infer from her questions about the corporation that she is money-oriented and wants to work for a company that pays better-than-average wages, gives bonuses, and has profit-sharing benefits for the employees.

Don't ask her to start working immediately. She needs to make the rounds and get the best offer. Also, she has to observe whether your offices are clean, pretty, and tranquil. If they aren't she won't work for you.

Now that the interview is over, let's first go to work for a Libra and thus see how Libra is going to fare as your employee, okay?

YOUR LIBRA EMPLOYER
What Does Your Libra Boss Expect of You?

If you're being transferred from one department to another, regardless of the reason, Libra will be kind and considerate — honey couldn't be any sweeter. He has a strong need to be liked by everyone and goes out of his way to be pleasant. He expects you to respond by being cordial, cooperative, and doing your job well.

This man is a regular fellow who will level with you and never give you a wrong deal. He trusts because he thinks that you are the same. Libra likes you to take the initiative because he's not the type to do so. He'd rather sit back and watch you do all the work. So the more get-up-and-go you have, the more you will gain his esteem. If you are rash and want to leap into something, he hopes that you will think ahead and weigh all of the consequences before taking action. He wants you to know what you are doing at every moment.

Libra expects you to give him your opinion about that latest deal he consummated, the possible merger that's pending and whether he should streamline the business now or wait until some future date. He wants you to know about the latest equipment available on the market to speed up production. It matters to him what you think. Your response is taken and analyzed from every angle.

This man wants you to be dependable. He expects you to be able to take on the responsibility of handling his business affairs when he's attending a meeting or away on a vacation. This man wants you to be a success because that means you will do everything in your power to make his corporation prosper.

How to Handle Your Libra Boss

Make sure that the colors you wear don't clash. Wrong combinations grate on his aesthetic sensibilities. Beauty and harmony of the right hues are as necessary to him as bread and water is to a hungry man. Never be loud, rude, use profanity or tell dirty jokes in front of this fellow. Good manners are an essential part of your job when you work for him.

Libra will be happy with you if you are tidy. Keep your desk neat and clean, dust the file cabinets, keep the cover on the typewriter when it's not in use, make sure nothing is lying down; keep things upright. All awards, certificates, and diplomas should be hung properly — fix them if they are crooked. If you have to leave some papers on his desk, don't pile them on top of anything. If you have to go into his office when he's not there, don't disturb his working area. This action causes confusion, which he dislikes.

Your Libra boss may arrive late most of the time, but that doesn't mean you have to mimic his actions or to take advantage of the fact that he won't know if you are tardy. Don't chance someone not telling him. However, if he does discover that you are not always punctual it won't upset him too much. But if you make a habit of it, instead of embarrassing you in front of everyone, he may ask you to come into his office so the two of you can have a private discussion. Don't panic! Remember he's a straight shooter. He isn't about to say anything to you that will make you dislike him. Explain why you are having difficulty getting to work on time. He's sympathetic but will take time to think about it.

Another day he may call you back to his office to give you his solution to your late arrivals. He gives good advice once he's had time to consider it. This man is not dictatorial and will not insist you obey him. He will say, "I suggest that you do_____." If you're off the beam this is one fellow who can get you back on again — that is, if you listen to him.

Make sure you've checked over your work thoroughly before you show anything to him. He's a perfectionist, but not a nit-picker. If you make errors, he'll tell you about it in a nice, kindly way because it's part of his job. Libra doesn't expect you to get a task finished in a jiffy. He wants you to take your time and do it right. He will not hold slowness against you, unless you are holding him up on an important project and he has to report with it to his immediate superior. But, even then, he won't goad you into quick action. Instead, Libra will butter you up with such charm, and a nice winning smile, that you'll pick up speed as if a demon on wheels was chasing you — and you'll try for accuracy, too!

Your Libra boss has sudden bouts of inspiration that come and go as quickly as those scales dip back and forth. However, one notion may be so overwhelming that he has to tell it to everyone he meets. So if he comes to you and sounds like he's high on something, just figure he's carried away with his "baby." Libra wants to hear what you think about it. Don't be afraid to speak up. He is considerate of the opinions of others regardless of whether he thinks you're wrong. If he goes to someone beneath you in position and also relates it to him, don't think he's gone wacky. This man is intrigued by the mental discussion of everyone's theories; therefore he'll make the rounds not only in his office but outside of it, asking everyone to give their opinion.

When your Libra employer gets these surges of creativity, and if you think the notion is valid and beneficial for the company, be sure and tell him so. But praise him in the process. Tell him that this new product could increase sales and make competitive corporations envious. Say, "How did you ever come upon such a brainstorm of an idea?" Flatter him; it's his weakness, but he needs it like a baby needs milk. Once he has your approval, he's partially reassured that the new product is important. Deep down he may not feel it, but he'll never let you see that side of his nature — the scales will never dip that far.

Before your employer will jump into mass marketing and producing this item, he will weigh the risks involved. So be patient with him while he goes through this painful process. If the scales tip too far down to the insecure side, he may be too fearful to indulge in this scheme. Or he may be just too lazy to follow through. This is where you come into the picture. Tell him you'd like to bring his product to fruition and that you'd feel honored if you could take over the responsibility of working on the details and the advertising campaign. Tell him that you believe fantastic profits can be made from his ingenious idea. Libra is easily influenced and once you've caught him in the trap of flattery, it's hard for him to spring loose.

There's still a hitch before Libra can take the final step of initiating his "baby." He has to weigh the possible gains and losses that can be attracted from bringing this product out. This man wants money to come easily and without undue personal effort; that's why you must make it all easy for him. Don't rush him. It takes him a long time to make up his mind. He'll change his mind several times while deliberating. You can speed this process up if you study the pros and cons and then present them to him. Of course, this ingratiating action of yours may pay off later. If Libra thinks that the end seems to justify the risk, he'll go full steam ahead.

If your Libra employer takes a loss on this product, expect him to have a philosophical reaction. He learns from his mistakes and believes the experience he gains guides him in future transactions. However, if he comes up a winner, so do you, especially if he promised you a bonus if it became a sensation. You can count on him keeping up his end of the deal. Not only will you get a generous bonus, but a substantial salary increase and may even be promoted to being his assistant. And to top it off, he'll share equal credit with you! So it's well worth your efforts to push your boss (without his being aware of it) to accomplish his inspirations. Sneaky? Selfish? Using someone to gain your own needs? It's actually employing good business judgment, and putting your own manpower behind it — you should be amply rewarded. Also it's auspicious for your employer and the company he owns. Everyone benefits — and that's a sign of success!

YOUR LIBRA EMPLOYEE
What Can You Expect from Your Libra Employee?

If she accepted employment in your concern, that's a clue that she approved of your office. It's neat, clean, and the color scheme and decor agree with her. Otherwise, she would have left before the interview began.

There are two types of Librans — the one who works because she doesn't have any other means of support and the one who toils because she likes money and wants to be successful. However, neither type will ignore a husband, boyfriend or fun for a job. Career takes second place (this also applies to the male Librans). Regardless of which one works for you, they both have certain traits that you can expect from them.

The Libra that's just there to earn a living is lazy and procrastinates. She doesn't put much into a job, but she's pampered and spoiled by coworkers who fudge for her, so you may never realize that you've got a lethargic employee on your payroll. The other Libra wants to be in a high position. Status is important to her. She will socialize on the job to get ahead. Both Librans are well liked by just about everyone. They have such lively smiles and are so easy-going how can anyone avoid catering to them?

Don't expect Libra to catch on the first time you show her how to do a new task. She's got a sharp mind (even if it isn't always obvious), but it's not fast. However, once she understands the logic behind it, she'll pick up speed. Don't be fooled into thinking she's weak and helpless — she's not. She's smart and knows what she is doing. If emergencies arise, she's calm, cool and handles them adequately, without rushing. Afterwards, she won't brag about it or belittle anyone who didn't pitch in. Most of the time, energy permitting, she'll try to do her best.

How to Handle Your Libra Employee

You will get the most out of your Libra employee if the office is tranquil. If she doesn't have a certain amount of quietude, she has difficulty concentrating on her chores. Libra needs an atmosphere conducive to work and she does her best when there's soothing music in the background. So bring in a radio or if you can afford piped-in music, that will suffice. It's best that her desk and chair are away from windows, especially if there's a pretty view outside for her to gaze at. Libra gets distracted very easily if the scenery is pleasing to her eye. If you notice that she's got a floating ethereal look about her, it's either that she's dreamy-eyed about a beau or enjoying the panorama outdoors, as seen from inside.

Libra likes everything new, bright, shining, and pretty. She doesn't like to work with dirty things or get her hands on anything that's not clean. Her love of beauty is seen in the way she dresses. You'll never be ashamed of her appearance. If you want to impress a client, she'll maintain the image you want. She may look like an executive. She's not garish or flashy, the makeup is just right and her manners are beyond reproach. If you are planning a party for a VIP, let her assist. This woman is an excellent hostess and has a good strategy for greeting and talking to people.

Let Libra attend business meetings. She may surprise you when she comes up with some dandy ideas, although when you glance at her sitting there so attractively attired and graceful, you may not realize the brilliant notions she comes up with later. But while she sits quietly, she observes and absorbs everything. Later, after she's had time to think things over, she comes up with policies, issues and changes that may flabbergast you because they are so ingenious.

Libra tends to arrive late to work quite often. It's because she has difficulty deciding upon what to wear and whether this outfit will blend with her scarf. It's essential that she has the right colors that mix-'n-match. Her decision making is done in her usual languorous style.

If you're vexed because she's tardy, do not reprimand her in front of anyone. Take her into the privacy of your office and talk to her. If you all work in one room, then take her aside and whisper to her. Tell her to either figure out what she's going to wear the night before or to set her alarm and get up earlier than normal so she can decide how to dress for the day.

Do not shout, scream, or yell at her if she's made a mistake. Noisy outbreaks and tension throw her off balance. Wait until the two of you are alone to quietly explain why you are angry. Point out her errors and suggest ways to avoid them. Libra needs logical explanations — later she will implement them. If you have a shortcut method for her to speed up production (because she's too slow), give it to her.

It could be Libra's indolent manner that burns you up. More than likely she's just recuperating from all those deadlines and stress you put her through the last several days. Although you're furious, you will probably forgive her because she's so sweet and she does try to obey your every command.

Libra is not given to physical labor. She needs mental work or work that involves communication. She's good at talking over the telephone. Libra is able to be in charge of an office and handle every problem tactfully. This female is a good troubleshooter and when difficulties arise she is able to diplomatically quiet things down. Give her all petty grievances to take care of and she'll charm the customer who is busy complaining. If there are any cases where there's a lot of red tape connected with a clearance on some funds for a client, let Libra graciously handle it. If there are any bottlenecks in the operation of the business let her have time to weigh the pros and cons and she'll come up with the right answer; she seldom errs if she's given the proper time to decide upon an issue.

This female wants to be paid fairly — equal to the other people in her same job classification. She'll all for the ERA. If she's not compensated equally, you'll see the other side of her personality come out — the scales of justice are now in the position of disequilibrium: therefore she will fight the injustice she feels she's received.

Can you imagine this normally affectionate and gentle soul suddenly turning bitchy? It may shock you, but don't worry about it. She never gets red-hot angry — just the color of glowing embers. Then she'll simmer down and swing into her cool mood. But don't fret, it won't be the ice cold of the Arctic in the dead of winter, it'll just remind you of a brisk autumn day. If she frowns, you'll know the scales are still tipped unevenly. But the moment she smiles, the scales are balanced — and she's back to being your Libra employee trying her best to be successful.

YOUR LIBRA COWORKER
What Can You Expect from Your Libra Coworker?

There are just a few basic facts to keep in mind when working with this fellow: he's noncompetitive, cooperative, pleasant, and courteous to a fault. This man looks only for the good in you. Expect him to encourage you to better your position. He treats everyone equally, therefore he will also try to inspire his *other* coworkers to get ahead. Libra is highly motivated but wants to get to the top in his own sweet time; he's just not about to rush for anything. Once he reaches the heights he may wind up with as much money as Libra-born Johnny Carson.

Libra doesn't get nosey in a personal way; he just likes to feel you out. So be prepared if he wants to talk to you; it's probably just to ask you how you think in general about a certain theory. From this conversation he can judge the type of thinker you are — and that's what interests him the most.

This is one individual you can confide in; he has a calming influence. Libra's a good listener and can keep a secret. If you need his assistance keep everything on an intellectual level because he's not an emotional person.

Don't ever tell him about any office gossip. However, it's easy to slip when you are in his presence because he is so friendly. Just remember he is your coworker and, although he may appear good-natured, he can turn around and surprise you with a cutting remark for being a tattle-tale. He believes scandalmonging is unfair because it doesn't give the other person a chance to give his side of the story.

Libra's quite social, especially at lunchtime or on the coffee break. Those are the moments when he may give you suggestions about how you can move up the corporate ladder faster.

How to Handle Your Libra Coworker

If you're new on the job you can expect Libra to be pleasant to work with. He's likeable so the two of you may become pals. This fellow can be relied upon to do what is proper. He's even willing to help you if you lag behind on a chore. Libra is quite flexible and finds it easy to shift from his task to yours. However, he tends to procrastinate; don't fret, he won't let you down. But if he's listless of body and mind, he needs a rest. However, that's not always possible, especially if the boss is around. If this is the case, he'll coast along and move slower than his normal snail's pace. Just be patient because eventually he'll get around to assisting you. And don't worry that he'll bungle your work — he won't, he's too skillful to botch up a job.

When the Libra scales are tipped to extremes, he's difficult to understand. He may be kind one moment, harsh the next. Just as you think you are pleasing him, he'll switch the other way; you'll wonder what you did wrong. You may be confused when he swings from cool to warm, optimistic to pessimistic. Five minutes ago he was sullen and now he's smiling with those twinkling eyes all lit up.

If he gets off balance his work can take a slide. Something is the matter. Ask him if you've done anything that has caused offense. If you had, he'll be truthful. If you hadn't, ask Libra if there's something you can do to solve what's bugging him, and not only affecting his work, but yours, too, since what you do is dependent upon his job performance. (Often unless something is brought to his attention, he's unaware that he's off balance.) Libra is susceptible to kindly overtures and will respond to you if you inspire it. Usually it's nothing personal because he leaves those problems at home (his thinking processes involve the scales tipping at opposite extremes; home and work are two distinct areas that are kept separate from one another); therefore his upset is coming from the business environment. Once you've helped him, his work — and yours — will improve.

You may think he's changeable and thus get confused with some of his actions toward you. Perhaps last month you pitched in and helped Libra get a report ready. If it hadn't been for you, it would have been late. Not only did he thank you with a bright smile, but he took you out to lunch and the next day brought you a chocolate candy bar. Now, it's a month later and you've noticed that he's lagging behind. You offer to lend a helping hand and he responds with a "No, I don't need your assistance. I can do it myself. That's what I'm getting paid for."

You may be perplexed and think, "Oh. I've insulted him. But those were the same words I used last month and he didn't act like that. So I guess he's angry with me for something." It's just the Libra scales dipping again — he forgets the past and lives in the present — two distinct eras. Therefore keep in mind that if Libra likes you for helping him today, don't expect the same treatment tomorrow or next month — because you do not know (and neither does he) which way those scales are going to be dipped. To avoid a repeat of this upsetting type of reaction, don't say, "Can I help you?" Instead say, "If you need my assistance, just ask."

If you and a teammate get into an argument, expect Libra to settle the dispute. When anger and chaos reign he feels he must bring peace to the room. Libra gets shaken up when loud voices, full of hatred, are yelling at one another — these antagonistic feelings are the opposite of his code: "Love your fellow man."

Libra's a good mediator. He'll listen to both sides of the argument, weigh everything and charm the two of you into being quiet, settling your differences, apologizing and shaking hands. Even though Libra may be buddy-buddy with you, don't expect him to take your side. He believes in fairness for one and all, and thus is going to do what is right by everyone. Because he intervened the boss won't get wind of this scene; therefore your job is saved and you still have a chance in this organization to get to the top.

YOUR LIBRA CLIENT
What Can You Expect from Your Libra Client?

This man is conspicuous when he walks through your store because he appears so elegant. Once you speak to him, you'll notice he's refined. He may make a remark about what a lovely place you have. Before you know it, you may find yourself in a fascinating intellectual conversation. Eventually he may look at a for-sale item, but he'll say, "I'll have to think about it." Don't be surprised if he stays and visits for a while; he enjoys making new friendships. And he may be back at a later date, if not to purchase an object, just to give you his regards so the two of you will keep in touch.

If you're a salesperson and call on Libra at his office, he'll be polite, serve you coffee, and make you feel right at home. He'll exchange pleasantries and then let you talk about your wares. Libra likes a relaxed atmosphere when conducting business. Now that you're both settled down, he's ready for you to proceed. While you are giving your sales spiel he will smile and look attentive. From his facial expression you may think you've got him hooked. But don't be so sure of yourself. Libra's not about to jump into a deal. This man needs time to deliberate before making a final decision. However, he is courteous and will listen to every word you have to say. Besides, he's also curious to learn about everything.

If he gets quiet suddenly, that means he's either considering it or thinking about a way to say that it's not for his company at this time. Either way he will not want to offend you and will try to find an easy way out. If he asks you to call him next week, that implies he's interested, otherwise, he may say, "I'll call you." In seeking success you have to take the bitter with the sweet.

How to Handle Your Libra Client

When you first meet Libra you may think he's shy, but he isn't. He's just waiting for you to talk so he can judge your character. If you are rough and tough acting and throw in a few cuss words to be showy, he'll shun you. If you are disorderly or erratic, hastily running to and fro, it throws his Libra scales off balance; he gets confused and may leave in a dither apologizing for his behavior as he goes out the door.

But if you made a favorable impression on him, he'll stay and converse with you. When selling your product, don't exaggerate. This is an extreme and Libra gets thrown off balance when you go too far in one direction. Keep your sales pitch at an even tempo and not that of a barker in a sideshow.

If Libra comes to your business address, take him to your private office or a room that doesn't have the noise of the jungle inside. If the environment is ugly or sordid, Libra may make up an excuse and graciously depart before you even had a chance to talk. If this occurs, as he's leaving, make a future appointment to dine in a fancy restaurant. Thus you still have a chance of getting his signature on a contract.

Go to a small, uncrowded (he needs air to breathe, not smoke), intimate restaurant that has soft lights, quiet music in the background and gourmet dining. Don't be tight with the budget; lavish spending makes it hard for Libra to say no to your proposition.

Don't hurry him through a meal. Avoid business talk for a while. Discuss the opera, theatre, ballet, art, music or the latest fashions. Slowly get around to your reason for this luncheon. Explain everything clearly and logically. If it's a modernization plan, tell him how others have benefited. If it's a product, show him an portfolio of neatly arranged pictures that he can take with him to look at in his spare time. Do not rush him into making a decision at that time. If he does make one, expect it to be changed later. Any time Libra leaps into something, he reconsiders it many times for the next few days; most of the time, he'll cancel an order that he made in haste.

You will get annoyed with his indecisiveness (it also bugs him). However, his kindness makes you forget his inconsistencies. Don't be surprised if later he calls you and says he has delved more deeply into it, and has decided to give you the okay to go ahead as previously arranged.

Libra notices everything you say and do. He can't stand anyone to cheat him or treat him unfairly — that brings out his temper. But you can calm him down with some flattery (he loves approbation) and tell him how he can increase his profits. This will put you "in" with him and you'll be headed on the road to becoming successful

YOUR LIBRA PARTNER
What Can You Expect From Your Libra Partner?

Be thankful you teamed up with this woman because she has soft manners, natural intellect, alert reasoning and is adaptable. She's got the understanding of a Dr. Joyce Brothers, the ability to communicate of a Barbara Walters, and the charm of the late Helen Hayes — all Librans. So you may be in the winner's circle with this woman.

Your Libra partner can't stand squalor so expect to see everything in your office shiny and bright. The office will be elegant pastel colors. The furnishings may lean toward the ornate but everything will be in excellent taste. Libra beautifies your office with her very presence — her eloquent voice, good manners and charisma. She dresses well — designer clothes; her jewelry is expensive and genuine.

This woman takes long and leisurely lunches so don't expect her to rush. She seldom brings her lunch; she prefers eating in a first class restaurant. She'll take clients there and take it off of the expense account. This could be a daily occurrence so don't be alarmed by it.

Libra needs to be associated with people. She can't be confined or work alone — companionship is essential. This woman accomplishes more when there's someone alongside of her — she's just not a loner. Expect her to share equally in all decisions and actions; she wants to participate in everything, otherwise she feels left out. She'll never be disrespectful. You can depend upon her to smooth the way for you and everyone else. And in any kind of a venture, this helps toward being successful.

How To Handle Your Libra Partner

There will be moments when your Libra partner will exasperate you. She will agree to spend exorbitant sums on a project, sign the papers for the bank loan and really be gung-ho about it. Then just as suddenly, before the project gets started, she pulls back and cuts the budget in half so she can save money This woman hates to hurt your feelings but may do so without being aware of it. In business deals expect her to make a promise and, later, think about it and renege. She won't think she's being unkind — she sees it as good business management.

You may wonder what goes through her mind when she pulls stunts like these. Libra must sort and assemble all the facts about the project, even discussing the pros and cons with you. Once she's alone (in times like this she prefers solitude) she questions whether it's logical and makes common sense. While she's going through this weighing process, she's trying to be fair to everyone concerned. Libra can't stand to take advantage of anyone. She comes to a conclusion many times before she finally decides upon an impartial decision.

Libra doesn't want you to be extravagant and, yet she's a lavish spender. Her reasoning is that the bank will think that you're not a good credit risk if she stops spending. However, her thinking is ambiguous because her credit rating isn't so hot — she charges things, goes into debt, is late making payments. In fact, she's delinquent most of the time because she hates to pay bills. This woman always *tries* to balance the checkbook, often she's off balance and in the red.

Most of the time Libra puts the fun, pleasure and entertainment of the customer first and the earnings gained from it is of secondary importance. Never try to be practical with her — she just doesn't understand the meaning of that word. But do try to guide her to use discretion when entertaining a client. You probably won't complain because she's able to consummate enormous deals while socializing — it really is her forte.

If you lost company money on a negotiation that fell through, Libra doesn't care about how you feel about losing it, she'll want to know *why* you lost it. This woman weighs the facts, not what's beneath the surface of human feelings. She doesn't sympathize that much with the emotions or rely upon them. It's the intellect she believes one can count on, if it's used. Therefore, give her the details so she can figure out where you really erred. Once she knows, she'll clue you in so you won't repeat this mistake on a future transaction.

Before you do anything impulsively, first check it out with Libra. She loves to give advice. This woman will weigh all the possibilities of the venture against the disadvantages. She doesn't want you to goof. Don't tax her mind to make a quick decision. She needs time to analyze everything properly.

This woman prefers an aggressive partner because she lacks get-up-and-go. She needs to catnap; if she doesn't get her proper rest she becomes irritated and makes mistakes. So be understanding of her need to relax. She's either all work, no play or all play, no work — that's how those Libra scales dip back and forth — it seems she has difficulty balancing them. And she really feels off balance when everything is topsy-turvy. At that time she may escape to a peaceful spot — inside or outside of the office. In the midst of all of this hullabaloo, don't ask her to make a decision she can't under these conditions.

If money doesn't come in as fast as Libra desires, she may want to dissolve the partnership. Encourage her to be patient and wait for the pending deals to culminate. Tell her how much you need someone as talented as she. Feed her vanity, and once she receives this attention, she'll reconsider it. Handle her with velvet kid gloves and you'll be on the road to success.

Sun-Sign Compatibility

This section deals with each sign of the zodiac in relation to a Libra Sun-Sign. By knowing how your sign blends with a Libran, you go one step beyond understanding his personality and one step closer to knowing how to handle him in any business situation. Greater insight is invaluable — it not only helps a business prosper, it encourages peace of mind on and off the job.

The following Sun-Sign compatibility summaries, with the exception of Libra/Libra, *are from the point of view of the person dealing with Libra. Note:* For the Libran's point of view, see the Sun-Sign chapter of the person Libra is dealing with, i.e., Aquarius — refer to the Aquarius chapter explaining how Libra thinks about Aquarius.

ARIES/LIBRA

Your Libra boss is easy to work for because she lets you run the entire office your way. She seldom interferes with any of your ideas. Those raises she gives you are great too! But your Libra employee makes you furious because she dawdles and takes forever to complete a project. If she doesn't start to improve her job performance, you just may fire her. You need hard and fast workers in your employ.

You need to compete with someone and with your Libra partner it's impossible — she's too lazy. She holds up your deals while she tries to make the right decision. This woman is too lethargic for you, especially when she naps instead of working. But she does follow through fastidiously on the ideas you have initiated so you can't complain about that.

Your hard-working talents are utilized to the fullest in your estimation. Your Libra counterpart falls by the wayside time and again. However, she knows how to give you the attention you crave; her flattery can keep things balanced.

You are impatient where she's patient. You both have assets that the other lacks and needs, Eventually you may be promoted or get angry enough to ask for a transfer to another department; thus the two of you can remain friendly. As partners, you need a financial advisor because you're both big spenders.

TAURUS/LIBRA

Just as you're ready to tell your Libra employee that his shiftlessness doesn't belong on your company's payroll, he suddenly becomes extremely productive. His changeableness puzzles you. But he is pleasant and likeable.

You don't like owing money and want the bills paid on time. Libra irks you because he's just the opposite. His splurging rubs you the wrong way; he's just not practical enough for you. But the major problem is his indecisiveness; it's bad enough he contradicts himself all of the time, but to make a decision and not stick with it is more than you can bear. You need a partner who is steady and level-headed, like you — but with Libra you never know where you stand.

Taurus and Libra are basically not that good a combination, however there are some good points about it. Both of you are charmers and socialize where it pays off. You have many things in common with your love of the arts; perhaps in this area you two could be extremely successful together.

Libra is not earthy enough for you, especially when his ideas are mainly up in the air. Both are interested in material gains. However, Libra may prefer spending his profits on something that, in your estimation, is wasteful. You'd rather reinvest the money in the business.

GEMINI/LIBRA

It's a joy to work with Libra because she's got such a winning smile even though she can be sullen, just like you, on occasion. Her moods change as swiftly as yours but most of the time you find her great to be around. The conversations you two have are fascinating — real high-brow stuff. Sometimes you don't get as much done because you are too busy talking — but you don't care, you'll make up for it later.

Your Libra employee is intelligent and comes up with some good logical solutions that have been beneficial for the company. She works fast when it comes to deadlines but you've noticed some slack once the pressure's off.

Your Libra boss is fair. Often you've made some real errors and she didn't get angry; she was quite kind in bringing them to your attention. And when you're late to work she doesn't say anything. Perhaps that's because she is tardy herself most of the time.

The two of you are an excellent team. Both are intellectuals and enjoy airing your thoughts to one another. If they are put into reality, tremendous gains may be earned from them. However, both are changeable and may not follow through on original ideas; plans could be altered continually, one could replace another, and none are developed — they just remain a figment of your imagination.

Both of you are adaptable and can give and take orders. Therefore ego problems don't exist in this relationship. Just put action behind your thoughts and success can be yours!

CANCER/LIBRA

You are insecure as it is, but with Libra as a partner you've become worse. His spend-thrift ways are going to cause a breakup if he doesn't change them.

Your Libra employee is not very helpful when the company is running behind schedule — you'd think he'd pitch in and work overtime, but he's never interested in working late; unless he gets paid for it.

Yours is not a very compatible relationship. You are a feeler; Libra's a thinker. The sympathy you crave is on an emotional basis; Libra's on an intellectual basis — thus you just don't meet on common ground. You need the understanding that Libra can't give — this involves your slowness, penny-pinching and all the daily upsets that occur.

Libra's lengthy deliberations aren't disturbing as far as the time element goes, but once he makes a decision he doesn't always stick with it. You are more tenacious than he; if a deal takes a year to culminate you'll see it through whereas, Libra is ready to abandon it — that's what upsets you about him.

LEO/LIBRA

Your Libra boss is a cinch to deal with, especially after she promotes you. It doesn't seem to disturb your associate when you take center stage and run the entire operation by yourself. It seems she enjoys having you make it a little easy for her. It sure is a relief to have a partner who doesn't cry about the budget — she's as willing as you to risk an expansion at this time.

Your Libra employee never questions your authority. She is agreeable even when you've criticized her for an error. It's a shame that the rest of the help doesn't have her same considerate manner. The two of you are a perfect team — you the leader and she the follower. This is one person who dotes on your every word, which you find builds your ego even bigger than it already is. She listens to you talk and admires your drive; you respect her considerably.

If you are in business together the office will be like a palace. Her taste in art and decor is as lavish as yours. Sculpture and paintings that are valuable will be sprinkled here and there. Neither one of you can count the cost — but the corporation will pay it — it's tax-deductible!

VIRGO/LIBRA

Your Libra boss sure is easygoing and easy to work for; he doesn't make demands and lets you be in peace so you can concentrate on your work. The atmosphere is peaceful and there aren't any rush jobs. Too much conflict in your working environment upsets you and affects your nerves. So since you've been working for Libra your health has improved.

You are so tired of telling your Libra employee to be punctual; his being late upsets the schedule. He does admit he's in the wrong, and in such a charming way, that you are almost sorry you spoke so harshly to him.

Libra is just too lazy for you. If he doesn't get more pep and stop spending those ungodly sums of money, you may dissolve the partnership. He argues that you are not fair, but you think you are being reasonable and that he expects too much of you. And what's more, his indecisiveness about everything is getting to you.

There are pros and cons in this partnership: the pros — both of you are tidy, love cleanliness, and think carefully before making a decision. Also, the two of you are perfectionists, adaptable, flexible, and want to be proper — including good manners.

The cons — Libra procrastinates, you don't. Libra is not industrious, you are. Libra wants to enjoy a personal life and not sacrifice it for work; you put the career and all it entails before your private affairs. Because of these differences the scales dip heavily toward you putting in the hard labor and Libra reaping the rewards without much effort.

LIBRA/LIBRA

It's a pleasure working for your Libra boss because she's so understanding. If you're a few minutes late she doesn't mind. And the office atmosphere isn't hectic, it's calm and peaceful. It's delightful having an employee like Libra who is as fashion conscious as you are. She's always up on the latest style. You are tickled pink having a Libra coworker. She's flexible and it's also a relief to have a person beside you who doesn't mess up; you abhor filth and everything topsy-turvy — it throws you off balance. You enjoy conversing with her because she's an intellectual.

Your Libra partner is a joy. Neither one of you likes to see anyone mistreated so justice plays a major part in all transactions. You always put yourselves in the other person's shoes. Both are mercenary and love money, but not to the extreme that you will take advantage of another — that is in your opinion; sometimes other people think differently.

You may not be a productive team because you both are lazy and take the easy way out with projects. You need to put forth more effort in your work rather than relying so much upon your beauty and charm. Havoc may result when both are too indecisive to make a decision with a new proposal or client.

SCORPIO/LIBRA

There isn't much of a challenge when you work for Libra: he's a pushover. You've got him under your control, so he does things your way. You aren't afraid of him when he gets a little bossy because you'll know in five minutes he'll swing the other way — you've got his number all right.

Your Libra partner is great for the socializing part of the business — something you shun. He doesn't interfere with your plans although once he got upset because you didn't carefully consider the pros and cons before buying a machine that turned out to be a dud. But you are not about to let him tell you what to do. He'll do it your way or else! And you are not going to waste your time pampering him either.

As long as Libra is out in the field making new contacts and calling on old clients, the relationship has a going chance. Otherwise, you will demand that Libra be productive and will push him to hurry and get off of his behind. Arguments will follow. Libra will think you're unfair; you'll scream back that you are too fair. And the battle will be on until Libra finally gives in and agrees that you are right.

Libra's inconsistencies drive you berserk; he needs your solidity. Keep him out of the office; let him drum up trade while you remain at headquarters and manage the technical operations of the business.

SAGITTARIUS/LIBRA

It's a ball working for your Libra boss. She's so easygoing that if you come in late, take a day off, or goof off a little she's quite lenient. You don't mind doing her favors like bringing her a sandwich, pastry and cup of coffee back from the deli at lunch time. It's a shame she has to stay in and catch up on some extra work.

You get a kick out of working beside Libra. She is smart and you enjoy discussing philosophy, the arts, and other subjects when you should be doing your various tasks. Learning something interests you more than getting a paycheck.

You are overjoyed to have Libra on your staff. Her congeniality fits in perfectly with your organization. You must admit though, that she is a little slow, but she's competent and seldom makes an error. It's a relief to run a business without a lot of hassles and nonsmiling people. When you make a mess of things, Libra's always straightening them out — she's so neat.

The two of you have similar traits; both enjoy fun, being out front, and are big spenders. However, Libra tends to be more balanced than you — seeing both sides of the coin. You are more impulsive than Libra and jump into hot water financially so fast that Libra has to come and rescue you as best she can.

You are more energetic than Libra; thus while she dawdles you are completing chores and starting new ones. It's not a bad partnership, both are easy to get along with, but it may disturb you from time to time that Libra doesn't do more. You believe in fairness and think that the work load should be fifty-fifty, not as it is with you taking care of most of the responsibilities.

CAPRICORN/LIBRA

Your Libra employer irks you by continually disrupting your routine because he changed his mind about the way the project should be handled. And what's more irritating is that later, he's back to his original plan. Everything is too much up in the air with this boss; it just doesn't suit your way of managing a business.

If your Libra employee doesn't start being more punctual, you'll have to let him go. You've got a business to run, not some party that he thinks he's coming to.

Your Libra partner lets you manage most of the company's affairs. It's quite a challenge, especially the way you have to make him stick to the budget. You like being the one in authority and Libra staying in a subordinate position. He respects you too — so does everyone else, and that's important.

This is a bad combination. However, if Libra stays home and just puts money into the venture and lets you handle everything else (you put in less money but have main control), then it could survive and be a success. You are ambitious and have perseverance which are traits Libra lacks. You are tight with money and Libra isn't, so you will disagree on this subject and just about everything else. Possibly Libra could handle the customers and do the socializing but even then you may not go along with Libra's openness. You prefer negotiating slyly and you drive a hard bargain whereas Libra doesn't.

AQUARIUS/LIBRA

It's a pleasure to work for someone who lets your ingenious ideas be expressed. Your Libra boss doesn't mind trying out your new time-saving methods. And she's so appreciative when a project is completed in half the time it took previously. Her generous raise was a nice surprise but you really care more about doing something new and different than you do about making more money for the Internal Revenue Service to get.

You are fascinated with the knowledge that your Libra coworker has about classical music, literature, the opera, ballet, and arts in general. It's fun to engage in these interesting conversations while you work; it seems more like play than hard labor. You are pleased that she's neat, but her slowness makes you restless and impatient.

This is a great combination. The two of you can be successful together if you both follow through on your wonderful imaginative notions. Both are highly creative but tend to abandon things in midstream for something more interesting. You need more staying power, although you tend to have it more than Libra.

You are not as hyped up about money as Libra is; it's the experimentation of the different and original that appeals to you, whereas Libra wants to be a financial success — she loves money, especially to spend it.

PISCES/LIBRA

Your Libra boss is an easy mark; you can con him into letting you take time off whenever you get the urge — which is quite often. You enjoy being in a low-pressure office. It's easy for you to adapt to changes, which is fortuitous since Libra's constantly switching things around. Libra's easy to get along with too, and doesn't nag when you make an error.

It's delightful having a partner who is as flexible as you are. His two-sided nature doesn't interfere with yours. You feel you can breathe a sigh of relief because he doesn't push you into anything or rush you into hurrying. He's more mercenary than you when it comes to getting money owed the company, whereas you feel sorry for your debtors; but you keep quiet about your feelings.

This is not really the best team for success because both are dreamers, lazy and procrastinate. You may both initiate projects and abandon them; this action is not conducive to achieving prosperity or recognition. Persistence is needed and you both lack it, although Libra has more staying power than you do; but even then it's spasmodic.

You are an impractical and unrealistic spender and Libra dips back and forth between being practical and extravagant. If you are in business together you need a financial adviser who will assist you and enforce a plan of action that you both will have to abide by — otherwise, you may go bankrupt.

Chapter Ten

Scorpio Compatibility In Business

If you were born between October 23 and November 21, your Sun is in the sign Scorpio. However, you may also express Scorpio traits, if Scorpio is dominant in your horoscope (refer to the Introduction, Page 1), even if it is not your Sun sign. If this is the case, you should read this chapter just as if your Sun sign is Scorpio.

SCORPIO PROFILE
Getting Acquainted With The Scorpio Personality

The Scorpio man is *not* easy to get to know. Once you understand what motivates him, it will help when dealing with him whether he's your partner, employer, employee, coworker, or client. His very presence is overwhelming. He commands your attention with a penetrating stare that seems to be looking right through you — and maybe he is. You will never really know him because he won't let you get that close.

This man has tremendous energy. It's difficult for anyone to keep up with him. He makes every moment count. Deadlines are his "baby" and he will pressure himself and others to make sure that a task is finished on time. His demands are often earth-shattering. He'll attempt the impossible. He finds challenges exciting. He must be productive regardless of what it entails. His ambitions are never completely satisfied because when he reaches one goal he finds another. His desires are bottomless.

If a new machine has just become available, he will investigate everything about it, including the company who manufactures it. Once Scorpio's satisfied with the report, he'll buy it and may even risk everything he owns on it. Once it belongs to him he'll do everything in his power to make it profitable.

Scorpio is a man who refuses to accept defeat. He is a builder who can go to the top, but he can also destroy anyone who crosses him. So treat him right and you won't feel the Scorpion's (his sign's animal symbol) sting — instead he'll make you both successful in the world of commerce.

IF YOU ARE A SCORPIO

Because you are impetuous you may ask, "What more can I do to be in the top spot quickly?" Success can be achieved faster if, when you deal with others, you adhere to the following advice.

When dealing with an employer you must realize that you do not have control of the business — your boss does. It's almost impossible for you to be an underling (you certainly don't consider yourself one), but under the present circumstances that is your position and if you don't accept it, war may break out on the job and you'll end up fired. Therefore, let your employer handle his job instead of you trying to take over. Stick to the decisions in your own department. Realize that your success sometimes depends upon your willingness to take second place; however, think of it as a temporary condition — later you'll be in first place.

If you give your boss an idea and he thwarts your plans, don't resent his decision. Perhaps he has a good reason that is beyond your present knowledge of how his business is operated from a financial standpoint. Don't stop giving him your concepts — new ideas plus your enormous output on the job will lead to promotions and to all other objectives you desire to attain.

When dealing with partners, employees and coworkers be on guard against driving others as hard as you drive yourself. Everyone isn't as energetic or highly motivated as you are because it's against their natures due to the Sun sign they were born under. So, be understanding of this factor. Speak to them kindly when you want them to follow an order instead of blasting them with forceful words. When you insist that others do your bidding, it makes them obey but at the same time it attracts enmity from them.

You will not take a back seat to anyone and must have complete authority at all times. However, you should learn to be open and realize that others have suggestions too; their ideas could be quite valuable. Therefore, when someone tries to express an opinion, give the individual a chance to speak instead of tearing into him. You may think that stopping to listen to what the other person has to say takes up valuable time when you and he could be working. But what if he has a shortcut method of performing an operation that would cut production time down to half? You may be quite surprised at the opportunities that come from the lips of others, if only given the chance. Help others to succeed by giving them the courtesy to express their views and they'll help you be successful in your accomplishments.

When dealing with clients guard against being impatient with those who are indecisive. You always know what you want, therefore it's incomprehensible to you that someone else is not the same. Usually you are able to size up a person at a glance. So why not use your innate observation powers on this indecisive client? Ask him if he'd like to take some literature with him so he'll have plenty of time to delve extensively into whether said product is right for him. If he says yes, especially in a gleeful manner, you'll be assured your approach was the right one. However, if he doesn't seem too interested in doing as you suggested, give him the pros and cons of the product, dismiss yourself politely while he's trying to make a decision; tend to another customer or pending duties.

You are very exacting and hard to deal with in business, especially when involved in a negotiation. With all clients try to avoid using high-pressured sales techniques and don't rush anyone or you may not conclude that transaction you have your heart set on. You like to get results; if you don't, you'll find a way at all costs to you, or anyone else's. If this has caused a loss in the past, learn from your mistakes so they aren't repeated; then it's easier to gain the success desired.

To go one step further, once you as a Scorpian know or can recognize the sign your partner, employer, employee, coworker or client is, read that sign's chapter to know how best to deal with him as well as to understand his compatibility with you. If you wish to know what he thinks about you, read the Sun-Sign Compatibility section starting on page 151. The remainder of this Scorpio section deals with how others relate to you, what they can expect of you, and how they should handle you. So let's go on an interview with your sign, okay?

AN INTERVIEW WITH A SCORPIO

A Scorpio employer interviewing you: Your resumé will be quickly, but thoroughly, scrutinized. Scorpio is testy, so be prepared to answer a whole slew of questions. This is her method of making inquiries and she hopes it throws you off guard so you'll answer everything honestly. Also, she wants to see how well you stand up under pressure. If you do well that clues her in and lets her know that you can stand a heavy work load and meet deadlines. Answer all questions carefully, but as quickly as you can.

Don't expect to be hired immediately. Scorpio has to investigate your background. Everything on your application will be checked out for accuracy. She may question those you worked for slyly without your ex-boss being aware of what she is up to. (Scorpio is the sign ruling detective work.) This is one person who doesn't want any duds or liars in her employment; she wants top people who will help her attain the success she desires.

If you're interviewing a Scorpio applicant: If you keep him waiting for the interview, he'll watch your every move while he pretends to be reading a book. When you interview Scorpio you'll notice that he's quiet, serious, collected, polite, and polished. Your questions are answered briefly. He's close-mouthed and is only going to tell you what he wants you to know.

Scorpio may ask you a few harmless questions (so you think) but everything is filed away in a compartment for easy reference at a later date. This man likes to find out what makes you tick. If he's really interested in a job with your corporation, he may mention a plan to increase your company's product and thus increase sales in the world market. Scorpio's confident of his every move; he's performing for you just as if he's in a well-rehearsed play and this is opening night. He is in a hurry to go to work so if you want to hire him, do it immediately. Possibly he'll start right away; just ask him nicely.

Now that the interview is over, first let's go to work for a Scorpio, and then see how Scorpio is going to fare as your employee, okay?

YOUR SCORPIO EMPLOYER
What Does Your Scorpio Boss Expect of You?

If you're being transferred from one department to another because you've had a run-in with someone, made a blunder or decided it was time for a change — your bad record will go against you with your new boss, the Scorpio. She will be suspicious of you (she suspects everyone). She'll note your every action and inaction. If you slip once, you'll hear about it immediately.

This woman expects you to toe the mark and obey her instructions to the letter. She demands that you work as hard as she and be as productive. Scorpio will insist that you have the same devotion to purpose that she has; if you don't measure up to her standards and what she needs, she'll fire you.

She wants a job done fast, "right now," and the way she acts you'd swear she has an invisible whip in her hands. Scorpio will remind you of a female Simon Legree. This woman doesn't expect you to talk on the job; she wants you to mind your own business and *work*. If you chitchat or make any kind of noise, it disturbs her concentration.

Scorpio expects you to be a perfectionist and pay attention to the details. She wants you to keep your word. If you said you would work overtime and you renege, you'll be headed for real trouble. You can either count your days in her employ or be ready for her to get her revenge through giving you extra laborious tasks. She demands loyalty and heedfulness. Scorpio takes from people and transforms this sponged-up energy to attain success — so go along with her and you'll be on top too.

How to Handle Your Scorpio Boss

Your first day on the job you may think "This is going to be an easy job. The boss is nothing to be afraid of. She's pleasant and shows me how to do everything." Yes, she does seem congenial and harmony may exist, but just break one rule, make a bad mistake, gossip about someone or try to pry into her affairs and that's when Scorpio's magnetic facade — her good side — disappears. You may be dumbfounded when you see the bad side of this woman, but if you're not fired, you'll get used to it.

Never talk about Scorpio behind her back. She has eyes in the back of her head, she hears everything and you may never know who's a spy. Sooner or later, though, you'll be discovered and wish you hadn't ever said anything. If your work is sloppy or proves to be different than what she expected it to be (from the time she hired you) she will have no sympathy for you — regardless of your excuse. When she figures that you are a liability, she will have no mercy and will let you go. Don't, beg or implore her to keep you on. She can't stand anyone who is emotional because that shows you have lost control of yourself — and that is a real no-no with her. Scorpio expects everyone in her employ to be like her — hard as nails with a heart of steel. So if you haven't goofed up and are still in her employ, keep in mind that this woman puts herself — and all of her aims — first before you or anyone else for that matter. You are important to her when she can manipulate you or use you to her advantage and then you are going to be well worth your salary.

Make every hour on the job a productive one. Don't loiter — keep going at a quick pace. Do not linger away the time on a coffee break; be back at your desk right on schedule. Avoid coming to work late. Scorpio will not tolerate it. You may get one warning; don't risk taking a second chance. If she's busy working and not looking in your direction, don't let that fool you — she hears and sees everything.

When you goof up she may seem stern but she's efficient and wants to see everything in her organization running efficiently. Scorpio will not put up with any nonsense from the help and she'll let you know that when she speaks up and tells you like it is. If you have sensitive ears, her bluntness may hurt them. But she doesn't care. This woman has to be honest and tell it like it is. She's not afraid of being disliked.

If you have a brilliant idea to improve her business in any way, don't let her cool demeanor scare you into keeping quiet about it. By all means tell her, but not as a command or in an egotistical way. Don't say, "You should do this," or "I just got a brilliant idea for you." Let her make the decision whether she should use the idea. Instead say, "I have a suggestion that you might be interested in. If you think it's good it may make you lots of money." That will get her attention and make her more ready to accept it than the others. Keep in mind that Scorpio's obsessed with money and power and any time you can help her gain financially, that is going to be a feather in your cap.

If Scorpio wants you to work on the Fourth of July holiday weekend and you want to stay employed, you'd better agree to do so. This woman is selfish and puts her business plans first — before you or even her own personal life. Whatever she feels needs to be done — mailing catalogues, manufactured items to be completed or a deadline for a client on a printing job — it will be done come hell or high water (that's how she feels about it). Don't waste time giving excuses that you can't because you made plans to go away to a beach resort with your family; Scorpio couldn't care less. She has a one-track mind and can only think about her problems. If you decline to work, she'll be angered and you'll know it as she seethes. You'd better change your mind fast or you may not have a job when you return from your holiday outing.

Be alert to everything this woman does and says; don't let even the most minute remark or the way she glances in your direction pass you by. That one look reveals to her all that she needs to know — how productive you are. If she tells you that you'd turn out more work if you'd do — do as she bids, even if you think she's wrong. Never tell her that you disagree with her ideas. Let her find out on her own that she made a mistake. If you are in a brave mood, and know that you'll be put behind if you follow her notion, say, "Oh, I tried that before and it took longer, but if you want me to try it again, I will."

If Scorpio is your supervisor and you compete with her outwardly, you'll regret it. Never try to get her position unless it has been announced that she's been promoted. If this woman gets wind of your motives you'll be given so many difficult tasks to complete in a short time, that if you don't do it — that will give her a good reason to fire you.

If you go to the boss, over your immediate Scorpio supervisor, and report her actions you'll have a revengeful woman to deal with. In her way of thinking you've damaged (or tried) her reputation — and that is something no Scorpio will ever allow. This woman tries so hard to look good to everyone that she won't even get involved in an argument in front of others — because she doesn't like witnesses.

So as a result of your tattletale action, Scorpio won't give you the ax right away because it would look like it was done out of spite. Instead she will bide her time, letting you go about your regular duties as if nothing happened. This woman will let some time pass by (so her boss, and you, will not be suspicious of her motives) and about a month after the "blabbing incident" Scorpio will give you some complicated task to perform. When you are unable to do it correctly, or maybe not at all, that's when you'll be notified that you are no longer employed for this corporation.

If you have an ax to grind, never go over Scorpio's head. Either get transferred, or look for employment elsewhere. If you try to iron it out with her, it's a hopeless battle — she won't listen to reason. This woman's stubborn and not about to change her views about anything, especially when it's coming from a subordinate. You're better off looking secretly for a job elsewhere. That way you may get a good reference from Scorpio; otherwise, if you've had a run-in she will blacken your record but good. Now that you know what to do you won't make any mistakes; being armed with this knowledge it's now easier to become successful.

YOUR SCORPIO EMPLOYEE
What Can You Expect from Your Scorpio Employee?
He is loyal and it's not just because you're the boss; it's because you are fair, honest, and treat him right (that's when you get this fellow's respect). Scorpio has an inner confidence that makes him sure he can tackle any job asked of him; he isn't a show-off, just self-contained. He has brains and knows how to use them. Ask him to do a complicated task and it'll get done. Scorpio doesn't make up excuses or alibis about anything; he performs what is required and will do his best to see that defeat never occurs. This fellow may surprise you with the poise he has at all times and under any given circumstance. If there's an emergency he can be relied upon to handle it calmly and quickly.

He may not appear as the friendliest employee you have on your payroll, but in job output most likely he's tops. Scorpio maintains his detached air because he figures that if he's aloof no one will disturb him and then he can concentrate on the work that has to be done. He's turned off by idle conversation; it's a waste of his time and detracts from his productivity (an obsession of his). Scorpio believes that if he's getting paid to work he should be doing just that and nothing else. Therefore he won't goof off or socialize with anyone on the job. He wants to excel so you will notice him and give him a raise or promotion or both.

You can expect a serious and extremely industrious employee who keeps his love of power hidden. Scorpio is goal directed and never loses sight of his objectives. The dedication to attain his aims is mind-blowing. He will not allow anything to interfere with his plans for success. This fellow will try every means to get to the top — but you won't be aware of it; his approach is subtle.

How To Handle Your Scorpio Employee
Never ask him personal questions; that's an invasion of privacy that he resents — he's there to work, so let him. Don't criticize (usually it's unnecessary), insult, or be discourteous to this employee. You'll regret it because someday he'll get even.

Give him a position of trust and responsibility and you'll be glad you did. Scorpio takes his job seriously and turns in professional work. Keep him busy because idleness bores him and makes him disagreeable. This fellow has a compulsion to finish all chores he starts. Once his tasks are completed, if you haven't given him any new ones, he'll find something to do; however, it'll be job-related — probably something that will improve production, which when it's made perfect, he'll present to you.

Let him handle all the work that requires an analytical mind. Give him a challenge. He can organize ideas and plans and he is never fazed by difficult problems. In fact, he's elated when he gets them because he's confident that he can solve them. Scorpio can accomplish tasks that others give up. There's nothing slipshod about him. If you have a program or system that has a defect or weakness he can usually point out what's wrong with it. Scorpio thinks quickly and has excellent judgment. He will give you a clear-cut, objective verdict. He sees the overall picture of a project and that is the key to the success he desires to attain. So the tougher jobs you give him, the happier he'll be and the better your business will be.

Scorpio doesn't seek praise so don't waste your time giving him any unless you think he's done something extra special. Compliments puff his ego up. In fact he may be suspicious of you if you commend him for some worthy task. He may think that you have some ulterior motive in mind and want to use him for something.

This is one person who doesn't like to be babied, pampered, or have you grant him favors on his way to the top. Avoid these actions like the plague. However, be on guard because he'll use you cunningly. He doesn't like to be obvious — that way at a later date you can't say that you were instrumental in helping him reach his goals. Scorpio doesn't want to owe anyone a thing; a clean slate is a necessity.

To handle Scorpio properly, it's important that you understand the way his mind works. Probably before he ever came to work for your company, he checked out your operation's growth potential. It's also likely he made inquiries about you, the officers of the corporation, the salaries paid and a newcomer's possibilities in your organization. This fellow doesn't waste time working for a company that can't be useful to his plans to be in a high position.

Scorpio knows he has success potential. He's never doubted that since the day he was born. He knows that it's up to him and his talent to get to the top. He *will* use stepping stones (this is where you come in) to help him advance. But he walks softly along the way, never hurting anyone. You won't even be aware that you've helped him reach a goal because he appears like he wants nothing from you. But he needs you and your knowledge so he can learn his trade well enough to better himself. Scorpio knows that he has to make sacrifices along the way, but he's not afraid of the cost and he'll pay the piper and never ask for special concessions or anything else. He's secretive and has a definite purpose in mind that you probably won't even guess. If you can help fulfill his ambitions, he'll use you to do so but he won't knock you down in the process.

This man is in no rush to get to the top. He will go along with his duties but he will not submit to any man or woman. He's his own person and has to be true to himself. Scorpio will scheme to get what he wants (he tells himself that you are playing in his hands) but he knows the difference. In other words, he is putting up with listening to your commands because you are paying his salary and that's why he has to go along with you. He will be faithful to you as long as he's getting his weekly paycheck.

If you're Scorpio's supervisor, be on guard against his wanting your job; however, his operation to get it is put into effect gradually. Perhaps he'll work overtime, pick your brains and ask for explanations of things he doesn't understand. He'll get advice from you and information for his use and learn about your contacts — when he's finished he'll know your job thoroughly. During the process he'll be cooperative and may willingly offer his energy or time to help you whenever you need his assistance. When he makes himself too useful to you that will be a giveaway. If you block or hinder his progress, or he feels that he'll never get your position, either he'll ask for a transfer or he'll leave the company. Don't plead that you will give him a substantial raise if he stays; once he's made up his mind to go out the door, he's gone.

YOUR SCORPIO COWORKER
What Can You Expect from Your Scorpio Coworker
There are just a few basic facts to keep in mind when working with this woman: she's competitive (without it being obvious), moves fast, is dictatorial and self-motivated. The Scorpio female is dynamic and accomplishes anything she sets out to do — and that's plenty. If you are slow she won't mention it to the boss; she'll pitch in and help you out if her job is dependent upon yours.

A Scorpio is a taskmaster and may practice until she is perfect as does Scorpio opera star Joan Sutherland. And someone born under this sign doesn't allow anyone (and that means you too) to interfere with her plans or job. She has a high moral code and principles; she follows them. If she makes a mistake, she won't blame you for it — she takes full credit for it.

You can expect Scorpio to mind her own business and never contribute to office gossip, games, parties, gift buying/swapping. She appears standoffish and keeps busy; her mind is only on her tasks. This woman is smart enough to know that if she stays out of things, no one can say she interfered or took part in anything that could cost her a promotion, raise or the job itself.

Scorpio doesn't trust people; she sizes them up instantly. She's not two-faced, if she doesn't like you she'll keep her distance and won't speak to you unless it's a necessary part of the job, in which case her facial expression will be that of a cold fish — her voice tone may be the same. If she likes you, she'll nod when spoken to or say a few brief salutations. She can be loyal and a friend, especially if she knows you're on her side and helpful to her on the job. That's when she'll take you under her wing; when she gets a higher position, she'll ask for you to work beneath her — she'll treat you fair and square.

How to Handle Your Scorpio Coworker

Be competitive with her (inwardly, don't make it obvious); it makes her plunge even more zealously and enthusiastically into her work. Don't interfere with her schedule (the one she's mentally made for herself) by talking to her because she wants to make every mental and physical motion count. This woman will stay up all night to meet a deadline; she wants everything done on time. Scorpio is indefatigable; you may get exhausted trying to keep up with her. If you are on her team and help her, she'll encourage you to get ahead; however, she prides herself on not letting you know that she's after the top spot.

Scorpio can be tough so don't get in her way or cross her. If she doesn't like you, look out! You've got an enemy for life. Her eagle eye never misses anything, so don't do anything sneaky on her. She is full of resentment when you've done something behind her back — like talking about her to someone else. Scorpio is a sly troublemaker and her maliciousness can be harmful to the position you hold. It's advisable to be a pal rather than a foe. Scorpio is in complete control of herself until she's ready to strike. This woman's capable of almost any outrage as long as the two of you are alone together. She doesn't want anyone around to watch so later if you report her to the boss it will be her word against yours. Scorpio loves to quarrel; it's the excitement of an argument that she loves. But you are better off being peaceful and not tangling with her.

Don't ask Scorpio personal questions or be testy with her in any way. Those tricks are hers; however, her technique is not obvious. Be prepared for her to grill you slowly and deceptively. She will do most of the conversing during a coffee or lunch break. Scorpio will get you to talk about yourself as if she's genuinely interested in you as a person. She knows how to probe to get you to spill private and professional secrets. Perhaps her innocent-sounding questions will sneak in while something else is being discussed. Maybe she'll ask about your plans: "How far do you want to go?" "Do you enjoy working for the company?" "What do you think of the boss?" "How do the wages compare with the rest of the industry?"

She may ask one question at a time over a period of months before she has a handle on what you think and know. You won't suspect anything, but now that you've been warned, you'll be aware of her underhanded approach.

This woman wants power and gathers this information about you so she can have it in case she needs it at a later date. For instance, what if you get angry at her and have a quarrel and go to report her to the boss? She will threaten you with, "If you do, I'll tell everything I know about you and you'll get fired." So this is one way that she would use her knowledge — blackmail, a typical Scorpio trait (the negative side of Scorpio being expressed). Or another way she could use this knowledge she has about you would be if she needed to have you back her up on something and you were against it. Or if she got promoted and needed a favor from you, she could use this information if you didn't play ball with her. Because the negative side of Scorpio can do any or all of the preceding, now you know why she doesn't want to talk about herself — she thinks that if she has the capability of being sneaky to get facts about someone, so can the other person do the same to her. A person expressing the positive side of Scorpio would not stoop to these little tricks. But it's best to be forewarned of all possibilities rather than made an innocent victim without this knowledge.

You may be afraid of Scorpio because you can sense the power that just emanates from her. Just be kind, do your job and *don't cross her.* If you'd rather not work with her, ask for a transfer or work elsewhere. Perhaps you can wait until she's promoted to a higher position — as long as it doesn't involve your department, you're safe. A Scorpio using the positive traits of her sign may be an enjoyable coworker. But either way, this woman is unfathomable. Now that you've been clued in, though, it should help pave the way toward your becoming successful.

YOUR SCORPIO CLIENT
What Can You Expect from Your Scorpio Client?
This woman comes in so quietly you may not even notice her unless the store's empty. She's cool, detached, and has steady penetrating eyes that seem to be sizing you up instantly (and she is). Scorpio will look quickly at your wares on display. Expect her to ask you some questions about an item. She's curious and enjoys probing.

This isn't anyone you have to push. She only buys what she likes at the very first glance and the price is no object. She's a compulsive spender. It's as if she *must* have that object at all costs. Don't be surprised if she says, "I'll take it," before you've had a chance to start your sales spiel.

Once Scorpio has placed an order with you, expect her to demand instant delivery. If you say, "That's impossible," she may cancel the order. If you agree to follow through as she desires, and the goods haven't arrived as scheduled, don't be surprised if she calls and threatens never to do business with your company again. This woman gets extremely disturbed by anyone who doesn't keep his promise.

If you are involved in the negotiation of a contract with Scorpio over some bid that her company is making, expect some shrewd bargaining to take place. This woman has strong self-control, appears placid, and is calculating. She will let you make the first offer and like a poker player, she'll cover up her feelings and try some bluffing. More than likely Scorpio has had your company investigated thoroughly — she likes to know everyone's weaknesses and strengths because with this information she knows just how to deal. Also it gives her a certain power that she loves. Scorpio is ruthless and if you've got something she wants, she'll find a way to get it. And she usually does — so be ready for her and you'll be just as successful as she.

How to Handle Your Scorpio Client
A Scorpio client isn't easy to deal with because she is demanding, dictatorial, and highly critical and sarcastic if she's not pleased. She wants you to jump to attention when she gives you an order. If you want her account, do it! Also, when she walks in a room she expects you to stop whatever you are doing and cater to her needs. So that's another factor you can keep in mind when dealing with her.

Make sure you have an appointment with her before ever calling on her. Nothing irritates her more than a salesperson who drops in just because he happens to be in the neighborhood. First, she doesn't believe you, so your dishonesty (in her mind) gives you a minus point. Second, she won't stop and talk to you if she's busy with her job — and most likely she will be smothered in work. If you have an appointment with this woman, be on time because Scorpio dislikes anyone who is not punctual. If you are late, and it disrupts a project she's working on, either she'll ignore you and make you wait or she'll tell you to reschedule another meeting, but the next time, "Don't be tardy or I won't deal with you in the future."

If you are making a sales call on Scorpio in her office don't waste her precious time with nonessentials like talking about the weather or asking her, "How are you today?" Just discuss the reason why you are there. Avoid flattering her just to get her business. This is one person who's on to deceptiveness and will never trust you again nor come back to your business establishment. She likes honesty in all transactions. Therefore, avoid telling her that you will slash the price in half, or reduce it, just because you want to do her a favor, or whatever other excuse you use. Scorpio has a suspicious nature and will think that either you are cheating her, the article isn't genuine, or you have some ulterior motive in mind. However, always tell her the cost right out; she can't stand salespeople who beat around the bush.

When selling to Scorpio, appeal to her desire to speed up production and increase her profits. This woman wants to hear the practical side, how much money it can bring her over a certain period of time and the mechanics of the operation. She's got a mind that can grasp all of these angles quickly. Don't talk slow but at a speed that doesn't appear like you are rushing her. Also give her the details without floundering around; get to the point. When dealing with Scorpio remember to always speak quickly, intelligently, and act fast once she's put an order in. As a result you'll fatten your bank account and have a good customer you can serve — all of this leads to becoming successful.

YOUR SCORPIO PARTNER
What Can You Expect From Your Scorpio Partner?

You may think you did the right thing when you teamed up with this man because he's self-starting, resourceful and has a fertile imagination (but is logical with his ideas). He's got the knowledge of a Dr. Jonas Salk, the creativity of the late John Keats (the poet) and the investigative ability of a Dick Cavett (all Scorpio's). Success is engraved in his soul, and with him, you can't fail. She won't quit even when he's hanging on the edge of a precipice. His persistence helps him reach the summit of prosperity; he's a daredevil that's not afraid of anything. So hang on and take the ride to the top with him.

With all of his outstanding traits, and count all of his numerous faults, is he worth putting up with? The decision is yours and yours alone. It will be easier to decide once you understand the Scorpio personality. This man will be in total control, not you. He *must* be in control of every situation and every human being. You will feel it and know it the first day your operations start. His confidence is *power* and it oozes out without a word or gesture — you just sense it. So if you don't mind his making all major decisions, then you're in business -- and it's not peanuts — it's gigantic. Your Scorpio partner is capable of running twenty large corporations simultaneously as did the late J. Paul Getty who had Scorpio "dominant" in his horoscope. So get on the bandwagon with this self-reliant, positive and relentless man who doesn't take the easy way to a goal, but never allows himself to be distracted from the road he's chosen.

How To Handle Your Scorpio Partner

Scorpio's not afraid to take a risk. This man's a real compulsive gambler and leaps in once he's given it some careful thought. He's fearless and gutsy and may owe a fortune to the banker, but let him make the moves because he knows what he's doing. However, if you're afraid to be in debt, then think twice about being in a partnership with this man.

Obstacles do not frighten him, in fact he's fascinated when barriers are put in his way. He enjoys mapping out a plan of action so he can attack a project with all of his might. You can try to make his route a little easier by making a suggestion such as, "Have you ever thought of doing it this way _____?" But don't be bossy. Be prepared for his not listening to your advice because he really likes to face problems by himself. Second opinions are not his style of doing things — however, you never know when he may be in a quiet mood and just listen and later improve upon it. He is capable of changing his train of thought if he thinks it'll get the desired results he wants. Scorpio feels assured that he'll make the right moves; usually he does, he has excellent judgment.

If you have any money transactions, discuss them. Be aboveboard and open, tell him how you feel about everything — but don't do it angrily or demeaningly — be kind. Scorpio can be conservative and go on an economy kick but don't expect it to last. In an office he's *not* out to impress people with furnishings; so his will be kept simple — so it's best you do the same. This man believes it's better not to flaunt wealth, but to keep it hidden. In his way of thinking the less people know about you, the better. When it comes to money he is greedy.

Scorpio is clever and shrewd and likes to outwit others. If he's quiet, leave him alone because he can't stand distractions when he's concentrating on his schemes. He may hold back a fact or two and not let you know what he's got up his sleeve. When he does tell you his plans, don't thwart them. If you do, you'll see an iron will in full display. Once his mind is made up, he resists change; if you force it upon him, he'll rebel. Try to realize that this man is a good organizer and isn't about to make a mistake. His decisions are going to be to his (and your) advantage. He makes good business deals and he's not about to renege on his word. You can't butter him up — instead do nothing, and let him follow through with his plans.

By now you know that he's a man that likes to have things his way or not at all. Scorpio takes his business earnestly and expects you to do the same. He is interested in modernization and getting the latest machines and equipment operating in the business. Don't balk him in this direction; he's all for speeding up production because it'll increase the bank account.

Scorpio makes sudden decisions. He's able to act quickly under any type of situation that may arise. If a computer breaks down, he'll move so fast that you'll think he's a streak of lightening. When Scorpio gets through talking over the telephone to the person in charge, another machine will be rented, leased or the repair man will be there in a jiffy.

Scorpio has fiery emotions that are bottled up straining to be released at the slightest provocation. He keeps his temper under control; it's as if he's wearing a mask. Don't ever get your partner angry at you, if you do, that mask will be pulled off and you'll see how vicious he can get.

Once you two have made a habit of fighting, Scorpio will block you out of his mind and sight and will treat you as if you didn't exist. He'll make you so miserable you'll be ready to offer him anything to dissolve the partnership. Once he's had it with you, he can discard a business, build up another one, and take on new people. If he loses a few partners along the way to the top, he doesn't care — he just keeps heading for his ultimate goal — success; so why don't you try it too? — that is if the two of you are compatible — and you think you can handle him properly.

Sun-Sign Compatibility

This section deals with each sign of the zodiac in relation to a Scorpio Sun sign. By knowing how your sign blends with a Scorpion, you go one step beyond understanding his personality and one step closer to knowing how to handle him in any business situation. Greater insight is invaluable — it not only helps a business prosper, it encourages peace of mind on and off the job.

The following Sun-Sign compatibility summaries, with the exception of Scorpio/Scorpio, *are from the point of view of the person dealing with Scorpio. Note:* For the Scorpio's point of view see the Sun-Sign chapter of the person Scorpio is dealing with, i.e., Pisces — refer to the Pisces chapter explaining how Scorpio thinks about Pisces.

ARIES/SCORPIO

Your Scorpio coworker is constantly challenging you so you try to show her how fast you can work. In fact, you try to outdo her. This woman just doesn't talk. She's so secretive it's as if she has something to hide. You can't stand her dictatorial nature and the demands made on your time. She treats you as if you didn't have an ounce of brains in your head.

You both are too temperamental to be in a partnership together. You may be so busily engaged in open war between yourselves that too little time will be devoted to the business. The two of you love competing with one another but both want to be the boss and that may be a major problem, especially when you both try to make major decisions without the other one's okay.

If Scorpio works for you, you'll fire her during the first yelling and screaming argument that takes place. If you are employed by her, she'll probably throw you out the first time you look angry. So, it's just a no-go team regardless of the relationship.

TAURUS/SCORPIO

Your Scorpio coworker moves faster than you do but you aren't about to speed up just so you can compete with him. If he wants to chance making a mistake, let him. It's not worth it to you to rush and wind up with a sloppy, inaccurate report.

You like the money you're getting paid, but your Scorpio employer is too high-strung and forceful. And your Scorpio partner makes you see red when he wants to spend over the allotted budget. However, he does have some brilliant ideas that are logical and can increase your earnings fifty percent. If he would just give you time to think it out carefully, then you could be sure that he is on the right track.

The two of you could make a fortune together if you would resist holding Scorpio back from disbursing funds for modernization and advertising purposes. Both are workaholics; although you go about a task differently — you're slow, he's fast. It's a toss-up as to who is the most stubborn. Business may be brought to a standstill because you both refuse to change an opinion. This type of action can hinder success and neither one of you are the type to give in. As a result you could both argue vehemently, but Scorpio's sarcasm is much more deadly than yours. If you could control your bad points, the good ones might give you the chance you both need to make a bundle of money.

GEMINI/SCORPIO

Your Scorpio coworker isn't any fun to work with because she won't talk while she's on the job. But Scorpio does keep your curiosity aroused, especially because she's so secretive. You have to admit you had your smarts when you went into partnership with Scorpio. She's good at handling the details that you can't stand. Also, she's so persuasive that you don't mind giving in to her demands. You do wish that she had a sense of humor, but you can't expect her to be perfect.

Your Scorpio boss looks over your shoulder a little bit more than you feel comfortable with. She restricts your desire to be free and come and go as you please. You like to move about; confinement drives you berserk — every time you set up your employer wants to know where you're going and why. If she keeps this up, you'll quit.

The two of you have so many opposite traits and yet you can be a good team if you don't get into each other's hair. Both agree to spending money on new equipment, only you may leap in without thinking things through, whereas Scorpio goes through an investigative process before making a commitment.

Both of you are intelligent and can talk to clients in a way that can bring the business in. You get bored easily and may take off on a sudden whim; that will not meet with Scorpio's approval. However, you need her steadying influence and she needs your ideas for change and experimentation.

CANCER/SCORPIO

Your Scorpio coworker is wonderful because he doesn't talk to you while you are trying to concentrate on your tasks. You appreciate it when he lends you a helping hand because you've gotten behind schedule. When you get uptight, he calms you with a few soothing remarks.

You think very highly of your Scorpio boss; he seems to understand your need for variety because he's always giving you a conglomeration of things to do. He certainly has won your confidence and respect with his working as hard as the rest of you.

You are glad you hired Scorpio; he's dependable, works fast and finishes a task before the deadline. His suggestions have proved invaluable; his ideas for expansion and getting that new machinery have speeded up production and increased sales. This is one person who has been worth his salary and then some.

Your Scorpio partner is ideal. He runs the business his way and keeps all of the problems away from you. This man doesn't bother you with lots of idle conversation. He is protective of you and always looking for better methods to improve the business. You feel safe and secure with him and know that the company is going to grow. He has never been angry with you but you've seen his temper displayed on others. Scorpio sticks by the rules, just like you do, so you are delighted with him.

You are a perfect combination. Both are tenacious and will wait for a business to prosper: however. Scorpio is a little more impatient than you — but it doesn't interfere with the plans the two of you make. You are a team that understands one another; neither one pries into the other's affairs.

Scorpio spends money fast on big deals and takes wild chances, which normally would frighten you: but with him you somehow feel that you don't have a thing to worry about — and you don't. Loyalty is important to both of you and it is to be found in your relationship. Success is practically guaranteed when you two get together.

LEO/SCORPIO

Your Scorpio coworker sure is difficult to get along with. You don't like it when she tries to dominate you. And ever since Scorpio has been working under you, you've felt that she's been out to get your job.

Your Scorpio boss is sure demanding. You don't know how much longer you can put up with it. And if she criticizes you once more you just may quit. The money she's paying isn't as important as your pride. You think she's mean on purpose. Maybe she's jealous of you.

Leo and Scorpio are just not a good combination. Although you are both dynamic and success motivated, you belong on separate teams because you both are types to be at the head of an enterprise. There will be constant quarrels and disagreements. You two may have difficulty communicating. Both are stubborn and neither one will give in; thus deadlocks will reign daily.

Both of you want to have a hand in making policies, changes, and operating the business on a large-scale level. The two of you spend money like it's going out of style, but may not agree on what the sums should be dispersed on. There are just so many bad points that you'd both have to overcome to be a lasting team — but will your inflexible natures let this come to pass?

VIRGO/SCORPIO

Your Scorpio coworker gets a little bossy but it doesn't bother you. He's much faster than you in completing a job, but he doesn't rush you.

You respect your Scorpio employer because, like you, he's not afraid of a heavy work load. It's wonderful how he comes up with so many ideas that cut the work in half.

You think highly of your Scorpio employee because he is able to handle his job and everyone else's, including your own.

The two of you are a good combination and should attain success without any hitches. Both are interested in business first, private life second. You are workaholics, excellent planners and stick to projects initiated. Both love detail, have analytical minds and are critical.

You and Scorpio both are reliable and will get the work out as promised. Schedules are a must for the two of you and will be followed by the letter regardless of whether you, or other people, make them. By combining your talents, you should be able to make a fortune.

LIBRA/SCORPIO

Your Scorpio coworker sure is a help when she pitches in and does some of your tasks because otherwise you'd never get done in time for those deadlines you abhor. You do wish she'd be a little more sociable instead of just slaving away as if every second counted.

Your Scorpio boss is too pushy for you and she rushes too much. Her temper upsets your equilibrium, so rather than anger her, you manage to tell her things that she wants to hear. At times you think she's unjust, asking far too much from her employees.

Because you are so indecisive you're delighted to have Scorpio as a partner. Your job is easy now that she makes all the decisions.

Your laziness and Scorpio's workaholic nature don't mix well together. You like to socialize. Scorpio doesn't. If you handle the party business and she the humdrum part, the two of you have a good chance of being successful. Scorpio may not like your being late or unreliable. You will have difficulty maintaining the same pressure that Scorpio can withstand. If you stay home after every deadline to recuperate and get your strength back (because you were worn out) eventually this could cause a break in the relationship. Physically, Scorpio's grind will be too much for you.

SCORPIO/SCORPIO

You enjoy competing with your Scorpio coworker; usually you finish a job at the same time. It's a relief to be working with someone who doesn't hold up production, especially since your work is dependent upon his. You hope the boss promotes you instead of him.

You are very pleased with your Scorpio employee. He is industrious and can be useful to your organization. If he continues to perform his job this well, he'll be promoted to a position right beneath you.

You are proud of your Scorpio partner. He's as ambitious and driven as you. This is one person you know you can rely upon. Of course, he is just as pushy and temperamental as you, so sometimes you clash. But you think that a good fight clears up the air, so you are glad you both are the types to get everything off your chests.

Both of you are materialists and obsessed with achieving your goals at all costs; therefore, with this attitude and your perseverance, you can attain your desires. However, you will have to watch little jealousies that may spring up if the two of you are doing similar work in your organization. If you are handling one phase of the operation and your Scorpio partner another, then you should be able to surmount any difficulties that might arise. In this relationship there will be lots of stress and tension, which may lead to some violent quarrels — but since you both thrive on an argument this shouldn't deter your success too much.

SAGITTARIUS/SCORPIO

You admire your Scorpio coworker's ability to concentrate completely on her endeavors. However, you do wish she'd smile when you try to liven things up. She does get bossy but it doesn't faze you. This is one person who sure can be sarcastic when she takes something you've said the wrong way. But it's only words.

Your Scorpio boss sure is difficult to please. You don't like it when she hovers over you, watching your every move. Her rules are too confining also; you detest getting that glued-to-the-spot feeling.

This is one employee you don't mind being extra generous with: she's deserving of the big raises she gets periodically. Scorpio is always willing to come in at odd hours, help other departments and do more than her salary pays her.

Your Scorpio partner has brilliant ideas for expansion. You are glad that she, like you, isn't afraid of dangerous risks; in fact, you both find them exciting, especially when they are profitable.

This is a good team; both agree on spending money extravagantly. The two of you are impulsive; however. Scorpio can balance you somewhat because she will think things carefully through before leaping in. Both of you like activity and keeping busy; however leave the behind-the-scenes negotiations to Scorpio and you handle the out-front selling end of the business.

The two of you are always looking ahead toward brighter horizons and make your future business plans accordingly. Both have a never-ending fund of ideas that keep this relationship active and productive; therefore success is easily yours.

CAPRICORN/SCORPIO

Scorpio isn't nosey and is quiet enough that you can tend to your duties. He moves faster than you and frequently offers to assist you when he's run out of work to do.

Your Scorpio boss is reserved and aloof but you find that necessary because of his position. You prefer people like that to overfriendly people; the former, you trust; the latter, you are suspicious of.

You feel that you made a wise and shrewd move when you went into partnership with Scorpio. He's as driven by his ambitions as you are. You're glad that he keeps abreast of the latest developments in the industrial field. Also, it's great that he's not afraid to apply new techniques.

You two are a fantastic combination. Success is guaranteed from the moment you signed the partnership papers. Both of you are cunning, clever, determined, and will work night and day to get your heart's desires. The two of you excel in negotiations; however, you have more patience than Scorpio. Both of you make plans years ahead and are able to stick with them, allowing nothing to defer you from reaching the pinnacle of prosperity. Both conquer all obstacles put in your pathway; victory is achieved at the bargaining table. The combination of your two brilliant minds and untiring physical energy is enough to make anyone bet on the two of you to get anything you want.

AQUARIUS/SCORPIO

You can't stand it when your Scorpio coworker tries to dominate you, especially since you are equals at the office. It's nerve-racking to try and get along with her — she's so unfriendly. Communication is important to you and she just doesn't have anything to say.

Your Scorpio boss bugs you when she tries to get you to do all of that routine, detailed and confining work. You can do it, but only for so long and then you've got to get up and move about. But with her eagle eyes you feel like a prisoner. If she continues this restrictive treatment, you may just walk right off the job and leave her in a mess.

This is not a good working combination. The two of you are both stubborn and refuse to give an inch; thus a stalemate occurs and the business has even less of a chance to succeed. Your erratic spending and Scorpio's compulsive sprees just do not mix well together; both want to disburse funds in opposite areas so you seldom agree in many areas.

Your aims differ from Scorpio's; she's dedicated to career, power and financial success and doesn't care if she doesn't have time to indulge in a personal life with friends and family, whereas you are the opposite. This could detract from the ultimate goals that each of you desire. You're better off alone.

PISCES/SCORPIO

Your Scorpio coworker is tops; if it wasn't for him helping you out when you get behind, you'd never meet the deadline on time. He's quiet and never disturbs your daydreaming that you enjoy doing when you have a boring job.

It's such a comfort to have a Scorpio boss who takes an interest in you. His pep talk, because you neglected some of your responsibilities, was what you needed to make you get with it. However, you wish he wouldn't goad you to hurry

You realize that most of the time you are unrealistic so it's a feather in your cap to have a Scorpio partner that brings you back to reality. However, he has taken your dreams and made them workable. You don't mind his running the entire phase of the operations and making all of the decisions because you know that he's one hundred percent right all of the time.

You are a very good team. Your ability to promote and Scorpio's talent to negotiate make you a hard pair to beat. You should work out front talking to the customers and drumming up new ones; tend to the advertising campaigns and let Scorpio handle the finances, and all the behind-the-scenes activities. You can be lazy, so you need the aggressive Scorpio as a teammate. However, you have to watch out for telling fibs because this will make Scorpio burn and you don't want to see this man erupt like a volcano, do you? With your wheeling and dealing and Scorpio's management talents, the two of you could make millions.

Chapter Eleven

Sagittarius Compatibility In Business

If you were born between November 22 and December 21, your Sun is in the sign Sagittarius. However, you may also express Sagittarius traits if Sagittarius is dominant in your horoscope (refer to the Introduction, Page 1), even if it is not your Sun sign. If this is the case, you should read this chapter just as if your Sun sign is Sagittarius.

SAGITTARIUS PROFILE
Getting Acquainted With The Sagittarius Personality

The Sagittarius man is very easy to get to know. Once you understand what motivates him, it'll be a cinch to deal with him whether he's your partner, employer, employee, coworker, or client. He goes through life with a friendly, happy-go-lucky attitude. There'll be a laugh a minute when you're in his company. He is restless, always looking for something new to do, whether it's having a good time or with a profession. If you try to keep up with him you may get the impression that you're on a wild goose chase — and you just might be!

Sagittarius is bursting at the seams. He wants to do something to keep him busy on the job. He doesn't like to sit still or be confined. This fellow needs to be able to come in and out of the office (like a salesman) when he pleases. He thrives when everything is topsy-turvy, active. Sagittarius likes to get a job done quickly and he can handle pressures and deadlines with ease.

This man never looks back, so outdated methods turn him off. Sagittarius is a gambler who can get carried away with new ventures. Unfortunately, he has a bad habit of not thinking — or following — things through. This man is loyal and will stick by someone even when that person is in the wrong. He believes that everyone is his friend, even if it's a stranger he just met. Thus, be his pal and you'll be making the right step toward your being successful with him in business.

IF YOU ARE A SAGITTARIUS

Because you're always in a rush you may ask, "What can I do to get to the top quickly?" Success can be achieved faster if, when you deal with others, you adhere to the following advice:

When dealing with an employer you must realize that you are beneath him or her in status. It's difficult for you to be in an inferior position because you strongly believe that everyone is created equal and you live your life in this fashion. In a work situation, though, it's necessary that someone be in command. Your "I-don't-give-a-darn" attitude about the opinions of those in powerful positions is going to get you fired *often*.

If you disagree with your employer, tell him about it in a calm, cool, and collected manner. Avoid tactlessness. When you are bluntly honest, you can get yourself into a lot of hot water. You sound insulting instead of helpful, as you had intended. You need to learn diplomacy. There are ways you can tell a boss how you feel, but it should be done so it doesn't cause offense. You must learn to *think* about what you are saying *before* you open your mouth. By so doing, promotions and raises are easier to attain.

When dealing with partners, employees and coworkers be on guard against impatience. Realize that not everyone can move or perform a job as fast as you can. Avoid pushing anyone to "get with it." Be aware that speeding can cause sloppy and inaccurate work — something you've been guilty of before.

If you've discovered that one person is slow, it's best to keep it to yourself. (There are lots of worse things.) But whatever you do, refrain from blabbing about it in a room full of people. If you just must speak about it, take the individual aside and kindly discuss it with him. Ask him if he has a problem that's keeping him from going any faster. If it's part of his nature to be as slow as molasses then accept it. Be tolerant of his shortcoming. If he is disturbed by something personal, suggest that maybe he should seek help — a minister, family counselor or psychologist — depending on the nature of his difficulty.

Stop allowing little things to bug you. If you don't you'll hastily fire an otherwise good employee, dissolve a partnership that could make money, walk off a job or allow a coworker's slowness to hold you back from a better position. If you want to be successful, avoid reckless action.

When dealing with clients your main problem is eagerness. Avoid rushing transactions. Give a person time to think. Excuse yourself by politely saying that you'll return soon for his decision. In the interim, greet other customers or tend to some duties. Return to your client shortly and see if he needs to ask you any further questions about the product you are selling. Keep in mind that when you are intolerant of delay, chances are that you won't be ringing up a sale on the cash register.

If you're in a business where it's possible for you to slash prices and still make a profit — do so if it's feasible. This may be difficult for you to do because you're not the type who ever thinks of saving money on a deal — you're a lavish spur-of-the-moment spender. If the buyer is from a large corporation, and your instincts tell you that you could make a bundle if you play your cards right, follow through and give the company a bargain. More than likely this could put you in solid and fatten your bank account at the same time.

Avoid turning a serious situation, such as a contract discussion, into a joke. Leave the humorous moments for that first greeting or at the conclusion of a transaction.

Now, go one step further — once you as a Sagittarian know or can recognize the sign your partner, employer, employee, coworker, or client is, read that sign's chapter to know how best to deal with him as well as to understand his compatibility with you. If you wish to know what he thinks about you, read the Sun-Sign Compatibility section starting on page 170. The remainder of this Sagittarius section deals with how others relate to you, and what they can expect of you and how they should handle you. So now let's go on an interview with your sign, okay?

AN INTERVIEW WITH A SAGITTARIUS

A Sagittarius employer interviewing you: Your resumé will be glanced at quickly right after you've been greeted by an ear to ear grin. Now you can expect a few on-target questions. Answer them all without hesitation. Sagittarius is probing to see if you have anything to hide. This employer can see through phony people immediately. And when she does you'll want to run and hide because she'll embarrass you by letting you know it — regardless of who is present in the room.

Be on the up-and-up with her. Honesty is a must. She's mainly interested in knowing whether you are truthful, intelligent, and flexible. She thinks and works fast. This woman doesn't care if you are career-oriented, just want the money, or are interested in a title.

If she hires you right then and there (and the odds are ninety-nine to one she will) accept immediately. If you don't you're out of a job. She acts quickly and expects you to do the same.

If you're interviewing a Sagittarius applicant: Keep him sitting in the reception room for too long, and he'll be gone. If you get a chance to interview him, though, you'll immediately notice how friendly he is and how easy it is to talk to him. You'll like him from that moment he grins (everyone always does). He'll answer all of your questions briefly and throw in some candid remarks about your organization. Don't be surprised if he gives you some valuable tips on how to increase your sales — he's a real promoter. Sagittarius may even tell you how he envisions your business's future and what you can do to make it into a large-scale operation.

If he's convinced you (and he probably has) that he's the one you should hire, by all means do it right then and there. If you don't, he'll go elsewhere — he's too impatient and restless to wait for your telephone call saying, "You've got the job."

Now that the interview is over, let's go to work for a Sagittarius. Later, we'll see how Sagittarius is going to fare as your employee, okay?

YOUR SAGITTARIUS EMPLOYER
What Does Your Sagittarius Boss Expect Of You?

If you're being transferred from one department to another because you've had a run-in with someone, made a blunder, or decided it was time for a change — don't worry what your new Sagittarian boss thinks. She couldn't care less about any difficulties you experienced. That's the past and it's the future that counts with her. If you're coming to work for her because you want to do something different, she'll understand that motive completely — she's done that number a few times herself. All Sagittarius cares about is that you are happy in your new environment and that you try to do the best you can.

This woman wants you to be loyal — it's a must — and you can show her your loyalty by doing your share of the work. She expects you to be friendly and outgoing because she can't stand to have sourpusses in her department. Sagittarius wants you to tend to your duties but she doesn't mind if you talk and gossip at the same time — that is, as long as there are no big-wigs in sight and you don't make any errors.

She expects you to tend to all those menial tasks — the detailed reports, monotonous chores, and routine work that she can't stand. This woman doesn't like to be bogged down by the little things. Sagittarius is open-minded and wants to hear about new developments so she expects you to keep abreast of things and tell her about them; when you do she'll be elated that you're on her staff.

How to Handle Your Sagittarius Employer

Sagittarius doesn't like to be around anyone who is negative. She wants everyone to put on the same happy smile that she has. This woman wants an office that is alive and sparkles. She wants the customers to say, "It's a pleasure to come here. Everyone is so friendly. They look like they enjoy working here." Don't gripe or complain. If you do, Sagittarius won't have you around for long. If you are despondent, this woman will boost your morale and lift your spirits. Her words of encouragement are hard to beat. She knows how to build up your confidence. Smile as much as possible, especially when she's around. Laugh at her jokes and witty remarks — at least one a day is guaranteed.

Sagittarius is acquainted with people from every walk of life. Expect her office to be like open house — VIPs will drop by to discuss contracts, products, marketing, promotions, and to conclude transactions. Some of them will be there just to say hello. So make yourself useful — this will put you in good with your boss. If it puts you behind on your other work, just stay late and come in early the next morning. This woman likes to know that you are ready to respond without her having to request your assistance. She's extremely generous and that extra bonus in your pay check will certainly repay your effort.

On this job, you'll never know what is going to happen from one day or moment to the next. If you're newly employed, by the time the week ends, you may think your boss is insane. She does wild things — perhaps she'll read an ad about a new type of computer or word processor (she's already got one) and on mad impulse will want you to make her an appointment with the manufacturer. Sagittarius is always in a hurry so she won't want to wait until next week for an appointment, so make it for as soon as possible.

Don't be surprised if she buys the machine tomorrow and it's delivered the following day. Be prepared to learn how to operate it. And don't be shocked if a week later Sagittarius calls another company about a different computer or word processor that she saw demonstrated last night at a trade show. But even more astounding will be her purchase of this machine because she thinks it's better than the other one. Do you think she'll sell the others? *No,* she'll keep them all, in case one goes on the blink. (She hates to have things stop.) Get accustomed to things happening a little erratically and on the spur of the moment.

Be on your best behavior at all times because you'll never know when your Sagittarius boss is going to dash in a room; it may be when you least expect it. Maybe she left for a late lunch and five minutes later she's back because suddenly she decided that she'll skip a meal and go on a diet because she has gained too much weight recently.

This is one employer who doesn't mind if you are late to work in the morning or take a few minutes extra for lunch or on your coffee break. If you call in sick, she's understanding. If you want to take a vacation at an odd time of the year, just ask. She is usually quite agreeable and easy to get along with.

Very seldom does anyone ever have to ask a Sagittarian for a raise. This woman believes in a share-the-wealth policy; she's known to pay huge salaries, fat bonuses, and has fantastic benefits with health and life insurance, and profit-sharing; her raises may be shockingly large. She knows that you need money and that there will be more coming in all the time for her so she isn't going to miss what's paid out to you. Besides. she depends upon your services and believes if she treats you right, you'll be an excellent employee who she can depend upon always.

Promotions come just as easily as salary hikes. However, you won't get one unless you deserve it. Sagittarius may puzzle you because she's in such a hectic whirl that you don't know whether she likes you or not. Just as you think you are making headway, and think she appreciates all of your efforts, something will happen to throw you for a loop. Try to understand that this woman goes so quickly that she doesn't always think about you. Often when she's talking to you, her mind is racing off in another direction. So, chalk up her odd behavior to speed and you won't be so confused. If this woman didn't like you, she would fire you immediately.

If you've made a mistake, be prepared for Sagittarius to criticize you in front of the others. She's honest and tells you the truth so you won't make the same error twice — she wants perfection. Sagittarius isn't tactful so you may be embarrassed and have your feelings hurt, especially if you're the sensitive type (Cancer, Pisces). Try to understand that her rudeness is not intentional. If she realizes that she's upset you, she'll apologize just as quickly. Sagittarius just doesn't always know when to quit, how to remedy the mess or keep her mouth closed. Fortunately this woman doesn't hold grudges, she forgets and forgives instantly.

Sagittarius doesn't like to be kept in the dark about something going on in the office behind her back. Don't keep anything from her; she'll find out sooner or later. Either someone will blab or she'll walk in a room unexpectedly and overhear a conversation accidentally.

If you are prejudiced keep it to yourself. Sagittarius believes in hiring all types of people — including minorities and the handicapped. She's against people living off welfare and may hire uneducated employees just to give them a chance to better themselves. If this goes against your grain either look for a job elsewhere or don't say anything, just accept it. This woman will stick up for what she believes in and throw you right out if you criticize. To her it means you are being unfair and mean to another human being. So if you want to become a success sign for her firm, change your way of thinking.

YOUR SAGITTARIUS EMPLOYEE
What Can You Expect From Your Sagittarius Employee?

This fellow hopes for the best. He's a gambler who will take a chance on working for your company. When he first starts to work for you he sees everything through rose-colored glasses regardless of how dismal the environment may be.

Sagittarius is not a griper. He tries to make the best of things. If he doesn't like the vibrations or the way he's treated, he'll walk right out. When he quits a job it's because he decided that life's too short to have to put up with discordant conditions, situations or people.

If Sagittarius is on your payroll he will be extremely loyal and defend you staunchly to the bitter end if he believes you are right. He is the type who, if his job hangs by a thread because you are almost bankrupt, will go around and cheer everyone up, plus he'll stay on without pay until you are back on your feet again. During the interim, he will encourage you not to worry that everything is going to be okay. Expect him to keep you, and everyone else, in stitches — you may even call him "the company clown."

This fellow is ambitious even though he may not always appear so. He is a hard worker and finishes his tasks quickly. Expect him to be inquisitive and ask you lots of questions. Sagittarius enjoys learning knowledge and may ask you about every phase of your operation. When an idea pops into his head he gets so excited about it that he has to blurt it right out. So expect him to run into your office without knocking and enthusiastically tell you about it regardless of who is in the room at the time. If you immediately accept his suggestion for expansion, or whatever, this fellow is likely to jump up and down for joy.

How to Handle Your Sagittarius Employee

Keep him on the run so he can move about rather than confining him to a desk. Don't give him a schedule to go by because this takes away his freedom; he can't stand being forced to stick to a timetable. Sagittarius does well talking over the telephone and excels in selling. However, he can't, and won't, sell a product that he doesn't believe in. If he's a salesman, give him a huge expense account — he's a big tipper, splurging on food and drink. But it's worth it, because he wraps up a deal about ninety-nine percent of the time. Also keep in mind that he can't stand cheap people, and if you put him on a budget it'll cramp his style. Thus sales won't be up as much as they would be if you give him unlimited funds to play with.

If you give him instructions, explain them thoroughly. Make sure they are logical and make common sense. Also tell him why you are doing something in a particular way. If you leave something out, and he goofs because of it, expect Sagittarius in front of everyone present to loudly question you with, "Why did you pull this on me?" And he doesn't care if you are his supervisor because to him you're a human being, which makes the two of you equal. This fellow doesn't even stop to think that you may fire him for such an insubordination — he just must tell you what he thinks and that's all there is to it. Also he has a high opinion of himself and doesn't want anyone to get an idea that he's stupid; he'll expose the guilty one at all costs.

If you are angry with his frankness, just ignore it because he means no harm. Think twice before you blow your top. Let things pass rather than getting in an emotional stew. Sagittarius thinks it's his duty to be honest, and once his duty has been performed that's the end of it. If you argue, you'll be reinforcing it with additional energy. If you are vexed it won't be for long (unless you're Taurus or Scorpio and hold a grudge) because he'll console you with one of his smiles and bring you a gift and will act like you're the best of friends and nothing ever happened. By the way, this fellow calls his executives, employers, wealthy people, and customers "his friends." He's handy to have around because he encourages you, builds your ego (when he's not deflating it unintentionally) and is just a jolly person that everyone enjoys.

Don't ever promise Sagittarius a raise or promotion and renege on it. He doesn't let anyone get away with a lie. Before he walks out, he'll belittle you with a stormy and embarrassing scene. This fellow lives high on the hog and wants to get paid high wages. If you are stingy, he won't hang around.

Sagittarius can pull some big blunders that may cost the company enormous sums of reserve cash. But he'll turn right around and find a way to make the corporation more than he just lost. So how can you fire a guy like that?

If your business deals with other cities and states, send Sagittarius on trips. Or if you are thinking of expanding to other towns and countries, let this fellow represent your company. He loves to travel because it's a change of scenery — he gets bored if you confine him to the office. He meets new people easily. His gift of gab — he loves to talk about any subject — and his sincerity and friendliness, give him the ability to talk to anyone, including the president of a corporation, who you need to win over to your firm. Send Sagittarius into the field and you'll see what a real asset he can be to your company.

Often he promises more than he can deliver, so be on guard for this type of action, especially when he returns from these field trips in, or out of town. Sagittarius is too optimistic and sees everything coming up roses so if he tells you that you'll hear from these VIPs he just visited, don't get too carried away. Use caution. He's not telling a lie. His problem is that he's too sure of himself and the people he's dealing with. Also, he's gullible. Because he is honest and truthful he expects everyone else to be the same. Later, when he finds out different, he's shocked. But then again, you may be surprised and hear from these VIPs sooner than you had anticipated. When you have a Sagittarian in your employ, be ready for anything — including success.

YOUR SAGITTARIUS COWORKER
What Can You Expect From Your Sagittarius Coworker?
There are just a few basic facts to keep in mind when working with this female. She's enthusiastic, kind-hearted, moves like lightning, enjoys a challenge, and can give and take orders. Sagittarius is energetic and if she's not bored, can follow through and accomplish her chores. She does it quickly because she likes to get tasks done and over with, so don't worry that she's being competitive with you because she's not. This woman will help you if you fall behind. It's important for

her to be liked, so to attain your good will she'll go out of her way to do favors for you. Expect her to volunteer her services, whether you want her to help you or not. Sagittarius abhors stagnation and if your job is dependent upon hers, and you are holding her up, she's likely to be on the verge of a nervous fit.

This woman dislikes seeing anyone treated unfairly. And, like Sagittarian Jane Fonda, she'll fight for a cause, or to have outdated company policies and rules changed, even if it means her job in the process. For instance, she may want to wear jeans to work when it isn't allowed; but her work is behind the scenes so she can't see why she shouldn't be allowed to work in comfort. And, because you're a coworker, expect her to try and recruit you to join the crusade against the boss.

Be prepared for a "good morning" smile that will snap you out of a bad mood; her happiness is contagious. You may laugh a little at her awkward movements when she bumps into a machine, knocks an electric pencil sharpener off the desk or clumsily hands you reports that fall and scatter all over the floor. Usually she's so busy yakking that she isn't paying any attention to where she's going or what she's doing. Sagittarius also does things so quickly that she makes a mess and slops ink all over her white blouse. But even with these little mishaps you can see that she's still a delight to work with.

How To Handle Your Sagittarius Coworker

If you can control your temper when she plays jokes and pranks on you, you'll avoid clashes. Sagittarius is as bubbly as a glass of champagne. When she's bored or feels the job is confining, she'll think of some mischief to get into and it may be at your expense. This action can be avoided if she's kept active with any mental and physical activity; therefore, give her some of your work to do or a puzzle that will challenge her mind.

Generally she is pleasant to work with, considerate of fellow workers and doesn't try to do anything that would make you angry. But she does these crazy antics in the spirit of fun and just doesn't think about how it affects you, or your work, so let her know that you're disturbed by her behavior and that you can't afford to chance getting fired. Sagittarius will listen to reason and, besides, she wants to keep in harmony with you — she can't stand to make enemies; it goes against her grain. Often she just needs to be spoken to in a kindly manner. This woman will not condemn your viewpoint although it may differ from hers. But by all means, speak up, because she is understanding and flexible. If she's run out of work to do, instead of pestering you, she may look for work in another department until things pick up in her own. Or don't be too surprised if she just ups and quits!

If you have a bad trait about yourself, don't point it out to Sagittarius. Perhaps it's nothing more than you're thinking that your ears are too big; however, others you've asked through the years have told you differently. So now you decide to see what Sagittarius has to say; when you ask her, you are really being gutsy. She's honest and just may come out with a loud, "Yes, you're right. Your ears are too big. why don't you save your money and see a plastic surgeon?" You may feel like going down under because everyone in the room turned around and looked at you. So now you know better than to ever ask a Sagittarian anything personal.

You will get accustomed to her frankness. In fact, you may be frightened that every time she walks into a room, you won't know what she may pull next — and you won't; what's more, neither does she! But just think of the excitement you'll have waiting to find out; at least you can't complain of a dull environment or boredom when you're working with Sagittarius.

This woman is sometimes too forthright for her and your own good. She bungles things in business by treating clients like she does you. Often she comes out with some humorous remarks; you'll laugh at the witty ones and cry when she embarrasses you with one of her Sagittarian arrows (her sign's symbol: the archer) that's always pointed ahead — right in your direction. She can hurt your feelings with her cutesy comments but try to understand that she doesn't realize she's doing it. If this woman is aware that something she said bothered you, it will upset her no end. Get used to Sagittarius, who can turn around and flatter you; she can touch upon your hopes with her words of praise and build shattered dreams into reality by helping you attain them — if not with physical actions, with her encouragement. So if you feel like clobbering her for saying something rude and too much to the point, think twice — because she really wants to be your friend as well as coworker.

Often Sagittarius may express her negative side and be unreliable and irresponsible. However, if you get angry and put her down for something she's not guilty of, expect her to flare up. She's got a bad temper that comes out when she's innocently accused of something. Downright lies infuriate her; she'll blab it all over the office. Apologize if you're in the wrong. Watch how fast she cools down. By tomorrow she'll be back in a buddy-buddy mood with you. Try your best to get along with her because this is an important factor that's instrumental to success.

YOUR SAGITTARIUS CLIENT
What Can You Expect From Your Sagittarius Client?
This woman will bounce into your shop with a hail-fellow-well-met attitude. Her smile, casual look, and impatience will be dead giveaways that she's a Sagittarian. She'll be friendly regardless of your position in the store. Don't be surprised if she has her billfold open within seconds saying, "I'll take that. By the way, how much is it?" If she's on one of her sprees you can expect her to buy most of your merchandise. It'll be paid for either by cash or a credit card — if it's the former, don't be shocked to see large hundred dollar bills pulled out (yes, she's that brave to carry that much money around); if it's the latter, she'll charge over her limit — if it's not checked with the credit card holder first.

If you want to show her some goods that you thought she overlooked, don't be surprised if she remarks flippantly with, "Oh, I saw that, but I think it's ugly." Her frankness and observance to detail may catch you off guard. Generally when Sagittarius enters your shop she knows what she wants ahead of time. Therefore, when she comes in the door, she notices everything with one sweep of her eyes.

And with that one glance she knows what she likes and wants. But when you watch her movements you'd swear that you don't know if she has any idea where she's headed or for what.

If you call on a Sagittarian in her office with the purpose of selling her a new product that will soon be available on the market, expect a quick reply. Don't be too stunned by her briefness. You may get a "What does it do? How will it make me money? When can I have it? How much is it?" And with your answers, if they satisfy her, expect an "Okay, I'll sign the purchasing order right now." She's an easy sale, if she likes the merchandise.

How To Handle Your Sagittarius Client

The most important point to remember when selling something to a Sagittarian is to talk quickly and get to the point immediately. She doesn't like to have her time wasted and she's sure that you don't want to dilly-dally either. Don't be afraid to tell her a price; so leave the hem-hawing at home. This woman is a good sport and will take a risk on something that is just in the experimental stages.

Never lie to a Sagittarian; she'll never trust you again in business. If you make a promise to deliver merchandise on a set date, keep it or call her and let her know why you have to change the delivery date.

Don't try to con her into buying something just because you want to make a fast buck and know that she's a quick sale. She senses intuitively when something is not legit, although often she doesn't follow her hunches and she gets stung. But don't take that chance. She is too trusting and when she discovers that someone cheated her, she'll be dumbfounded. Her belief is that if she's good and honest, how can anyone else be different?

If you have an appointment with her, don't be surprised if she cancels it. Sagittarius breaks dates on the spur of the moment. But her friendly smile and outgoing personality make up for it— and so does the large order she gives you when she does see you.

Don't get disturbed by Sagittarius if she doesn't remember your name; it's the face she recalls. Perhaps you met her at a workshop seminar last night and she said, "Drop by my office sometime and we'll talk business." If you take her up on it and you gave the receptionist just your name, you may not get to see her right away, especially if she's tied up in a conference. However, if you tell the receptionist to relate to her that you are calling upon her due to her request at said seminar, then Sagittarius will find a way to see you immediately. (That's when she remembers meeting you.)

If you are selling something personal to Sagittarius, don't waste you time or hers by mentioning how much money she's saving because it's a bargain or that tomorrow the price is going up and how lucky she is to be here today purchasing said item. Those lines won't interest her at all. Appeal to her desire to derive pleasure from the object and you'll wind up a fast sale.

If you are selling something that's business-related, appeal to her desire to speed up production and let her know the large amounts of money she can derive from purchasing said machinery, equipment, or a system, etc. That's the approach that is the most likely to wrap up a sale for you. And when you do that, you're headed in the right direction toward becoming successful.

YOUR SAGITTARIUS PARTNER
What Can You Expect From Your Sagittarius Partner?

You may think you hit the jackpot when you teamed up with this man because he's brilliant, self-sufficient, far-sighted, not easily discouraged and just plain lucky. He's got the humor of the late Flip Wilson, the honesty and frankness of a Phil Donohue and just may gain wealth like the late industrialist Andrew Carnegie — all Sagittarians.

This man is vivacious; his gregarious nature aids him in business. He has high aspirations and is constantly in search of new ways to make money. Sagittarius will follow up every lead in the pursuit of his goal. He thinks big and doesn't want anyone to keep him from chasing his dreams. He'll gamble for high stakes; and he expects you to come along for the ride. If he doesn't take a risk, he considers himself a loser. If the two of you have an actual loss, he'll tell you that it's a lesson you both had to learn. But be ready for the two of you to be back on your feet again because somehow just as you think the worst has come, your Sagittarian partner gets saved at the last minute. So expect him to keep on trying, he wants to make a fortune, therefore, why don't you, also, give it a try ?

Sagittarius may astound you because just as one goal is accomplished he doesn't sit and relax; he forgets he attained that objective; he's got another one that has to be achieved. He's never satisfied and doesn't think he's doing enough — it's his restless spirit that goads him (and you'll be in the act, too) on and on. He points that Sagittarian arrow to the future (he doesn't even think in the present tense) and follows his star as high in the sky as it shines. Follow along with him — you won't be sorry.

How To Handle Your Sagittarius Partner

This fellow has a here-today and gone-tomorrow attitude. He can't stand stale, stuffy rooms. He likes the fresh air, thus gets a whiff of it by being in and out of the office. So let him handle the part of the business that allows him the freedom to come and go; otherwise he won't seem to settle down for long cooped up inside all day long.

Let him dash off on trips and travel overseas; he enjoys expanding and having a world-wide trade so don't interfere with his big plans. You tend to the home office and let him make millions for the company drumming up new deals in foreign lands and obtaining loans from Geneva, Switzerland. Once he's in the swing of things he'll suddenly get the urge to go to Japan, even though neither one of you know anyone there. (He'll know loads of people before he leaves.) Don't worry that it'll be a costly trip in vain, it won't be — have the confidence in him that he has in himself and you can't help but be a winner. After all, if he's positive that you'll handle the business at headquarters real well, why can't you give him the same courtesy while he's in far-away places?

Sagittarius likes modern surroundings and equipment that is as progressive as his goals; so don't balk when he orders the newest digital or laser-beam electronic computer. It may be costly but give him a chance to explain his big ideas; they may be unbelievable but, if you'll take the same risk your partner's willing to take, they just may pay off. Also, when he wants to expand to larger quarters go along with him verbally, but suggest that the two of you consult with your accountant first; tell him that maybe the bookkeeper could make some improvement over his plans. When you appeal to Sagittarius intellectually, and kindly, he won't be so headstrong; he's likely to curb his impulsive desire to leap into some wild scheme he's just concocted.

Your partner is an extrovert with no inhibitions. He prefers being the boss but will call the shots in a jovial, rather than demanding, manner. So, hopefully, you don't have an ego problem; if you do, consider his commands as a game he's playing; usually he isn't even aware that he's trying to take the lead. However, he'll follow your orders, if you give them.

Sagittarius likes to be on the go constantly; so give him free reign. He does scatter his energies with so many projects that he wears himself out. As exhausted as he may get, he doesn't stop. You'll never have to be concerned with his staying out sick; he'll be there with bells on — but a warning, if he does stay home and in bed, that's a clue that he's seriously ill although he'll smile and say, "I'll be okay."

In business, Sagittarius makes more successful deals than unsuccessful ones. When he travels, or even on the home front, he's great at spreading goodwill for the company and is able to smooth over personal problems of those who are employed by the two of you or with the clients he contacts. Everyone seems to confide in him; therefore let him tend to this end of the corporation and you take care of the other tasks.

He needs you to control him when he makes rapid judgments and comes to quick conclusions. Don't waste time discussing trivialities or things that don't have to do with consummating a deal such as problems with an employee — that he leaves for you to handle. To Sagittarius there's nothing as important as the big deal he has going on at that exact moment. His reasoning is that he can always hire new help, but he can't always have the opportunity to make a quick buck like he's got going when you approach him. (He's never without a deal pending.) Therefore, whatever you want to say, make your point immediately — aim his Sagittarian arrow at him for a change! He doesn't like to hear about his mistakes and may ignore your criticism; but he'll think about it when he's alone.

His love of speculation may turn your hair grey ahead of time. Watch debts piling up with his foolhardiness with money. His "sky is the limit feeling" needs to be curbed — so arrange before you go into business to countersign all checks. He can't stand stinginess, but knows inwardly that he needs you to control his excessive spending urges — so with your help and combined talents, success should be achieved. After all, in the world of industry, Sagittarius can be a giant and make tons of money — so, hitch your wagon to a star, you won't regret it — maybe you'll make a billion dollars!

Sun-Sign Compatibility

This section deals with each sign of the zodiac in relation to a Sagittarius Sun sign. By knowing how your sign blends with a Sagittarian, you go one step beyond understanding his personality and one step closer to knowing how to handle him in any business situation. Greater insight is invaluable — it not only helps a business prosper, it encourages peace of mind on and off the job.

The following Sun-Sign compatibility summaries, with the exception of Sagittarius/Sagittarius, *are from the point of view of the person dealing with Sagittarius. Note:* For the Sagittarian's point of view, see the Sun-Sign chapter of the person Sagittarius is dealing with, i.e., Aries — refer to the Aries chapter explaining how Sagittarius thinks about Aries.

ARIES/SAGITTARIUS

You appreciate Sagittarius pitching in and tying up the loose strings you left dangle on the job that bored you. He sure makes your workday run smooth. It's good to have a coworker who just takes you as you are. If you yell or get bossy with him, he doesn't quibble — he takes it all in his stride.

Your ego gets a real boost when your Sagittarius boss admires and praises you for your various skills. You are delighted when he encourages you to enter into other and more productive endeavors. The confidence he inspires is almost overwhelming. You are glad that you work for such an easygoing person as well as one who gives you generous raises every time you do something extra.

Your Sagittarius partner makes you feel at ease because he respects your quick decisions and is not disturbed by any hasty or impulsive action on your part. In fact, he gets as excited as you do when you've got a new project on the agenda. It's a pleasure to be in business with someone who doesn't hold you back from accomplishing goals; instead he pushes you to do even more.

The enthusiasm that you two have should make you achieve your desires. You are a great working combination that has everything going for you. Both are hard and fast workers and won't accept defeat. There is no ego problem because Sagittarius is constantly taking a back seat and is blowing so much adulation in your direction that you feel like you can climb the highest mountain in the world and conquer it — and maybe you can. Both of you are outgoing and speak the truth whether it hurts or not. But there's seldom any criticism; when there is, it's taken more as a challenge than an insult.

TAURUS/SAGITTARIUS

Your Sagittarius coworker will just have to learn that you are not about to rush to complete a chore. She can just find something else to do while she's waiting for you to give her the report. How does she expect to get anything done with all of that talking she does?

Your newly hired Sagittarian employee doesn't do the neat and artistic type of work that you require. It she doesn't slow down, she'll continue to turn in sloppy work and that's when you will have to give her notice.

Your Sagittarius partner has so many new ideas that you can't keep up with her. Just as you've figured one out she dumps it for a better one — so she says. This constant changing of her mind is beginning to annoy you. Also, you don't go for her surprises, like bringing in a decorator without your consent.

The two of you have many opposite traits that could cause problems: your slowness and her quickness; your penny-pinching and her wastefulness. Both can work hard; however, it's best you stay indoors confined to the office and let Sagittarius be outdoors in the field meeting people and drumming up business. If you try to hold her back from larger-than-life ideas; you will have difficulties that could cause a dissolution of the partnership. Your wanting outdated equipment and Sagittarius wanting the latest "in" machinery is also a reason for the two of you splitting and going your own separate ways.

GEMINI/SAGITTARIUS

Your Sagittarius coworker is a delight. His fingers move almost as fast as yours. He never holds you up from accomplishing a task. His ideas are brilliant and he's gutsy enough to experiment with them right here on the job — that's what you like.

This boss sure is generous and easy to work for. Sagittarius isn't demanding and doesn't mind if you come back late from a coffee break. He's also intelligent and you enjoy the talks the two of you have. His openness to your modernization notions is really unusual for an employer, but you admire him for it.

Your Sagittarian employee sure has some clever ways for you to expand and increase your sales. If the latest one works as well as the last one did, you think you'll give him a promotion; he'd be an excellent assistant for you. His innovativeness tends to follow your own same lines. You are tickled pink that he is adaptable and can leap right into those changes you're contemplating.

This is one partner that spends as much money, and as quickly, as yourself. You think highly of his productiveness, he can gab almost as fast as you can. His happy-go-lucky personality is sure great to be around. You can't stand people who are always griping and complaining. Your Sagittarius partner makes sure the office is lively — you're so busy with other things that you don't have time to see to that part of the business; therefore, you're glad he tends to it. Together, the two of you can do very well in business!

CANCER/SAGITTARIUS

This is one boss who just demands too much of your energy. You just can't keep up with the heavy work load. You are coming to the end of your emotional rope and may look for another job that's not quite so strenuous. You need more free time.

Every day you get more frightened by the risks your Sagittarian partner takes. You try to talk her into using common sense before taking on these added financial burdens but it just doesn't do any good; she does what she wants. Her bluntness disturbs you, especially when she wisecracks with clients. If she isn't careful, you're afraid that losses will occur.

Cancer and Sagittarius is not a good combination; Sagittarius is too reckless for you, you'll get sick every time she wants to spend money on new equipment. What's worse is that the two of you disagree on the way a business should be conducted — you tend to be old-fashioned and she's futuristic.

You will worry too much about the way Sagittarius goes about everything from A to Z. Your negativity is something that will make Sagittarius very put out and when she gets through reading the riot act to you, most likely the corporation will be dissolved suddenly. It's best you don't work together, but remain friends.

LEO/SAGITTARIUS

Your Sagittarius coworker is lots of fun. He's always joking and making the day pass by quickly. This fellow pitches in if you get a little behind. He's also very loyal, never reporting you to the boss.

It's a lark working for a Sagittarian. He's always giving you so many compliments that you don't mind taking orders from him; besides, he does it in such a friendly way that it doesn't even seem like he's the boss. His open-mindedness may be helpful to your plans to get ahead — and his pay raises are fabulous.

Your Sagittarius employee handles his duties capably. He seems to be responsible although now and then he goes off on a tangent of being late — but you really can't complain because he makes up for it by staying late. You are very impressed with his honesty because you can't stand lies. Sometimes he's a little bit too frank but most of the time his remarks are useful.

When you signed partnership papers with Sagittarius, you knew you made the right move. The two of you are dynamic together — a real winning twosome. Goals are planned, reached, and more goals are schemed and achieved and so the cycle goes; neither one of you is content with resting on your laurels — you must continue earning more money and expanding into a huge conglomerate type of operation.

Both of you attract wealthy and powerful people into your circle; these are your friends who want to do you favors because the two of you go out of your way to help them too. The two of you are generous and probably the last of the big-time spenders.

VIRGO/SAGITTARIUS

Your Sagittarius coworker is so sloppy that you're afraid she's going to spill the ink on you just like she does on herself. And furthermore, you are so tired of telling her how to arrange the papers on your desk when you're not there. Why she can't remember, and be neat, is perplexing.

Your latest employee, the Sagittarian, is just about to drive you berserk. She's not very punctual but just grins about it when you tell her she's late to work.

However when you give her a job to do she is fast, but she's up and down so much during the process it disturbs your concentration.

You dislike the haphazard way your assignments are handed out. This lack of routine and schedule is not to your liking. This Sagittarius boss is a little too pushy for you. When she rushes you it makes you so nervous that you think you'll make a mistake; if this keeps up, you just may quit.

You are very put out with your Sagittarian partner who takes risks after you've disagreed with her on them; she sure is headstrong. The way she wants to spend money is shameful; it's a good thing those checks have to be counter-signed by you; otherwise, she'd be spending all of the reserve cash. This is not a good relationship for you unless you can curb Sagittarius from leaping blindly into deals.

LIBRA/SAGITTARIUS

Your Sagittarius coworker sure does work fast; he never seems to rest or sit still — you wish you were like that.

The happy atmosphere you have in your office has a lot to do with your Sagittarius employee. You are so delighted to have someone so positive and cheerful on your payroll. It's important to your peace of mind that you have harmonious vibrations in your working environment, so Sagittarius is really a godsend.

Your Sagittarius partner needs you to balance him when he gets those urges to expand. You know how to get him to listen to the pros and cons of a situation; also you avoid hurting his ego. He is an extremist, and when you nicely point this out to him, he admits it's true and that he can't help himself. His desire to make a bundle of money coincides with yours.

This is a rather good combination; however, you should let Sagittarius be out front more than you — although your charm, tact, and diplomacy (something your Sagittarius partner lacks) is needed with customers. You don't mind being confined because it gives you time to balance yourself; however, Sagittarius must be on the go constantly. So if you work this out, the two of you have a good chance to be successful. Both of you love learning knowledge and have an eye toward future trends, rather than past ones; therefore, streamlined operations will be important to the both of you.

SCORPIO/SAGITTARIUS

Your Sagittarius coworker sure amazes you with how she can laugh at everything — even her mistakes! It's a good thing she works fast and doesn't hold you up.

You have to admire your Sagittarius boss, her words are as much to the point as yours are when someone's goofed.

Your Sagittarius employer reminds you of yourself — she seems to have the same spurts of energy that you do. Her ability to handle stress and strain is needed because of all the job deadlines. She's pleasant because she never gripes or complains about her duties.

As a partner, you find Sagittarius is capable of great tasks. She's as gutsy as you. The woman is thinking constantly of new enterprises that the two of you can undertake. She's not envious of you and is encouraging to be around.

This is a good combination of talents, and success can be easily achieved. If you allow Sagittarius to travel as your goodwill ambassador while you tend to the home front, you won't clash. However, it'll be difficult to confine Sagittarius to any routine — so guard against trying that procedure.

Both of you are for modern equipment and systems and don't mind spending the money impulsively in this direction. Sagittarius won't mind if you want to have separate tasks to tend to; in fact, she welcomes them. You seem to see eye-to-eye on most issues, policies, and future trends of the world; therefore, you both know what world market to enter so you'll gain the most profits.

SAGITTARIUS/SAGITTARIUS

You are just tickled pink working for Sagittarius. He's so jovial and pleasant that it seems more like play than it does drudgery. You think highly of his nonscheduled way of conducting business. It's fun to have new chores to do on the spur of the moment.

You've noticed that your Sagittarius employee is just as restless as you; therefore, you give him tasks to do that keep him moving.

Your Sagittarius partner is as extravagant as you are. The two of you can reach the multimillionaire bracket (there are more millionaires born under your sign than any other) if you follow through on your commitments. You have to be careful of getting bored with a project and dumping it in favor of another. Persistence is needed in this relationship.

You both are spendthrifts and have to guard against going head over heels in debt. The two of you tend to do everything too impulsively and need to get an accountant's advice before making any big moves. Your optimistic and cheerful personalities can easily take you to the heights you dream about.

CAPRICORN/SAGITTARIUS

You wish that your Sagittarius coworker would tend to her job more and talk a little less. She does cheer you up when you're depressed, but when you have a job to get out, you dislike interference of any kind. However, you really shouldn't complain about her because she's always willing to help you whether you ask her to or not.

Your Sagittarian boss seems a little scatterbrained, although you must say pleasantly so. She certainly doesn't know how to handle finances with those generous raises she gives; however, that's good for your bank account so just let her go on being foolish.

The two of you could do well in business if you handle the money, negotiations, and serious side of the business; let her greet the customers and do some selling. But if you confine her to a desk and chair, she'll find excuses to leave her office and do something else that is less restricting.

When her salesmanship and your buying talents are combined, you've got a super-duper team that can't fail. Don't dampen her enthusiasm with your practicality — that turns her off and makes her lose interest in everything. You need to keep her busy so that her restless spirit won't make her dump the whole operation in your lap and walk right out the door.

AQUARIUS/SAGITTARIUS

It's a pleasure working with someone who rolls up his sleeves and gets down to work immediately, just like you. Your Sagittarius coworker finishes tasks in a jiffy and never holds you up with those designs that you need to complete. He's got a brain, too. His ideas are worth experimenting with; to some people they may sound too ahead of the times but to you they are logical.

Your Sagittarius employee approaches his duties in the same positive manner as you do; it's a shame the rest of your help can't do the same. His restlessness is understandable because you also dislike being confined to a single environment.

Your Sagittarius partner has the same wild imagination as yourself. His impatience with established customs and wanting to break away into new fields is right up your alley. The modern equipment and machinery that he wants to buy costs exorbitant sums of money, but you agree with his philosophy, "Progress is the key to the future."

The two of you are a team that could build an empire together with your innovative ideas and ability to put them into practical use — although you may have to curb the Sagittarian from being too enthusiastic and overdoing everything to an extreme; especially in financial areas.

Both of you have wonderful personalities with your magnetism and his hail-fellow-well-met attitude. You've got the business market cornered — who could resist dealing with the two of you? The only problem you may encounter is your desire to get involved in a crusade that takes you away from your tasks. If Sagittarius doesn't also get into the same type of scene, and can do your work while you're away, then there wouldn't be any difficulties.

PISCES/SAGITTARIUS

Your feelings are always getting injured by your Sagittarian coworker. One moment she's laughing with you and talking up a storm and the next she's verbally attacking you for being slow. You just can't help it if you have trouble concentrating on this dull job and, as a result, lag behind.

You are grateful for your Sagittarian employee who is able to manage some of your responsibilities. However, when she blabs to others that she's in charge because the boss is resting, you feel that the tone of her remark is sarcastic and is meant offensively rather than being informative.

Your Sagittarian partner takes so many chances that you are frightened that the two of you will go broke. You are a wreck because you never know what she's going to do next. Her bluntness is upsetting and has you in tears most of the time.

Pisces and Sagittarius are a very bad team. You are too sensitive to be in a partnership, or even work with, a Sagittarian. Her arrow will hit you hard every time you do something she doesn't like. You tend to be negative and she is positive, so your polarities are opposite — you drag each other down.

Around this partner, you need to move fast, have lots of energy and not rest or be lazy — if you are, that's when Sagittarius goes berserk and tells you like it is; she believes the truth will make you do something about it — change. But it's just not in your nature to be like her, so right there you have a snag in any type of operation you want to undertake.

Chapter Twelve

Capricorn Compatibility In Business

If you were born between December 22 and January 19, your Sun is in the sign Capricorn. However, you may also express Capricorn traits if Capricorn is dominant in your horoscope (refer to the Introduction, Page 1), even if it is not your Sun sign. If this is the case, you should read and treat this chapter just as if your Sun sign is Capricorn.

CAPRICORN PROFILE
Getting Acquainted With The Capricorn Personality

The Capricorn man is not easy to get to know. Once you understand what motivates him, it will help you deal with him whether he's your partner, employer, employee, coworker, or client. Capricorn may seem a bit of an introvert but don't let that fool you. He's clever and observant in his own quiet and reticent way and he can outwork and outlast most people. He's even-tempered, and he never gives his feelings away — his emotions are enclosed in a solid sheet of ice.

This man is a climber, ambitious (like the mountain goat — his sign's animal symbol), who wants to reach the heights of success. He may fall back a little after making some headway, but this doesn't stop him for long. He's always quickly back on his feet and ready to continue on that upward path toward his goals (actually his gods) of prestige, power, and wealth. However, it's not obvious because he prefers keeping his objectives a secret. Capricorn believes that the less people know about him, the better off he and his dreams will be. He's afraid that if someone else gets wind of his plans that person will steal them or try to deter him from achieving them. So he plods along secretly and attains his desires gradually. Capricorn's never in a hurry. This man is patient and knows that in the final wind-up, he'll get what he wants — and he always does! Capricorn is an asset to anyone in business and if you understand him and treat him right, you can join him on that upward climb to the pinnacle of success.

IF YOU ARE A CAPRICORN

Because you are extremely zealous you may ask, "What more can I do to get to the top?" Success can be achieved faster if, when you deal with others, you adhere to the following advice:

When dealing with an employer guard against being so pushy that it's obvious you are trying to use her to get ahead. When your boss notices that you are trying to wield your way in, don't be surprised if she fools you by giving you a phony opening just to test her suspicions. (A typical Scorpio or Capricorn boss would pull this stunt.) If she discovers that you're an opportunist, you may be without a job (especially if she's your supervisor, because she could be afraid if she gave you too much rope, you'd hang her and not yourself — thus you'd get her position).

You take your career so seriously that most of the time you go around with a long, drawn and sullen facial expression that is taken either for snobbery, unhappiness, or lack of confidence. Your gloomy appearance makes others feel either uncomfortable, threatened, or inferior. Try smiling more often; it may get you that raise and promotion that you long for.

You can be difficult to get along with when you're depressed. Under this circumstance you may gripe, complain, and be critical of others. This type of action can hinder the success you wish to achieve.

When dealing with partners, employees and coworkers, be on guard against being so self-centered that you can't see beyond your nose when others are having difficulties. Your callused indifference, with those who are in your vicinity arouses hostility. Take an interest in those you work with.

Listen to the ideas of others; don't be so narrow-minded that you miss the boat. If you are the type of Capricorn who lives in the past, and are afraid of moving ahead to the future, break those ties rather than clinging to them. Don't be frightened of what tomorrow may bring. Avoid being too conventional in business and sticking with the old rather than becoming involved with new ways, modern equipment, machinery, and systems. It's easy for you to get stuck in a set pattern because you resist changes and are fearful of taking chances. Realize that change is progress and progress is change.

Avoid placing limitations on your abilities. Be confident that you are tops and others will feel the same about you. Often you are deeply dissatisfied because you don't feel you're advancing. When you get in this self-pitying mood you are being destructive to yourself and this lessens your chances for success. Therefore snap out of this state and get involved in so much work that you don't have time to think; this constructive action can bring you your heart's desire.

When dealing with clients your main problem is your personality. You are too reserved and need to smile or at least give a grin. Customers are attracted to friendly shopkeepers who give them a relaxed feeling. You do have a dry sense of humor and even a witty remark might save the day and ring up a sale.

Avoid devoting too much time toward watching all the customers in the store to see if they are going to steal something. You can be so cautious that you don't pay enough attention to the client who you're waiting on because your eyes, nose, and mind are elsewhere.

If you visit a customer who's in a bad mood and she starts crying the blues, don't chime in and agree that life is rotten and rough! Encourage her that there's always a reason for everything and that perhaps tomorrow everything will look brighter. Try to lift her spirits with words of encouragement that will take away from the negative thoughts and make her more interested in doing business with you. Otherwise, you'll just add to her discord and she probably won't give you as large an order as she would if she was in a happy frame of mind. It's difficult for you to be optimistic because usually you're pessimistic. Therefore, plan ahead of time some inspiring words that can be used when you need to help someone — remember this in turn may be to your benefit also.

To go one step further, once you as a Capricorn know or can recognize the sign of your partner, employer, employee, coworker, or client, read that sign's chapter to know how best to deal with him as well as to understand his compatibility with you. If you wish to know what he thinks about you, read the Sun-Sign Compatibility section starting on page 189. The remainder of this Capricorn section deals with how others relate to you, what they expect of you and how they should handle you. So let's go on an interview with your sign, okay?

AN INTERVIEW WITH A CAPRICORN

A Capricorn employer interviewing you: Your resume will be carefully examined. Your former job descriptions will be checked over for accuracy. You may be tested along these lines. This employer may ask you questions to see if you use logic and can handle responsibilities. She may want to know how disciplined you are and whether you can stick with routine. These are the signs she's looking for in an employee — to her they are signs for success.

Be pleasant. Avoid being too friendly or chatty. Keep your distance — be a little aloof, but not as much as she. Answer her questions but don't tell her any more than you have to, especially about your previous jobs. Don't talk against another company because she'll get the impression, you'll do the same thing to her if you left her employ. Be calm, cool, and collected. Capricorn is affected by sound judgment and common sense.

Don't expect to be hired right away. This woman must take time to consider your application and qualifications as compared to the others applying for jobs. Patience is needed.

If you're interviewing a Capricorn applicant: If you keep him waiting he won't throw a fit. Capricorn is there to be hired regardless of how long it takes. When you interview this man you'll discover that he's sagacious when it comes to business. His solid reasoning ability shows up when conversing with him. Capricorn may ask questions about your corporation; he's concerned with whether there are growth opportunities here. His desire for security shows when he asks about the company benefits — medical, education, bonuses, profit-sharing. He'll also want to know his chances for advancement; if new departments will be opening up — especially if the corporation is planning to expand.

You can tell that he wants the security of a lasting job with growth potential and salary hikes, and that a title interests him. It's his ambition and drive that makes you hire him — you can just sense this man's going to go to the top. He's very obedient and will start work whenever you ask him.

Now that the interview is over, let's first go to work for a Capricorn and thus see how Capricorn is going to fare as your employee, okay?

YOUR CAPRICORN EMPLOYER
What Does Your Capricorn Boss Expect of You?

If you're being transferred from one department to another, regardless of the reason, Capricorn is suspicious and will notice every move you make and word you utter although it will seem that she's standoffish. But don't be fooled by her aloofness. This woman wants you to be as competent as she is; however, she doesn't want you to try and get the job away from her.

Capricorn doesn't want you to be late to work or take long lunch hours. Don't be surprised if she has a time clock to be punched; she likes to run her business on schedule with every moment accounted for. This woman dislikes wasting time so she'll expect you to be productive; in your spare moments, she'll keep you engaged in either helping another department filing reports, moving machinery, or assisting her.

Your boss will want you to obey her rules and tend to your duties. Capricorn will frown upon your talking while you work. Office gossip is a real no-no, so don't let her catch you doing it. Personal phone calls aren't allowed except in extreme cases of emergency. She is paying you a salary and expects you to work for it. This woman doesn't want you to gripe and complain on the job. She wants you to pay attention to details, avoid making errors, complete tasks and be a perfectionist as much as possible.

Capricorn is extremely industrious and she expects you to be diligent. If you don't work hard, she'll crack the whip if you don't improve, she'll fire you. She's inwardly disciplined and expects it of you — no goofing off with this woman; everything has to be businesslike.

How to Handle Your Capricorn Boss

Capricorn wants you properly dressed for her office; a neat and conservative look is preferred. Therefore, don't wear colorful or gaudy apparel — jeans are out generally, depending upon the nature of the business and locale. Don't go around with chipped fingernail polish on if you wear nail polish; keep your nails manicured. Make sure your hair is neatly in place.

This woman wants you to use a formal approach when speaking to customers. Be courteous. Don't run in the office, walk — carry yourself with class. A reserved appearance will keep her happy. Don't raise your voice. Capricorn expects you to speak calmly, firmly, and with eloquence. She can't stand familiarity; therefore, at all times be proper and address her by Miss or Mrs. Capricorn likes everything kept current, therefore don't let your work pile up. Promptly execute all documents, reports, papers, designs, and keep everything filed so she can find it if she needs it in a hurry. She has a horror of waste, so don't throw office supplies into the wastebasket that are still good; she may surprise you with an inspection. Your desk should be kept tidy; if it's messy she'll tell you. This woman is dominating to her staff members; she's the boss and continues to remind you of it by the way she treats you.

Don't tell her about your personal problems. Capricorn doesn't want you to bring family troubles into the office environment. She's there to tend to business and expects you to do the same. This woman is selfish and only thinks of your job performance; when you come to her with your private heartaches, she considers you to be wasting her, and your, time, because you could be working instead of talking about yourself. She's only interested in you professionally; therefore, don't mix your home life and business. If you do, it'll be a mark against you with this woman. Don't cry; she's unemotional — tears don't move her, they bring disgust.

Never walk into her office without being announced, calling first, or knocking on the door. Capricorn gets very disturbed when her privacy is disturbed. If she's in conference and tells you to hold all phone calls, do just that — regardless of a caller who says that it's an emergency. If a problem occurs in the factory, put it on ice until she's available; if it's something that is in urgent need of being solved, you are taking a chance if you interrupt her and disobey an order. However, if you are born under the sign Cancer, Scorpio, Sagittarius, Aquarius, or Pisces, follow your hunches because your intuition is usually accurate. And instead of getting bawled out, you'll be complimented.

Capricorn doesn't like it if you ask her for a raise. She believes in giving it to you when she thinks you've earned it — and not before. This woman keeps a tight control over her money; she is frugal, although you may call her stingy. Don't expect a bonus for extra favors or work; if she's the real cheap type of Capricorn you won't even get a Christmas bonus. She does pay you well if you prove extra valuable, however, generally this woman pays according to the common wage scale. If you travel for the company, she's thrifty — you'll go economy class. She considers it a waste to pay extra money for a first-class ticket when you'll get there at the same time regardless of the price of your fare.

If Capricorn thinks you have a lot of personal responsibilities (you've discussed them with her perhaps when first hired) and are handling them to the best of your ability, this will put you in good with her and could get you extra raises and promotions if your work, at the same time, is excellent. This woman admires anyone who supports their parents or relatives — she understands the self-denial and sacrifice you go through and how rough it is to take care of others and yourself; probably her empathy stems from her having gone through a similar experience.

When she delegates work for you to do don't disappoint her; stick to the timetables she's allotted you. This woman insists that you follow her plans to the letter. She is a disciplinarian and prides herself on running the office smoothly and systematically; therefore, don't throw her schedule off. In spite of her telephone ringing constantly, she'll still check with you to see if you are adhering to her orders. Capricorn works tirelessly and ploddingly to do her job plus keep tabs on everything else. She knows everything going on at all times; it's as if she has eyes in back of her head and on the sides as well. And yet, she'll appear like she's not noticing anything; therefore, don't get fooled by her poker face.

Your employer's occupation plays center role in her life. Solid achievements are a must. She's in a position of authority because she's capable of assuming responsibilities. Capricorn wants you, and everyone else for that matter, to be under her control so you'll respect her — it gives her a sense of power. She wants recognition for her diligent work, how she shoulders burdens, works long and late hours; it's important that you understand her position and give her courteous consideration of her opinions. So compliment her for her accomplishments, and praise her for how hard she works; avoid a sympathetic approach — one of admiration and holding her in high esteem is what she yearns for. This type of flattery will put you "in" with her. Don't B.S., that's one of her tricks.

It's important for Capricorn to have a good reputation; therefore, don't make mistakes that she may be blamed for, avoid taking off sick too often and don't do anything crazy in your personal life that could reflect upon your job — these antics not only give you a bad name but she's afraid that it will cause a problem with her superiors and bounce back on her because you are in her department.

Never criticize her, especially in front of anyone. Don't surprise her with new ideas. She's set in her ways and won't budge. Avoid shocking her in any way; she dislikes being caught off guard — she likes to maintain her dignified appearance at all times.

Your Capricorn boss never mixes with anyone who is in a subordinate position, so don't waste your time trying to get friendly with her. However, if you know important people or executives from other companies. and introduce her to them, she'll make the most of the opportunity that has come her way. But don't expect any special favors, although she'll be much kinder than before. This woman uses people to get what she wants and throws them aside later after she's moved ahead. It's best you perform your duties as industriously as you can and you'll be on the right road toward becoming successful.

YOUR CAPRICORN EMPLOYEE
What Can You Expect from Your Capricorn Employee?

Capricorn may neglect family, friends, and associates because he puts his ambition first; however, he won't sweep anyone aside who may be useful to his career — contacts connections, etc. He prefers working quietly behind the scenes, but don't let that fool you into thinking he's content to stay there — he's not. His ultimate aim is to be on top in a high position — his eye could be cast on your desk. So don't let his shy appearance lead you into thinking he's going to remain in a subordinate role.

This fellow will seldom take sick leave; he doesn't even like a vacation. He's a real toiler who enjoys laboring long hours; luckily he's got the endurance to withstand fatigue. He will never be idle or late. He's conscious of his responsibility. This is an employee who is loyal and trustworthy don't be surprised if he stays for years on a job that's before he's decided he's ready to make his big move, which is a better job elsewhere or his own business.

Capricorn does painstaking work, he wants everything correct. This fellow enjoys routine and can stick to a regular schedule like glue sticks to paper. He doesn't mind doing humdrum, boring work because he knows that someday it'll pay off and when that occurs, he'll be in a higher position giving orders to others.

You can rely upon Capricorn to take charge of the office while you're away. His duties are handled sternly with his usual rigid, but kind. manner. This fellow keeps to himself a lot and is a man of few words. He shuns office gossip; his activities go unnoticed because he keeps a low profile — he doesn't want anyone to know a thing about him. Success is his goal and he won't allow anything to interfere with that.

How To Handle Your Capricorn Employee

Give him some prestige with the job; something where he can be in authority so others will respect him. If he's in a position that allows him to assume command, and that he finds challenging as well as having some esteem attached to it, he'll stay in your employ. Also, the salary has to be good; if it isn't, but the job meets his other qualifications, he may work for you until he's saved a lot of money (also income coming from another job, nights and weekends). and then he'll figure he'll be in a better bargaining position with you for that salary increase he desires. So be ready to negotiate with him when he reaches this point — at least, you are now alerted to the fact that he's not in a poor state — and may just have the upper hand, that is if you want him to continue working for you. Capricorn never does anything unless he feels secure that he's in the driver's seat.

This fellow has great skill in handling just about any situation; nothing seems too tough for him to handle. Give him a chance to use his foresightedness — this may involve land you want your company to invest in, or new techniques and developments for your corporation. His ability to rely upon reason, and make far-reaching decisions, plus his innate talent in the field of negotiations. make him an asset to your business. He knows value when he sees it, and if you'll just realize *his* value, you won't regret it.

Capricorn is not original nor creative; he lacks imagination. However, he's got an excellent memory and can rattle off statistics, facts, and information so fast it might make your head reel. Give him work along these lines and you'll satisfy him as well as yourself. He can be trusted with company secrets. He may astound you by knowing the figures of your corporation's profits this year as well as five years ago. This is where his foresight comes in handy again. Ask him what, in his opinion, will be the future profit potential of your firm. His answer will be as good as any financial adviser you might have hired, if not better.

If you don't give Capricorn more responsibilities and raises along the way, he'll be dissatisfied and look elsewhere for employment. He likes to be well paid — fear of financial insecurity drives him to work hard. He gets panic-stricken if he runs out of things to do. So keep him busy at all times. This fellow knows how to put things together (he uses logic) and he enjoys keeping records. If your office needs organizing let him do it. He can rearrange furniture, equipment, desks, filing cabinets, and machines so everything is more efficient and handy to get or reach. When he's finished you'll marvel at the common sense he used; you may wonder why you didn't think of it. If you are afraid to have the office disrupted while he puts his sound methods into practice. don't worry; he'll labor for hours steadily in such a way that everything will be in tip-top shape while he's progressing; he won't make or leave a mess.

Capricorn gravitates to the commercial world as if he is born into it — and maybe he is. If you want your firm to become involved with the international trade and interstate commerce, this fellow may have some good suggestions; just ask him. If you want a good mediator, use Capricorn. He will do his duty because he sees it as a trust that you have for him. You can count on him doing the right thing.

If your corporation has certain traditions, Capricorn will honor them respectfully. If you need to entertain VIPs or want to give a company party, let this fellow be in charge; he's good with dealing with catering services and getting service and food at a price that is within your budget; in fact, you may be shocked to find that he saved you lots of money — he knows what to say to caterers so they'll come down on their fee. He figures by saving you a buck, it puts him in good with you — thus he comes closer to his goals.

He dislikes wasting time; however, he will not hurry for anyone. Therefore, don't goad him, let him push himself — he knows his speed and how long it takes him to execute a plan. Often he's all work, no play, and forgets to eat his lunch because he's so bogged down with heavy responsibilities — but that's the life he loves. He may complain about chores that aren't going to pay off; however, most of the time he's too weighed down with a pile of reports, etc., to even feel sorry for himself.

Capricorn is prepared for every emergency and contingency that may arise. Nothing is ever lost — all important documents, as well as the office keys, are kept intact. He knows where everything is at any given moment. This fellow's not absentminded — he's on the ball twenty-four hours a day.

Don't send Capricorn off on trips, he prefers to stay put at headquarters; in other words he likes to keep the home fires burning. He doesn't mind traveling if it involves deals with VIPs and gives him prestige and power. He'll journey to a convention because of the important contacts that can be made there; perhaps someone may be of use to his future plans that revolve around one word — success. If you treat him right, he'll be an asset, and bring you prosperity also.

YOUR CAPRICORN COWORKER
What Can You Expect front Your Capricorn Coworker?

There are just a few basic facts to keep in mind when working with this woman — she's dependable, cautious, moves slow, and is a workaholic. Capricorn is inordinately desirous of power, honor, office superiority and plans to get her aims achieved through hard work and using anyone she can along the way. She's not in a hurry to get to the top but she's confident that her patient effort will reward her eventually. If you try to interfere with her schemes, keep in mind that although she seems subdued, she can be cruel and ruthless; therefore, it's best you leave her path clear on her climb upward. This woman may wind up being as famous as Capricorn Mary Tyler Moore.

Capricorn doesn't smile much (you may think she's on her way to a funeral) because her mind is on her business. She doesn't meddle in your affairs and expects you to give her the same fairness. Don't expect her to join in with any office frolics — telling jokes and laughing heartily; when you do, she'll give a sign of disapproval and with that one sour-faced glance, you'll know she's going to keep her distance. This woman's not about to risk getting fired for some prank-playing that just isn't her cup of tea anyway.

She is unapproachable, although she's not rude. Capricorn may give you the impression that she's got her nose in the air because she's got a Queen-like walk that gives a stiff and reserved appearance. However, her inbred nature gives her this haughty air — don't let it disturb you. She is shy, sensitive, and covers her feelings up. You may not become pals with her because she enjoys socializing with those in power who can be of some use to her. She's the type who may marry your employer's son. So with her working beside you, just do your job and try to be successful.

How to Handle Your Capricorn" Coworker

If you're new on the job don't let her quiet disconcert you. She'll let you get to know her on coffee breaks — that is if and when she takes one. Capricorn is suspicious of others so don't come on too strong and friendly with her. She's distrustful because she thinks that you're out to use her or take advantage of her — that's what she does when she wants something; she thinks everyone's the same. This woman enjoys being in the company of those who have power and influence. If she discovers that you come from a prestigious family or that you're related to the owner of the corporation and are learning the business from the bottom up, then she will become buddy-buddy with you. However, that will not be so much during office time, but after hours.

If you're not just starting to work for this company, and Capricorn is, she will be pleasant. If she thinks you are about to be promoted, and will be above her in position, this woman will try to get in thick with you. Otherwise, if she sees you are just a person who is doing a job, without a desire to get ahead, she'll treat you nicely but not go out of her way to be friendly.

Capricorn is a slave to a job. She may come in early, leave late, and be there on weekends. Work gives her a safe and secure feeling. She believes it's going to give her the benefits she wants in the long run, therefore she figures it's worth her time to put in all those extra hours. She is dedicated and doesn't mind plodding along — don't be alarmed if she asks for more chores than what you have to do. Most people can't endure her pile of tasks, therefore if you try to compete with her, you may become quite exhausted.

Your coworker is conscientious, wants to do a good job and can't stand to make mistakes. So don't start yakking to her while she's attending seriously to her duties. Try to emulate her attentiveness to her work, and you may wind up at the top. Don't ask her personal questions or waste her time with nonsense. If you lag behind, she may help you out — but if she does, don't be too shocked if she lets the boss know that she assisted you. This woman will step on your toes in order to make a gain, regardless of how small it is. She wants recognition for her every effort — so think twice when you ask her to help you. She knows that the more she does, the better her chances are to get a raise and promotion.

Capricorn is obedient to the higher-ups. She bows to those in authority, so if you try to get bossy with her, she'll ignore you. This woman will use diplomacy and tact with you, or anyone else — she doesn't want you to think badly of her because you might say something that would damage her good record. Her goals are planned secretly and you may not even think that she's aggressive or will ever make a million bucks. She's inconspicuous and thus may fool you into thinking that she's not a threat. However, take heed — don't get lax on the job, give it your all. Capricorn likes to stay put with one company and advance slowly; however, if she sees that you are getting the breaks because of seniority, she may go to work elsewhere.

If you are having difficulty making a decision, ask your coworker. She weighs everything carefully from every angle. Her judgments are sensible and she's impartial. Accuracy and consistency are used in all undertakings even if it's something that she's assisting you with.

If you ask Capricorn to go Dutch-treat lunch with you, don't get your feelings hurt if she turns you down. She's the type who brings a light snack and a thermos of coffee. To save a buck she avoids vending machines and company caterers. Capricorn is insecure about work (she worries she'll lose her job) and money. Therefore she saves every penny she can. Don't try to talk her into changing her mind — she's stubborn. Her one goal — success — goads her into making many sacrifices; she considers them all necessary. Be understanding and watch her because you'll learn plenty from her. What she teaches, if applied, could take you to the top also.

YOUR CAPRICORN CLIENT
What Can You Expect from Your Capricorn Client?
This woman is inconspicuous when she walks in the store, although if you glance her way you will notice that she's properly dressed, appears reserved, and has a solid look about her. If she stops to speak, she may strike you as being gentle, with a touch of timidity. Her speech is clear and she's polite. If she handles an object, she'll be very careful and will seriously scrutinize if from top to bottom. If the price isn't on it, she will ask the cost immediately.

If you mention, "It's beautiful, isn't it?" she may answer with a, "Yes, but so expensive." Don't expect her to say much because she's looking for a bargain. She hopes that you'll slash the price. However, don't expect her to buy it right then and there. She's a comparison shopper who'll make the rounds till she finds the best deal in town. She has great self-control, and as much as she may want something, she'll repress her feelings. If your shop is the last place on her list, she will wait till she's sure you have the cheapest price. Then she will purchase the item. She's undemonstrative, so don't expect to see her get excited during the sale.

If you're a salesperson and call on Capricorn, don't expect a cheerful client. If she's in her black mood, you may not get past the door. But if she's accessible, it'll be a hard sale. This woman is interested in new products or even in modernization, if you can explain to her why she needs it. She's not about to risk her hard-earned money on a whim. Perhaps in the past she made a mistake (she never forgets the bitter lessons she learns), so anything you have to offer her will just remind her of her former loss and that will make her leery of trying anything unless you can convince her of its solidity.

How to Handle Your Capricorn Client

Are you wondering "How do I deal with such a serious and unenthusiastic person?" Don't let her demeanor fool you. If you have something for sale it may be something she can find extremely useful; therefore she is a willing listener. This woman never lets anything pass her by.

Capricorn is a realist who will buy something that is indispensable or requisite, especially toward the attainment of some end she has in mind. Therefore, appeal to her practicality. Check out her company before visiting her office and you'll know what she needs and why. Do not use any high-pressure sales techniques on her — she can catch a con and is suspicious of people who go to extremes or come on strong. To begin with she's not very trusting, even if you've been there before and made her happy.

Let her know that you are interested in her success and if your product or system can help her, you both can gain. She likes honesty, though if the negative side of Capricorn is expressed she isn't always on the up-and-up herself — perhaps that's why she doesn't trust others. Security is a must with her so appeal to that. She doesn't hide the fact that she's interested in profit and gain. If she doesn't buy your machine today, she'll analyze the pros and cons until she's sure she's going to profit. Then she'll want to *trade* her old machine for your new one. This is a point you could offer to her to help her decide.

If you are involved in a negotiation with a Capricorn then you are in for an experience. This woman can be cold and callous and once she sets her mind on something, nothing will discourage her until she gets the contract worded her way. She will hammer away until she's made her side clear — and a point is made. Capricorn is willing to bide her time and can patiently wait for her plans to mature. She's determined to succeed in her own time and in her own way. This woman has the capacity to endure hardships and setbacks, but in the end she's going to win. She will use all of the contacts she knows, accept favors from those who can help her, and regardless of a delay or a restriction, she'll find a way to get past everything. Once you've given in, you can count on her to hold up her end of the deal as negotiated.

If you're in a business where customers come to you, keep your place clean and tidy; she 's impressed with neatness and simplicity. Be courteous, don't raise your voice, speak softly and intelligently. Avoid impatience. Realize that she's a difficult person to sell anything to but nothing is impossible. Try your best to handle her in the right way; by so doing, that goal at the top will be closer to achieve.

YOUR CAPRICORN PARTNER
What Can You Expect From Your Capricorn Partner?

You may be elated that you went into partnership with this man because he uses common sense, makes excellent plans and will achieve his aims in spite of great odds. His ambition is limitless and so is the money he can earn in his lifetime. He has a goal to be a winner like a Mohammed Ali and he has the business ability of the late Conrad Hilton (Hilton Hotel chain founder) and may wind up with wealth like the late Howard Hughes — all Capricorn's. You can't help but succeed with this man.

Your Capricorn partner is materialistic. Don't expect him to take any foolish or frivolous risks; he's conservative with the way he handles finances — every dime will be accounted for; he's miserable if he loses a penny. Expect him to insist that the two of you have a reserve account — a nest egg — that is to be used only for a rainy day. He's practical but you may call him a tightwad.

He will not go all out for the' swankiest office decor; he may be a little old-fashioned and have a cozy place that will remind you of a fuddy-duddy. It will be comfortable because he may spend most of his time here. He's the type who works late in the office or,he takes papers and documents home and spends every moment until the wee hours of the morning going over them.

Capricorn will buy the latest equipment and machinery on the market if it will bring in enormous dividends. He is an economist and won't overdo anything. He has an inkling about how world affairs are going to affect business in general, therefore he's prepared to make his moves accordingly. As a result he'll make money either way the tide turns. So go along with him — you want to be successful, don't you?

How To Handle Your Capricorn Partner

This man eats, sleeps and lives with business just about every moment of his life; it's in his blood and there's no stopping him from achieving his goals. Go along with him. Let money be important to you, too. Capricorn will work hard to build up the financial resources of the company; you should do the same — don't stand in his way, he makes excellent decisions and is interested in things that have a value here and now.

If he wants to assume most of the responsibilities, let him; but also do your share of the work — if he wants to be in authority and you don't allow it, the two of you will clash and he'll plan to buy you out at a later date. He wants everyone, including you to bow at his feet — no one but him can be in that top spot, and yet he's not an egotist or show off; he likes recognition that is justly deserved, and the power to make or break someone — that's his ultimate goal.

This man admires people who've made it big, especially on their own without being born into the lap of luxury. He chooses his friends carefully; bankers who can help him get that loan he may need someday, executives whose knowledge and contacts he can use, politicians to give him that "in" he needs with certain deals, the society crowd who gives him the status he enjoys. If you want him to remain your partner, socialize with the V.I.P.'s also. Because Capricorn lives well, impresses others with his position, it costs him lots of money. But as a result he has the respect of the community his friends and family and it is glory, prestige, respect and the title that goes with it that makes him strive onward and upward to the top of that mountain. Go along with him on his journey and you'll share the same rewards.

Capricorn sits behind his desk stiffly as he firms up deals, ties up details and loose strings. Let him take care of the management part of the business; he's good at making arrangements, buying, leasing and renting — he'll get a bargain or whole-sale price every time. Let him do the negotiations, he'll get such a deal that you'll be flabbergasted how anyone could pull off a stunt like that.

If there's trouble with a machine, ask Capricorn to fix it; he just might surprise you. Let him handle anything that is snarled. He is calm as he examines a mess that an employee or anyone else, makes. If you have a problem for him to solve, be quiet while he's thinking about the solution. This man can sort out tangles that are complicated to most people. He can reorganize the whole factory and make it more streamlined and efficient. He's neat and orderly, so don't get anything out of place — and keep your office the same. Avoid throwing reports on top of other documents on his desk. If he's in a hurry, let him go at his own pace. Compliment him when he's successful and be as diplomatic as he is.

Sun-Sign Compatibility

This section deals with each sign of the zodiac in relation to a Capricorn Sun sign. By knowing how your sign blends with a Capricorn, you go one step beyond understanding his personality and one step closer to knowing how to handle him in any business situation. Greater insight is invaluable — it not only helps a business to prosper, it encourages peace of mind on and off the job.

The following Sun-Sign compatibility summaries, with the exception of Capricorn — Capricorn, *are from the point of view of the person dealing with Capricorn. Note:* For the Capricorn's point of view, see the Sun-Sign chapter of the person Capricorn is dealing with, i.e., Taurus — refer to the Taurus chapter explaining how Capricorn thinks about Taurus.

ARIES/CAPRICORN

It's relaxing for you to know that you can depend upon your Capricorn co-worker to get a job done, especially when it's something you didn't take the time to finish. You admire his ability to laboriously attend to details and make exact plans.

Your Capricorn employee meekly obeys your commands, which pleases you. Often he lacks confidence in his ability but he does his regular duties despite muttering under his breath. He's displeased because he wants a larger raise than what you just gave him.

Your nerves get on edge when your Capricorn partner is so slow to make a decision. When he waits too long to decide upon an issue, that's when you get furious and let him have it. However, you do respect his final judgment; he's always on target.

You are not really a good team although the two of you together are extremely productive and can accomplish a lot. The problems happen when your personalities clash. Your bad temper makes you burst out with some angry words that are better left unsaid. You do need Capricorn's dependability and diligence to attend to tasks.

You are open and honest, where Capricorn is silent about his intentions of elevating himself. If he uses you on the job to step up the ladder of success, you'll be vehement. Or if you operate a company and Capricorn learns your trade secrets, then later opens his own establishment with your clients he lured away, you'll have a fit. You'll wind up bitter enemies as well as competitors.

TAURUS/CAPRICORN

Your Capricorn coworker is easy to work with because he is orderly, neat, and doesn't rush you — he moves almost as slowly as you. It's a relief to have another perfectionist in your midst, especially since your work is dependent upon one another's.

You're very pleased that you hired Capricorn; he's a hard worker, tends to his business and accomplishes all of his chores exactly on time. It's a good feeling to have someone so obedient on your staff.

Your Capricorn boss sure is rigid with those regulations he enforces, but you admire him for making them — you'd do the same if you owned a business.

Taurus and Capricorn are a perfect team with so much in common: ambition, materialism, conservatism — and you are both workaholics. Both of you are plodders, but this dull perseverance of yours will pay off. You approve of Capricorn's plans and are willing to go along with all of his schemes.

All affairs will run smoothly. Both can handle people with tact and diplomacy. Any enterprising venture that is shared should be an enormous success — both are excellent at management. Budgets are followed to the penny. The two of are excellent negotiators; your patience will win out over those you deal with.

GEMINI/CAPRICORN

Punching a clock is not your idea of the perfect job. This Capricorn employer just can't understand that being a few minutes late on the job isn't such a catastrophe.

Your Capricorn employee is just dandy; you can rely upon her to manage the office when you're out.

You two are not the best combination; however, when the practical Gemini twin pops out the two of you will get along fine; it's the impractical twin that causes an uproar in your relationship. Your wild schemes are frowned upon because you talk rather than produce (often, not always), and Capricorn wants to see action, not mere conversation. Profits are her "baby" — not the dreams they are made upon.

You are an Air sign and always are building mental castles in the sky; Capricorn is an Earth sign and wants to construct those buildings on the ground. Come down to earth and let Capricorn turn some of those fantastic ideas of yours into reality. Stick with it and you two could be a successful team.

CANCER/CAPRICORN

You think very highly of your Capricorn coworker. It's amazing how anyone can sit still for so many hours — from early morning until late evening (long after you've gone) and turn out so much work. And she's so helpful; when you're behind, she catches you up so you don't get in trouble.

You certainly admire your Capricorn partner's business know-how. Her plans for renovating meet with your approval. She has your respect for the way she handles the employees. Her cost-saving methods for next year's expansion plans are ingenious. You agree with her economizing measures. You look up to anyone who can be so cautious in the management of a company's finances.

Your Capricorn boss sure puts you through some tough assignments, but you'll show her you can do it. although you wonder if you'll have the strength to pull through. Her cautiousness seems to equal yours when it comes to trying some newfangled device that's just been made available for business use.

This is not a bad combination because you two have many things in common: both can be tight with money, worry a lot about security, and are afraid to take risks. Your hunches, combined with Capricorn's reasoning ability, could prove valuable to a company if utilized. Perhaps you'll get a gut feeling that this is not the time to increase expenditures and Capricorn will have to come to the same conclusion by applying logic. Thus you both agree although your approaches differ. Both of you deplore extravagance; a low profile is kept by the two of you. Your persistence is an aid to success.

LEO/CAPRICORN

Your Capricorn partner holds you back too often because he insists on pondering too long. You can see the advantages of his sound business policies, but you like to handle everything in a more prompt manner.

It's quite a challenge competing with your Capricorn coworker. He s got just as much staying power as you do. However, you don't think you have to worry about him getting that promotion away from you because he doesn't have your outgoing personality: furthermore. he doesn't seem interested in being in the top spot — he's so quiet and unassuming.

You were real smart when you hired Capricorn. It's comforting to have a subordinate who is so willing to please. He handles all that dull, routine work magnificently.

You two can be a very good combination for success both seek it avidly and earnestly. Your ego drive doesn't bother Capricorn. He lets you take center stage while he stays quietly in the background. Thus neither one of you interferes with each other's desired roles.

You are both leaders and want to be in authoritative positions; therefore a clash can occur. However, Capricorn may patiently wait until he's piled up enough money to go into business for himself, and that's when he'll want to dissolve the partnership — at that point, you'll see a humble person turn into a powerful figure.

VIRGO/CAPRICORN

It's pleasant to have Capricorn as a coworker because she's quiet and doesn't disturb the harmonious surroundings that are so necessary for you to work in.

Your Capricorn employee is going to go places in your company. She's methodical, systematic, and puts in lots of overtime without asking for extra wages. You've noticed that she has management possibilities because she handles everything properly and with a certain amount of authority.

You enjoy doing the tasks that your Capricorn boss assigns you. She doesn't mind that you take your time to do neat and perfect work. You are well suited to the routine that Capricorn has outlined for you; timetables are fun — it's like a game. You know how long it takes to complete each part of a job and you enjoy testing yourself along the way.

You are a winning team that can go as far as you want. Neither of you do anything in slipshod or haphazard manner. A blueprint is made. stuck with and both of you roll up your sleeves and work until you're exhausted. The office is home for the two of you; business comes first, personal matters second. And the way Capricorn cuts down on costs is amazing.

Neither of you likes to waste time, especially when entertaining. However, Capricorn does best taking the clients out to lunch, whereas you enjoy staying right at your desk tending to those chores you feel must be done. So with the endurance and perseverance that the two of you have, success should be attained just as planned.

LIBRA/CAPRICORN

When you get home at night you are exhausted from the grind that your Capricorn boss has put you through. You don't know just how much longer you can continue putting in those long hours. This isn't a fun job; he's watching you every moment so you can't socialize with anyone.

Now that Capricorn in on your staff, everything is running more efficiently. He is easy to get along with and doesn't cause any trouble for anyone. You do think he's too sullen and wish he'd smile a little. But you are glad that he takes his tasks seriously. When someone is that silent, you wonder if he's got problems on his mind; he sure keeps you puzzled.

Both of you use tact and diplomacy so you *can* get along — but deep down there's friction. This man is industrious whereas you're lackadaisical. In a partnership Capricorn would be doing most of the work although you, as well as he, likes to have a hand in making decisions. But even then, your views are opposite; you're liberal, he's conservative.

You are both even-tempered and dislike arguments. However, you may disagree over the disbursement of funds. Because he is more stubborn than you, you'll give in to his demands — later you may be glad you did because of the money he saved the corporation. Business is his chief objective and it's not yours — this could cause problems in the relationship.

SCORPIO/CAPRICORN

Your Capricorn coworker is hard to beat. She's as dynamic as you. She's not competitive but she does her job and doesn't hang you up waiting for things.

You've always considered yourself clever and shrewd but your Capricorn boss appears to be your equal with the way she handles the firm's negotiations. Those reports she gives you to go over are good deals for the company. She's standoffish but you think that's how an employer should be.

It sure is a pleasure having Capricorn in your employ; she obeys all of your rules and sticks to the schedule better than anyone else. Under stress she can be relied upon and when an emergency occurs — and you are out — she takes over and does exactly what you would do in a similar circumstance.

Your Capricorn partner is an organizer just like yourself. You are delighted that she can't stand to waste time and feels committed to make every second count. She's got good reasoning behind her every action and doesn't do anything without first discussing it with you. It's remarkable how her insight matches your own. You are glad that she's as driven as you to be rich. With her resources and your talents, the two of you can buy the world.

Success! Success! Success! It's written all over both of you. You both know that nothing and no one can stand in your way!

SAGITTARIUS/CAPRICORN

You admire your Capricorn coworker for being so industrious. He is dutiful and finishes every task. Often he gives you orders but you don't mind. You wish that you could settle down and stick with your chores the way he does.

Your Capricorn employee is extremely capable of managing your business when you're out. He enjoys those numerous responsibilities that you've given him — it takes a load of work off your hands and gives you time to drum up new accounts.

This job keeps you busy hopping; you like the variety it offers. Your Capricorn boss listens to your ideas but doesn't commit himself to any of them — he says he'll think about them. You get so impatient with some of the routine tasks that you wish he'd let you handle the bigger things — like selling and talking to the customers.

This is one partner you are proud to be in business with. Capricorn knows all of the angles; he's really intelligent and can maneuver better than anyone you've ever seen. You just let him handle the buying end of the business; he manages to get things at cheap prices — something you don't have the patience to fool with.

You are a good combination even though you are opposites. You are impatient whereas Capricorn's patient. You are a spendthrift whereas he's a cheapskate and you like large-scale operations from the onset, where he wants to start small and expand.

Your personalities differ also; you laugh a lot and always have a smile on your face. He is the reverse. You're an optimist, he's a pessimist. But. even with all of these differences the two of you can make a good team; what one lacks. the other has — and that's a lot!

CAPRICORN/CAPRICORN

This is one employee who seems to be as much a slave to the business as you are. Capricorn seldom complains about the heavy work load you give her. You are delighted when she volunteers to work overtime. You don't quite trust her because she's too good to be true; perhaps she's got her eyes set for your job. You'll keep watch over her to see what she's up to.

You are suspicious of your Capricorn partner although you sense that the two of you could make a fortune together. You aren't sure whether you are using her or she's using you. But you agree with her arrangements to organize the business into separate departments — that way you'll both have control in different areas.

This could be a team that could wrap up a million bucks or more if you could learn to have faith in each other. Both are schemers who may be dishonest on occasion. Low profiles are kept; you don't want any skeletons in the closet to be used against you — therefore, when you communicate it will be strictly about business, which you both adore.

Both want to be in the top spot; neither likes to share — the two of you are selfish. Power can be held only by one person in your estimation; therefore, you'll be vying for it so much that it could cause a break in the partnership when one of you leaves to go it alone. However, the other one is smart enough to be prepared for such action, so she's not left dangling in thin air.

AQUARIUS/CAPRICORN

This is a sensible partner you have although you wish he wasn't so stiff and would open up a little. Capricorn's old-fashioned ideas are the opposite of your futuristic outlook. This fellow is afraid of change and that's your key to living; if he doesn't shape up, you'll just walk out on this whole deal.

Your Capricorn coworker seems half dead as he slaves away on those reports that have to be out. It seems he's lost his zest for living; that disturbs you, especially if he's allowed material gains to be more important than friendships and the pursuit of intellectual activities.

This is one boss who sure is strict; you're ready to rebel if he takes too much of your freedom away.

You never try to dominate your Capricorn employee but he's very humble in your presence. Although you are in a superior position because of the job, you still feel one with him and wish he'd treat you more as an equal. However, it's not your right to try to change his personality.

Both of you can be stubborn and deadlocks may be reached if you disagree about a clause in a contract. If you are in a partnership, let Capricorn do the negotiating while you tend to bringing in new customers. If travel is involved with your business, it's best you leave Capricorn with the factory and you make the trips. You need a change of scenery, he doesn't.

Capricorn's desire for sameness and your desire for change may clash. You have a wonderful imagination; Capricorn doesn't — however, he can pick out the flaws in your creative endeavors. Allow him to find a way to bring your fantastic modernization plans to fruition in a practical sense; this will aid success.

PISCES/CAPRICORN

You've got a coworker that amazes you with her productivity. Capricorn works so hard that you feel sorry for her. You bring her little gifts for helping you with your tasks.

Capricorn is so methodical and systematized that you hold her in high esteem and can't help telling the boss how clever she is.

Your Capricorn employee is quiet and tends to the tasks you assign her without a squabble. She runs out of things to do so fast that you have to loan her out to other departments. Capricorn is conscientious and always does everything to perfection.

Your Capricorn partner runs the entire operation while you sit back and do the promoting end of the business. You adore this arrangement. She's a genius with finances, management, and can negotiate as well as any top union mediator. She listens to your ideas but says they are too impractical to put into operation at this time — but she's saving them to use at a later date.

This is a winning combination. Pisces, you will be Capricorn's slave, doing everything as she bids. You don't try to take her prestige or power away from her — you hand it to her on a golden platter that shines so brilliantly that she seems to glow in the reflection of it.

You are not money-oriented like Capricorn, nor are you as ambitious and hungry for success as she is. You do not interfere with her or stand in her path to the top of that mountain; your words of encouragement can reestablish her faith in herself and aid her to gain her heart's desire — and you'll benefit also.

Chapter Thirteen

Aquarius Compatibility In Business

If you were born between January 20 and February 18, your Sun is in the sign Aquarius. However, you may also express Aquarius traits if Aquarius is dominant in your horoscope (refer to the Introduction, Page 1) even if it is not your Sun sign. If this is the case, you should read and treat this chapter just as if your Sun sign is Aquarius.

AQUARIUS PROFILE
Getting Acquainted With The Aquarius Personality

The Aquarius woman is easy to get to know on the surface but not deeply. Once you understand what motivates her it'll be a cinch to deal with her whether she's your partner, employer, employee, coworker, or client. You'll never know what to expect when in her company because she does and says everything spontaneously. She thinks for herself and refuses to follow the crowd. This woman moves quicker than a bolt of lightning, so you may find it difficult to keep up with her.

Because Aquarius is intrigued by things new and different, she gets bored with humdrum work. She needs a job that will hold her interest. This woman needs unusual chores that she can do on her own without someone breathing down her neck. She needs to move about freely; confinement will drive her bananas. Aquarius has lots of nervous energy that has to be expressed by keeping busy; if she's idle, she'll quit without giving notice.

This woman is in the avant-garde. She's the first to utilize unorthodox or revolutionary concepts or techniques in a business. Aquarius delights in taking risks and getting involved in new ventures. She's not afraid of the cost — her mind is centered on how others will benefit from her ideas as a result of the chances she takes.

Aquarius is idealistic; her dreams need to be put into reality. She may need you to help her. If you try to understand her complex personality (she's also a bundle of contradictions) and treat her right — that's a step toward your being successful with her in business.

IF YOU ARE AN AQUARIUS

Because you're always in the forefront, you may ask, "What can I do to get ahead?" Success can be achieved faster if, when you deal with others, you adhere to the following advice:

When dealing with an employer you must realize that you are beneath him or her in position. Because you are an individualist you set yourself apart. To your way of thinking the so-called "employer" is your equal. Your refusal to be subordinate and obey the rules is going to get you fired often and loudly. (This is the negative side of Aquarius being expressed; not all Aquarians are like this.) You don't like to take orders from anyone, but in a work situation it's necessary. Because you're getting paid for doing a specific job, you must adhere to the instructions of the one in charge. Although you have your own set of laws and beliefs, you are expected to follow the regulations of your company. If you continue getting sacked, you won't be able to find a job. Be smart (your sign is) and adaptable. Save the money you earn, invest in your own business and when you're your own boss do as you please.

When dealing with partner, employees and coworkers be on guard against being abrupt with people — this action hurts the feelings of those who are sensitive (Cancer, Pisces). Avoid arguing just for the sake of being contrary — this is a waste of valuable time when production could be in full swing. Often you are tactless and say whatever comes popping out; think first before you speak and then you won't blunder. Don't be rude enough to interrupt others. Give them the courtesy of listening. Avoid impulsiveness when presenting ideas. Use your excellent reasoning powers and you'll see things in their practical light.

People who are slow-moving, talking, and thinking drive you berserk and bring out your erratic and high-strung nature. You are highly impatient with people who get bogged down with details and give lengthy explanations. Try to realize that if you stop to listen to every minute thing you just might learn something you didn't know.

Watch against getting involved in so many crazy and way-out things that these activities interfere with business. Some of your radical ideas in the world of commerce may be too ahead of the times or just plain eccentric. Give others a chance to express their opinions; perhaps they might have an idea that will help you be successful in the accomplishment of your desires.

When dealing with clients your main problem is impatience. You get out of sorts with people who take a long time to make a decision. Those who have no imagination also get on your nerves. Keep busy with other customers or activities when you have someone who thinks at a snail's pace. When someone is unimaginative try to be patient; draw a diagram, picture, or show one if you have it; use visual means rather than the thinking processes. Taurus, Virgo, and Capricorn have difficulty concocting images in their mind's eye; they are realists who need to see on paper, in black and white — or color — what you are talking about.

Try not to be unreliable with clients, If you promised to be at someone's office at a specific time, be punctual. Also avoid being careless and have the courtesy to call or show up. Irresponsibility doesn't lead to success, it detracts from it.

If you have an idea of a way you can save a client money, once it's spoken, don't drop it and go off in another direction — this action causes confusion and your customer won't feel confident with you if you continually change your mind. Avoid fixed ideas and learn to be flexible, especially when discussing finances and methods of payment. Openness and adaptability are helpful signs for success.

To go one step further, once you as an Aquarian know or can recognize the sign your partner, employer, employee, coworker, or client is, read that sign's chapter to know how best to deal with him as well as to understand his compatibility with you. If you wish to know what he thinks about you, read the Sun-Sign Compatibility section starting on page 208. The remainder of the Aquarius section deals with how others relate to you, what they can expect of you and how they should handle you. So now let's go on an interview with your sign, okay?

AN INTERVIEW WITH AN AQUARIUS

An Aquarius employer interviewing you: Your resumé will be briefly scanned. A few to-the-point questions will be tossed at you. Answer them quickly and intelligently. This employer wants to see if you're fast and alert. He may ask you if you have any theories about his business. State them if you can — this could get you hired. Talk about modernization and the new device, machine, or technique that you just read about. If Aquarius knows you are interested in advanced technology and anything that's just out or to be available in the near future, he'll be eager to have you join his staff.

Don't be surprised if he hires you immediately. If he asks you to go to work right away, do so; that is if you haven't made other plans. If he really finds you fascinating, because you are knowledgeable in the areas that interest him, don't be shocked if he invites you to lunch. Keep in mind that this man will give you your walking papers as quickly as he hired you.

If you're interviewing an Aquarius applicant: If you keep Aquarius waiting for too long for the interview, she may have disappeared by the time you get to her. However, if you get a chance to interview this woman, it won't take you long to discover that she's got an ingenious mind. She may ask you all sorts of questions about your company, and then quickly give you suggestions for improvement and expansion. Perhaps she'll surprise you with some eccentric notions or way-out ideas that you may have thought about at one time but discarded as utter nonsense.

You notice that she's quick with answers and questions; also you are impressed with her innovativeness — perhaps that's the key that leads you into hiring her. She's restless and in a hurry, so ask her to start to work when the interview is over; otherwise, you may risk losing her. If Aquarius had something else planned, she won't care — she just won't show up there. Instead she'll say, "Okay, I'm ready to begin."

Now that the interview is over, first let's go to work for an Aquarius, and then see how Aquarius is going to fare as your employee, okay?

YOUR AQUARIUS EMPLOYER
What Does Your Aquarius Boss Expect of You?

If you're being transferred from one department to another because you've had a run-in with someone, made a blunder, or decided it was time for a change — don't worry about your new boss holding anything against you. All she cares about is that you become a productive employee and be happy in your new environment.

This man doesn't believe he has a right to tell you how to dress. He thinks that you should be true to yourself. Therefore, if you wear long or short dresses, jeans, shorts, slacks, evening clothes, or colors that don't match, or even odd combinations — Aquarius doesn't mind. He won't even be shocked. If your hair is unkempt, you haven't shaved, or you're a girl with a crew cut or a boy with long hair — it doesn't matter. Just be yourself and be happy — that's what this Aquarius boss expects of you.

Aquarius dislikes nine-to-five workers and comes and goes as he pleases. He does expect you to be punctual though because he may not be there and he wants someone in the office to attend to the telephone calls and customer's. This employer doesn't want you to goof off. He's paying you to work, so that's what he expects. He believes that if you've committed yourself to be in his employ then you should follow through all the way.

He has high principles and is ethical. He expects the same from you. If you steal from petty cash he'll fire you. Or you can get axed if you are at the typewriter supposedly typing a report for him and he catches you working on a manuscript — such as a play you're writing. So tend to your job and make him glad that you're on his payroll.

How To Handle Your Aquarius Boss

Try to be mentally alert at all times because you never know from one moment to the next what to expect. If he's giving you instructions, hopefully you're fast, and can catch his quick and to-the-point words, since "bing-bang-boom," he's disappeared. Aquarius can't stand to repeat anything chiefly because his memory is poor. He rattles things off as they pop out — he's an ad-libber and if you ask him to tell you again what he said, he may say something entirely different. So have a tape recorder handy or a note pad and jot everything down.

If you like routine (Taurus, Virgo, Scorpio, Capricorn), you'd better learn to be different because with an Aquarian boss everything gets disrupted and changes are the order of the day. He may even forget to tell you that project has been canceled because (a new one you never heard about) needs to be initiated today. In his mind he takes care of everything and he's already thinking about something in the near future; therefore, he doesn't tell you about it. Perhaps he believes you are intuitive because he is.

Be ready for surprises and don't balk if your desk has been moved to another room or by the window (maybe he thinks the fresh air would be good for you). Aquarius has peculiar ways that catch you off guard. When he moves the office furniture (the night before) it may just be to experiment; there's really no reason why he does these things — so don't ask; just adjust.

Don't be too startled if you come to work and find your old typewriter gone and a word processor in its place. If a machine speeds up production or a system does, this man will buy or lease it. He can't stand the clutter of antiquated equipment or the detail and lower output that's involved when you use something outdated. If you don't know how to operate the word processor, he won't care. He does think you'll learn it overnight (he thinks you're fast or brilliant or he wouldn't have hired you in the first place) and if you don't he'll be patient. It's best that you go to night school and, on Saturdays attend classes — the sooner you learn it, the better off you'll be. Meanwhile, you need a typewriter, so ask him to rent a late model — he will.

Your Aquarius boss has a favorite word — *improvise* — although you may not hear it said out loud. (Improvisation is ruled by this sign.) If you are the type who does everything according to a set pattern, and change throws you for a loop, then you shouldn't be working for an Aquarian. You'll fall by the wayside when he asks you to do something on the spur of the moment. Perhaps material normally used is not available at that time; don't mention it to your boss or ask him to draw a picture of what you should do. He wants you to think for yourself (and hastily too) and improvise whenever it's necessary.

Be prepared to drop the work you're doing because he may at any moment spring a surprise on you and give you something entirely different to do out of the blue. Be flexible even if you have to work overtime to finish. Don't ask him why he wants the other job set aside temporarily and don't be dumbfounded if it gets canceled. He doesn't like to explain anything. Just do what he says and you'll keep your boss satisfied.

Aquarius doesn't usually care if the office is a mess; so you don't have to worry about being orderly. There is a type of Aquarian who is fastidious, so in case you've got him as a boss, don't take chances, be neat. His office may be turned upside down as he hectically answers the telephones, dictates to you, searches for a cuff link that disappeared, looks at new designs, shuffles through reports, and has interruptions constantly — it may resemble a madhouse. This man enjoys this electric excitement in the air. If you don't like hullabaloo, think twice before going to work for him.

This is one employer who is unpredictable. He may seem a little strange or way-out when you walk in after lunch and find him playing around with your new word processor. He likes to see how it operates, like a kid with a new toy. Anything with push-buttons that operates electronically fascinates him. He may hit the wrong keys and jam the wires or the circuits. Be ready to call the repairman the moment you walk in the door and see him fooling around with your machine. There will never be a dull moment with this boss.

Aquarius may see the mailman leave and about five minutes later you look up and there goes your boss dashing down the hall, elevator, and out the front door running after the mail truck. Just as he nears it, he bumps into a telephone pole, falls down and injures his knee. When he returns with the letter he had wanted to give to the mailman, he looks like an erratic person — he is. Tell him you'd be glad to take the letter directly to the post office on your lunch hour — that will please him. However, don't be flabbergasted if he tells you that it's not that important, it can wait until tomorrow!

If you've worked overtime, he'll be silently appreciative. If you've done something special, and he thinks you've deserved a wage increase, you'll get it. Don't ask him for a hike in your earnings unless it's been long overdue. His mind is so preoccupied with a million and one things racing through that he doesn't always think about your salary and whether you should get more money. It may dawn on him suddenly that you haven't received a raise in a year; that's when he may shock you in your next pay check. He goes to extremes; he may be cheap or generous. As you know by now, you'll be kept guessing from day to day with this man.

If you do inferior work, he'll give you your walking papers pleasantly and when you least expect it. Aquarius will not fire you because you are dating another employee, or because of anything you did, or are doing, in your personal life. He figures it's your life, and that's it. This man is unbiased. If you are mysterious, out of curiosity he may take an interest in your private life. Tell him anything you want. He likes to hear shocking things although he won't be stunned by anything. He won't criticize you or your activities — even if you're making love to his assistant behind closed doors before anyone else arrives in the morning. Aquarius considers that's your business and no one else's. He believes you are free to do as you please, to live the way you want and he's happy to see you doing just that. Aquarius takes everything in his stride, so you should do the same. Give the job your all, and that should put you on the right road so you can become successful.

YOUR AQUARIUS EMPLOYEE
What Can You Expect From Your Aquarius Employee?

This female may be bold or shy, responsible or irresponsible, agreeable or contrary, keen-minded or absentminded and she may have a swim-or-sink feeling — she's an extremist in one sense but in another, she's just unusual; others may call her crazy. But regardless of how weird she is, she's honest and won't steal from you. You can confide secrets because she's trustworthy. If you listen to her genius ideas, she may be an asset. But then again she may have some crackpot notions that should be dismissed.

Generally Aquarius doesn't ask for a raise because monetary concerns don't interest her that much. Money gives her the freedom to do as she pleases in her personal life. If she's saved enough it will be her passport out of the office and into her own business.

You can expect Aquarius to look at systems, projects, or programs in a unique way; she'll discover things that you or others can't see. This female is a clever reasoner. She has high goals but often doesn't put her plans into action. Aquarius can let things slide when she gets interested in new and intriguing undertakings on or off the job. She doesn't hold on to old and useless (in her opinion) values; this female must move ahead and make a better world — one of peace, harmony, and brotherhood. Therefore, don't be surprised if you see her on the television news waving a banner in front of the mayor's office. She can become so involved in demonstrations and causes that it interferes with her job. But don't worry, you probably have the type of Aquarian on your staff who doesn't participate in crusades and who tends to business — she doesn't goof off because she wants the security of a pay check and to be successful.

How To Handle Your Aquarius Employee

Guard against being dictatorial (authority leaves her unmoved). She doesn't like anyone to tell her what to do, especially if it's done in a bossy manner. Stay out of her personal affairs; if you don't she'll walk off the job. Avoid laying down company rules in a forceful way. Aquarius believes that conventional regulations don't apply to her; she'll break them. She doesn't like her duties shoved down her nose or to be subjugated to a role that infringes upon her freedom. This woman cherishes freedom and independence; however, she will take care of her responsibilities and work well with others if you don't violate her code — she adheres to her beliefs in the strictest sense.

Aquarius can't stand being caged up; therefore, don't confine her. Assign her duties that give her the liberty to move about. If you put her in a corner, she may leap out just like a cornered cat does. That's when you'll be looking for a new employee.

This quiet, brilliant, and friendly female may stun you if she decides suddenly that you're unfair about working conditions or wages. She may get a petition for the other employees to sign or picket your place. If you fire her, you'll still see her outside your establishment with her banner — she's protective of those friends she left behind who work for you. However, don't be concerned that all Aquarians are like this; the other type would just quit if things are not to her satisfaction.

Give this woman a job that is a challenge. If Aquarius gets bored she leaves chores unfinished. She becomes impatient when she has to follow a set routine, therefore give her a variety of tasks to perform. Aquarius can concentrate over a certain period of time on one project; however, she welcomes disruptions that break up monotony. If you give her the freedom she needs, she will stay on your payroll. However, if she finds the job unstimulating she'll look elsewhere for employment. She may switch to an entirely different field; even that may be a mistake, but it's something she had to do.

If you can make her work intriguing or if it's spiritually rewarding (perhaps some after-office-hours project you may initiate, such as raising funds for the hungry or creative activities for the aged or handicapped), she may stay on if you let her be in charge of it. A security-conscious Aquarian may stay rooted to a job until she's saved a sizable bank account. Then, for no apparent reason, she will flabbergast you when she gives notice — she may have been employed with your firm for ten years.

Don't ask her why, but if you must, Aquarius may tell you that she's got to job-hop until she finds the trade that's really for her. This female may move to another state or leave the country on a Peace Corps mission and help those in a distant land — she's interested in culture and humanity. If you give her a leave of absence (a practical Aquarian will ask for one) so she can investigate new possibilities, attend classes and see what there is to do, she may discover (after she's been through the mill) that she really enjoyed her job with your firm, and she'll return happily. However, even then you can't count on Aquarius staying. If you make a concession and let her report in at odd hours (yet put in a full day's work), you'll have a better chance of having her as a permanent employee.

Don't limit the jobs this woman can do; she is intelligent and is capable of doing a great many things .Aquarius dislikes working with details, but she's good at dissecting facts. Aquarius can plan complicated programs if given the chance. She has keen insight and can sense the coming trends. Perhaps the knowledge could be an asset to your company, depending upon the nature of your business. This woman is creative and inventive. Don't hold her back from experimentation if she suggests something to you. She can discover shortcut methods because she likes faster ways of doing her work. She's restless and gets her attention easily distracted if a job takes too long to perform or is repetitive — that's when she may work in spurts. Never let her be idle; she needs to be kept continually busy.

Send Aquarius to seminars, trade shows and let her attend meetings. She's full of surprises. This woman is able to take a conventional plan and revamp it into a modern program that will pay handsome dividends. If your company's got old-fashioned systems, let her bring it up to date. She can save your firm bundles of money if you listen to her original and unusual ideas.

Aquarius is a born innovator and can improve your business if you have an open mind and give her some leeway to operate. The changes she may bring into your corporation are astronomical. Most of her ideas are sane and concrete, but a warning — she does come up with some way-out notions. This woman is ahead of her contemporaries; she has flashes of genius that can see decades, and even a century ahead. So why don't you let her fabulous ideas benefit you? If you do, success might be just around the corner.

YOUR AQUARIUS COWORKER
What Can You Expect From Your Aquarius Coworker?
There's just a few basic facts to keep in mind when working with this fellow; he's noncompetitive, broad-minded, tolerant, energetic, and kind. The Aquarius man is progressive and accomplishes his tasks quickly. He doesn't like to give orders to anyone, therefore he won't tell you what to do. This man doesn't encroach upon your freedom and he expects you to give him the same courtesy. Aquarius has an innate sense of fairness. He believes that everyone should be entitled to the same privileges regardless of his religion, background, and race. So you are working with a man who is not going to interfere with your job or desire to get ahead — he'll be your friend.

This fellow loves excitement at a high rate of speed. He may be as fast-moving as Aquarian-born actor Paul Newman. Aquarius dislikes wasting his time when working; he is usually quicker than anyone else, getting his job done in half the time it takes others. If you lag behind and need him to help you, ask him and he'll be glad to assist you. Let him take over when the boss isn't looking; you can trust him, he won't snitch on you.

Your Aquarian coworker may dumbfound you daily. You'll never know what to expect — he may be selling raffles for a church, promoting a children's basketball game or taking a survey for a research company. These sidelines he may talk to you about on the coffee break or at lunch time. But keep in mind that Aquarius will not try to persuade you to change your actions, personal life, or views. He believes that you are entitled to your own opinion.

How To Handle Your Aquarius Coworker

If Aquarius can't find his stapler and asks to borrow yours, keep your eyes on it or you may have to search for it when you need it. This fellow is a little forgetful, and he may put the stapler on someone else's desk. So, if you want to find your stapler, and it's not on the Aquarian's desk, just look to see who has two staplers — I'll bet one of them will be yours.

This fellow is not afraid to try a new method or technique to improve his job. He believes in modern ideas. He may inspire you to go along and experiment with him on a new project. His ability to grasp new ideas and put them in terms that you will understand simplifies everything. So don't be afraid to give it a chance; however, if you have a family to support, think twice because if it fails and you lose your job as a result, you'll be in dire circumstances. Perhaps you'll feel a lot safer if you just let Aquarius go through trial and error stages.

Have you ever noticed that when Aquarius comes charging in that the air seems filled with an extra electrical current? If he comes near your computer, turn it off — that is if through experience you have come to realize that whenever he's near it, it goes on the blink. This man is magnetic and the electricity (ruled by Aquarius) in his body is so strong that he demagnetizes the electromagnet in your machine. If Aquarius uses anything that is composed of electronic elements, it will break down quicker when he uses it than if someone of another zodiacal sign operates it. So be observant and see if your machine goes haywire every time he's near it when it's turned on.

It seems that when you work alongside Aquarius that things are always hectic — emergencies occur with machines; disruptions take place because Aquarius finished the reports so fast that it's piled on your desk. Just about that time, the boss wants you to stop the project you're working on and start laboring on the pile of reports Aquarius just put on your desk. Often you wish that your tasks weren't dependent upon his. Get accustomed to a helter-skelter workday because with Aquarius as a coworker that is what can be expected most of the time.

You may think he's a little odd at times although you know from conversing with him that he's an intellectual. Often he pulls astounding stories on you that you think are too farfetched to be true. But Aquarius is honest and won't lie to you. You may start to think that maybe he likes to shock you because it gives him attention. This is not true — it's just that he's interested in the unusual and is being himself when he tells you about some weird happenings. This man believes in what he does and doesn't care for the approval of others — although he does want to be accepted and liked. Don't nit-pick just because he's a little eccentric; he doesn't do anything in the normal sense of the word — he's got to do things his own strange way. Even his abstract theories may sound wacky to you. Keep one thing in mind about Aquarius — he's ahead of the times. He's not only tuned in to you but he has an uncanny ability to see far ahead into the future — what sounds crazy now may not be then.

You may go through some strange experiences on the job with your Aquarius coworker. He may try to get you interested in a new fad; he may show up wearing an eccentric outfit. Or when there's a slack period he may discuss how he is worried about world starvation, the expiration of natural resources, the nukes, pollution; he may want you to join him on a crusade along these lines or go marching in a parade to get some law changed. If he's the radical type of Aquarian, he may be so frantically involved with his ideas that he'll neglect his job just so he can put his notions into effect. If he gets that carried away, you may be minus an Aquarian coworker. Either he'll be fired or he'll quit. So be ready for anything with this fellow — but don't let it influence you so that you dump a good job and go into debt. If you want to be successful, tend to your own work and leave the humanitarian causes for weekends or evenings.

YOUR AQUARIUS CLIENT
What Can You Expect From Your Aquarius Client?

Aquarius may come into your shop dressed in hippie clothes, the latest in fads, or elegantly attired; you just never know what to expect. He may saunter around or rush — depending upon his mood. His eye catches items that are original, different, and novel — that's the counter where he'll stop. Also, he likes antiques — old things, especially if they are only one of a kind; he dislikes reproductions in the antique field or wearing the same outfits that others wear.

This man has a magnetic personality; he's obliging, kindly, sharp, and knows how to use words that will simply charm you. Generally he makes up his mind quickly. That's when he's in and out of the store so fast that you may not believe he was really there. However, look in your cash register and you'll know it wasn't a dream.

If you have an appointment with him for a set time and go to his office to sell him a product or system either he won't be there and his secretary will have you wait and Aquarius will come dashing in late, or he'll be there busily engaged with several people running in and out of his office while he's talking to you and doing half a dozen other things simultaneously. The moment you mention that the system you're selling is going to be available soon, watch his eyes light up — that's a clue that he might be an Aquarian or have it dominant in his horoscope (Aries, Gemini, Sagittarius also might react similarly). Because this man lives in the future, in his mind's eye (although often he seems spaced out when you talk to him), he can see the scope of things to come. Therefore if your item is "big" to him, he'll purchase it immediately. Often this man will argue and debate with you over the product because he loves to take the opposite view just to be contrary — so it's best to expect anything and then you won't be too surprised with whatever he pulls.

How To Handle Your Aquarius Client

The first requisite in handling Aquarius is to become his friend — just about everyone is. This man becomes chummy with crackpots, drug addicts, neighbors, hippies, celebrities, salespeople, conventional blue-collar workers (although stuffy types turn him off), maintenance men, garbage collectors, members of the Mafia, and his employees. When you become his pal you are joining the ranks of the many he has collected from around the globe. He enjoys discussing all types of subjects — but his mind leans toward the bizarre. Tell him some fascinating stories; perhaps about UFO books you've read, ghost tales, music, the opera, or any cultural area. He's interested in new concepts and in learning as much as he can. Therefore, be ready to answer his endless array of questions. And of course, bring him back to the subject of why you are there — he gets off course but can be brought back to reality very quickly.

Be cordial and congenial even though Aquarius might appear a little detached. Often he's disengaged as his mind soars or is sizing up everything he can about you and making mental notes. He has various compartments where he places things related to you and your product. He does this with everyone so don't take offense. Don't talk about trifles — like the weather or domestic issues; keep it intellectual and impersonal. If he gets that faraway look in his eyes that is when he's not paying any attention to what you are saying. Aquarius is interested in space technology, and anything of a mechanical, logistic, computer, or scientific nature as well as new techniques and products. Therefore if your business involves these areas, he's an easy sale.

Normally his decisions are not made through analysis, but through his keen intuitive powers. It's at that time he will give you a quick yes or no answer. If he doesn't, then let him know that you'll leave and get in touch with him later. Aquarius will appreciate that because there are moments when he likes to be alone to do his thinking without interruptions or distractions. However, he can be forgetful if he gets carried away with some project, so be sure and follow up with a call — even if it's just to say hello. He dislikes giving orders and may ask other people their opinion about your product. This man believes that everyone has a view and something important to say — plus everyone on his staff should have a hand in it. Aquarius believes that ingenious ideas may come from those he least expects. Therefore, give him time to discuss it with lots of people — his friends.

If you are negotiating with this man, he has a decided tendency to break off too soon from deals, and thus may lose them — he gets impatient. Therefore, if you hold out until this occurs, you may win the contract. Once you make a commitment with Aquarius, follow through regardless of what it may cost you in time, energy, or money. He'll experiment with the new — so go along with him and sell him something unique. The end result may just make you both successful.

YOUR AQUARIUS PARTNER
What Can You Expect From Your Aquarius Partner
You don't know where she is because she didn't notify anyone that she had gone. Either she may call from London saying she wrapped up a deal or she may get back from New York City in time for dinner with you and excitedly tell you about the contracts that were signed in England. Therefore with her spur of the moment whims, she can be successful, and so can you, — you're her partner aren't you?

How To Handle Your Aquarius Partner

Don't tell fibs. If Aquarius catches you telling a falsehood, she could dissolve the partnership. Don't make a promise that you can't keep: if you make a commitment, she expects you to keep it. Avoid stealing money for yourself out of petty cash; that's dishonest and goes against the Aquarian principles. She wants you to be above board on everything; just like she is with you. This woman can't stand to have you take advantage of her, so keep this in mind with all dealings.

You've got a partner who is chock full of unexpected surprises not only during your working hours but also away from the office. Aquarius may wake up in the middle of the night with an ingenious idea. Therefore don't be angry with her if she calls you at two o'clock in the morning and disturbs your sleep. This woman gets so excited that she can't wait to tell you about it. Aquarius doesn't like to take the time to write it down — it's when she's talking that the spontaneity comes out and even more notions may come popping out. Many of her far out conceptions are so far ahead of the times that they are not practical because necessary tools, machines or equipment to process what she has in mind have not, as yet, been invented. But often when this woman gets a brainstorm those ideas are for the now — that's why it may pay you to answer the phone at odd hours.

Your Aquarius partner isn't always reliable. She may make plans and then cancel them, show up late for appointments with clients, or take off work during the middle of the afternoon to play tennis. But if she does goof off during normal office hours, she'll make up for it at another time. Often Aquarius brings home reports, documents, or designs to do over a weekend. However if she gets bored she may wind up dumping the whole thing and go to a lecture or a concert. Don't fuss at her for her spur-of-the-moment antics because any lost time is utilized at a later date. She likes to have her freedom and to work on her own terms; if things don't go her way, she may dissolve the partnership.

Let your Aquarius partner travel in connection with your business. She's interested in international trade and enjoys meeting people of different nationalities because it's part of her world-wide brotherhood plan to have everyone all over the globe communicating with each other. Therefore the foreign market is her "baby". Also this woman is great at thinking up new ways to present facts; she excels in sales, advertising and promotion — so let her handle this end of the business rather than being confined with menial tasks.

Aquarius will take risks and spend lots of money; however, if her practical side is being activated, she may hesitate on taking chances. Money comes in suddenly from out of the blue and somehow seems to go out the same way — that's the effect this woman has in the currency department. If you have the stingy type of Aquarian as a partner, she will try everything in her power to keep the cash reserve intact; however it's the erratic type who may do the opposite. Therefore get a financial advisor or accountant, that is if she won't listen to you, and have a meeting so she'll understand that you can't make a go of the business if she spends everything on some wild notion.

If Aquarius isn't careful, she has to watch overextending the company to the point where a bankruptcy is declared. By the way, she doesn't always learn from her mistakes — so if she ever was insolvent in the past (before she met you), it could happen again.

Your Aquarius partner has off-beat interests and a highly unorthodox attitude about most things. Often she will get fixed on some newfangled idea and refuse to change her mind. Don't try to talk her into altering a particular course of action, because it'll be like conversing with a blank wall. Be open and just maybe her unusual way of modernizing the firm will be to your liking — especially if it brings in lots of dollars.

Sun-Sign Compatibility

This section deals with each sign of the zodiac in relation to an Aquarian Sun sign. By knowing how your sign blends with an Aquarian, you go one step beyond understanding his personality and one step closer to knowing how to handle him in any business situation. Greater insight is invaluable — it not only helps a business to prosper, it encourages peace of mind on and off the job.

The following Sun-Sign compatibility summaries, with the exception of Aquarius/Aquarius, *are from the point of view of the person dealing with Aquarius.* *Note:* For the Aquarian's point of view, see the Sun-Sign chapter of the person Aquarius is dealing with, i.e., Gemini — refer to the Gemini chapter explaining how Aquarius thinks about Gemini.

ARIES/AQUARIUS

The day sure does fly by fast ever since Aquarius became your coworker. She reads a lot and seems to know just about everything. This woman is fascinating and it's easy for you to talk and work at the same time. Often it's difficult to keep up with her but you find it a challenge as well as a new experience.

Your Aquarius boss is quite often abrupt but that is understandable because it reminds you of yourself when you're in a hurry, which happens to be most of the time. Her quick orders don't throw you for a loop, although, your other coworkers get confused until you explain to them what she hastily said.

You aren't fazed by your Aquarian partner's stubbornness. Luckily you both give each other independence so when your views differ it doesn't interfere with the business. This is one woman who works as laboriously and quickly as yourself. And she's extremely intelligent, which you admire.

You two make an excellent combination. Neither of you is afraid of taking risks. In fact you find them exciting. Enormous amounts of money will be spent and on the spur of the moment. Aquarius leans more to the practical side than you do, though. Neither of you ever learn your lesson so will have to watch getting too carried away with spending, especially on modernization plans and new inventions.

Both of you are impatient and need to learn patience. Your creativity and interest in the novel should keep you both actively engrossed in the variety you love.

TAURUS/AQUARIUS

Your Aquarius coworker is erratic. Just when you think he's settled down, he's up and moving so quickly about that it disturbs your concentration. Aquarius gets bored so easily that he's always dumping projects into your lap while he goes on with something new — this bugs you. You get angry with some of his crazy notions and you are not about to try them out.

Your Aquarian employee shocks you with so many upheavals, especially when he changes the method of operation from the established way you are accustomed to.

It's not the greatest thing to come to work every morning and have your routine suddenly switched on you. Working for an Aquarian is too unpredictable and goes against your predictable nature. You refuse to rush a job and make an error or do sloppy work; if your boss doesn't stop pushing you, you'll quit.

You are not a good team; both of you are stubborn and stalemate conditions may occur daily. You are interested in the old and proven way of doing things whereas Aquarius is all for the new and untried. Your practicality won't set well with Aquarius, although he needs you to keep the creditors away. You are down-to-earth and he's floating around up in the sky with his dreams. It's possible you could stabilize him if he stopped long enough to listen to your views, but your slow speech disturbs him. He makes quick decisions whereas you make slow ones. It's best you seek partnership with someone more compatible than Aquarius.

GEMINI/AQUARIUS

It's lots of fun working with Aquarius; the two of you rush through your chores and have the most interesting conversations. She's got ideas as unique as your own. And what's more, she's gutsy enough to try them out on the job. This is one coworker who you never have to wait on.

Your Aquarian boss is tolerant of your restlessness. She seems to understand your need to move.

It's a relief to work with a brilliant person like Aquarius. Your Aquarius partner is great. She never looks over your shoulder or questions what you are doing. It's necessary for you to be able to do your own thing; thus Aquarius is a delight. You don't mind that she wants to spend a lot of money on a new laser beam computer. She always goes along with your ideas to expand. You don't get bored with this partner because she's as unpredictable as you.

Gemini and Aquarius is a perfect team that can be very successful together. The business will undergo a continual program of changes that involve modernization. Your intellectual conversations could turn out to be profitable if you two would take some of the subject matter and apply it to your company's growth plans.

Both of you like to travel, therefore this could be a problem. However, if you alternate trips abroad, or to short distances away, you'll both get a chance to get that change of scenery you crave.

CANCER/AQUARIUS

Your Aquarian coworker is intriguing and you find him interesting to watch. He's so unpredictable that you never know what to expect from him from one day to the next. You live vicariously through his wild antics; listening to his stories makes the work go faster. However, it puts you behind and that's when you are in dire need of his assistance, which he so nicely gives.

You don't know how much more you can endure working for an Aquarian boss. His abruptness hurts your feelings but you won't let him know that. He doesn't compliment you, therefore you are not sure that he's pleased with your work. You are thrown for a dither because he expects you to learn overnight how to operate the new word processor that was just delivered.

This is a partner that drives you berserk with the way he wastes money on ideas that seem so far-fetched. If this continues you'll go bankrupt. He just won't listen to reason and this exasperates you.

Both of you are restless but in different ways. You like to break up the monotony with a variety of tasks whereas Aquarius may dump the job for the day and get involved in a crusade. You are more interested in money than Aquarius is, although the practical type of Aquarian wants security.

The two of you are not a good team. There are just too many differences to make it a profitable relationship. You are an emotional person who lives by your feelings; Aquarius is unemotional and lives by his thoughts. Therefore he'd be too much for you to cope with on a five-day-a-week basis.

LEO/AQUARIUS

Your Aquarian coworker is not as punctual as she should be. You won't admit it but you learn a lot from her. Her newfangled ideas are interesting but you are reluctant to try them out. It's somewhat dizzying trying to keep up with her. You are glad that she doesn't try to tell you what to do.

Your Aquarian boss seems easy to work for because you have a lot of freedom connected with your job. She is open-minded when you give her your ideas to improve sales. You are glad that she's not domineering because that's the one type of employer you can't stand.

In all, though, you two, as partners, do not make such a good combination, although you could make a go of it if you both weren't so stubborn about issues and policies. You don't approve of the Aquarian's instability and erratic ways; you are stable and like to see things through rather than dumping them the way Aquarius does.

Both of you are kind-hearted and like to make friends in the business world; however, you may prefer stuffy and conventional people to deal with and Aquarius goes for all types. Therefore, if you deal with the type whose company you enjoy, and let Aquarius be around her type, then you'll both be happy.

VIRGO/AQUARIUS

Your Aquarian coworker drives you bats by rushing through everything and making a mess when she throws those reports on top of other important papers. You don't trust her shortcuts. You'll stick to your tried and familiar methods. She talks so much it's almost impossible for you to concentrate on the tasks that have to be done.

This is one employee who doesn't pay attention to detail and thus inaccuracies occur. You wish Aquarius could keep to that schedule you've got everyone on. If she doesn't start being a little more orderly and punctual, you'll have to let her look for employment elsewhere.

It's exasperating to work for an Aquarian. Your assignments are always being changed. Disruptions occur in the middle of a job and work is abandoned in favor of something else. It's like bedlam with so much activity going on that you can hardly think straight.

You are not the best combination possible, however you do have some good points. You should let Aquarius be out in the field, making friends, contacts, and bringing the customers in, while you stay behind the scenes, do the menial chores and run the business in your usual efficient manner.

You are a perfectionist and Aquarius isn't, therefore difficulties could occur in this department. You don't like to be the boss and Aquarius doesn't like to direct and give orders, thus this could be a hindrance to business success. You are difficult to please and Aquarius may drive you bananas with her helter-skelter existence.

LIBRA/AQUARIUS

Your Aquarius coworker is a delight. It's so pleasant to work with someone who is fascinating with all of his many ideas that make the job a little quicker. You're all for anything that will speed up drudgery. When you lag behind he is so gracious in helping you catch up with your chores.

You admire your Aquarian employee's ability to foresee future trends in technology. His visions are way ahead of what's being practiced now, but you do agree with him that they are not impossible. You'll have to think about it for a while and see if it's financially feasible for you to change to another faster system as Aquarius suggested.

Your Aquarius boss is fair-minded and doesn't do anything that interferes with your view of justice; he's always employing minorities and the handicapped. The freedom he gives you on the job is appreciated. When he wants you to shift from one operation to another, you are glad to do so. You wish though that there could be a calmer influence in the office than what exists. However the electricity in the air seems to give you lots of energy — therefore it's bearable.

The two of you can be a winning team if you apply most of your energies in tending to business rather than goofing off. Both tend to enjoy other things more than a career. As partners this could interfere with making money because you may prefer attending a social event and Aquarius may be involved in reform measures for some city law that he thinks is unfair.

Both are intellectuals and have stimulating ideas that could be put into practical use, especially if Aquarius lets you have time to weigh the pros and cons. You can be relied upon to take the proper action. Usually your decisions are logical; apply your charm and Aquarius will listen to you.

SCORPIO/AQUARIUS

The bouts you have with your Aquarian partner keep you angry most of the time. He's just too stubborn to give in to your views about how the corporation should be handled. Most of the time he's off attending to meetings with some New Age society instead of spending the weekends here working. When it comes time to negotiate he doesn't use your shrewdness; instead he is interested in being fair and giving everyone a chance to make a buck. He doesn't seem to realize that you've got to be smarter than the other guy.

This is one boss you don't know quite how to sum up. Aquarius certainly is odd and trusts everyone. But he's in and out of the office so much it's as if he's not even running a company. When he is here, he just lets everyone do their own thing — that's not the way you'd be if you were in control.

Unfortunately the two of you are not a good team. Your goals differ — you are driven toward the top and Aquarius isn't interested in climbing the heights of success. Thus you'll dedicate all of your time and talent to the firm and Aquarius isn't about to do that.

You excel working behind the scenes and can't be confined to a single environment; Aquarius can't hack it. He's got to be out where the people are and moving about; therefore if you two each do your own thing, perhaps it could work out. However your personalities don't jell.

SAGITTARIUS/AQUARIUS

You sure have a lot of laughs talking to your Aquarius coworker when you're supposed to be working. She's got a good sense of humor just like yourself. Nothing you tell her ever shocks her — and you've told her some whoppers. The two of you are great together because you both get everything done ahead of the deadline.

Your Aquarius boss is fantastic to work for. She never encroaches upon your freedom and gives you duties that are not confining. Your restless nature is satisfied with this job because there are always disruptions, new chores to perform and nothing is set to a timetable. Aquarius lets you experiment with your innovative ideas and has some fascinating ones herself.

This is one partner who certainly improvises every time you turn around. It makes the business seem more like an interesting game rather than something that's serious. There's never a dull moment; everything is topsy-turvy but somehow all transactions seem to be consummated. You are all gung-ho for those futuristic ideas that the two of you have concocted.

It's a God-send to have Aquarius as an employee. She's quite intuitive and your listening to her has paid off. It doesn't take her long to do her assigned tasks and you certainly can rely upon her. You can tell by her straightforward remarks that she's honest, so you feel you can trust her handling the money when you're away on a trip.

This is a wonderful combination of two people who understand each other completely. Both are lovers of freedom, independent, and tell the truth. Friendships are made easily; it seems like the two of you call everyone your pal. Thus business deals are transacted in good faith and usually turn out fortunately for all parties.

You need a financial adviser or accountant because the two of you are impossible when it comes to money — you spend extravagantly and Aquarius erratically. You get along so well that it would be difficult to control each other, chiefly because you agree on the expenditures.

CAPRICORN/AQUARIUS

Your Aquarius partner frightens you with the way she forges ahead with wanting to spend money on streamlining the business when you disagree. Aquarius and you reach deadlock positions on this issue every time it's brought up; if she doesn't come to her senses you'll dissolve the partnership.

You pride yourself on doing your tasks correctly and being free from errors. However, your Aquarian boss is always trying to rush you and she doesn't care if there are a few mistakes. You want to build a good reputation and be known for quality work, but if Aquarius keeps interrupting you, it'll be difficult for you to hold the position desired.

Your Aquarian employee has difficulty sticking to a humdrum work schedule. Often she's late when returning from lunch, which is something you frown upon. If she doesn't start getting more ambitious, you may have to give her the ax.

Capricorn and Aquarius are not the best combination because you are opposites in some areas: you prefer old things and Aquarius new. However, she can blend the two together and come out with a profitable venture — that is if you aren't too obstinate in your views toward her notions.

Aquarius can be stingy or a spendthrift, depending upon her moods. However, you are always practical and dislike parting with a dime. Therefore you may not agree half the time in financial areas. She is too erratic for your calm nature; thus when she's ready to leap into new projects you have to hold her back from taking risks.

AQUARIUS/AQUARIUS

Your Aquarian partner and you do well together in business. Neither one of you takes the other's individuality away. You believe in letting him express himself in the way he sees fit. Luckily you both agree on the projects that are undertaken on the spur of the moment. It's great having someone around who can improvise when emergencies occur.

It's a relief to work for someone who doesn't have a list of conventional rules and regulations that you have to abide by. Aquarius is a boss that understands your need to roam about and to get routine work done quickly so you can do other chores that are new — especially when you help out another department.

You don't care how your Aquarian employee dresses. If he wants to wear his hair long and dyed, you couldn't care less if that's the real him. His private life may be full of wild escapades but as long as he puts in a day's work that's all you are concerned with. Often he's unreliable but not frequently enough to fire him.

The two of you can work well together; however, both are unyielding and if it's on the same issue in business difficulties might occur. The other main problem you have to watch in a partnership arrangement is that if you both spend more time to getting the laws of the land changed than you do to making money, you may not be in an auspicious position as far as finances are concerned.

You both are all for the new — have foresight and can see the changing trends decades from now. Your knowledge of computers or electronics can take you both far.

PISCES/AQUARIUS

Your Aquarian coworker has you magnetized with her interesting conversations and far-fetched notions; everything that she says appeals to your imagination. It makes the work day go speeding by even though you may not do your chores that fast; but you can always count on Aquarius to lend a helping hand

Whenever you get a little down your Aquarian partner lifts your spirits up. She's such an inspiration to be around. You are always in awe of her fantastic ideas and you yourself have wonderful ways to promote these brainstorms so they are lucrative for the both of you. You worry about all that money she's spending, but somehow you psychically sense that she knows what she's doing, therefore you never criticize her.

The day you hired Aquarius was a day you struck it lucky. She's always making the office exciting when she comes in with the latest "in" dress. Her pep talks are good for the morale of your other employees. She's never without an idea for you to make more money by using shortcut methods in production.

Your Aquarius boss is a delight to work for; she gives you chores that are interesting, easy, and have lots of variety. There's so much activity going on all of the time that there's never a moment to get bored. It's as if the air were full of sparks flying every time Aquarius enters the room.

You two could be a good team if you'd stop being frightened by your Aquarian partner's risk-taking ventures. Your anxiety can be perceived by Aquarius, who has the ability to sway you in the opposite direction. Often she may be abrupt and bring your sensitive nature to the fore; however, if you learn to accept it and just say she didn't mean to hurt you, then you'll be able to live with these daily occurrences.

Aquarius is very intuitive and you are extremely psychic; therefore if you both follow your hunches you could do well together — especially if you both tune in to identical things at the same time.

Chapter Fourteen

Pisces Compatibility In Business

If you were born between February 18 and March 20, your Sun is in the sign Pisces. However, you may also express Pisces traits if Pisces is dominant in your horoscope (refer to the Introduction, Page 1) even if it is not your Sun sign. If this is the case, you should read this chapter just as if your Sun sign is Pisces.

PISCES PROFILE
Getting Acquainted With The Pisces Personality

The Pisces man is easy to get to know. Once you understand what motivates him, it'll be a cinch to deal with him whether he's your partner, employer, employee, coworker, or client. When you first meet him you'll notice his shy smile, plus an elusive something about him that may puzzle you. Once you get to know him, you'll realize he is gentle, sweet, and has a sympathetic soul. He's always ready to listen to your problems and inspire you to do great deeds.

There won't be much commotion or pandemonium going on with him in the office. He's quiet and tends to his business almost in a daydream. His actions spring from his moods — he can experience the highs (increasing inspiration) and lows (depression) within minutes. He dislikes a job where there are pressures or decisions. With the latter he finds himself at loose ends and becomes indecisive and is likely to escape his responsibilities by building castles in the air.

Generally Pisces has a lack of interest in worldly ambition. He drifts through life without a goal and, along the way, he searches for his ideal occupation. This man is easily bored with a job unless it allows him to use his imagination, emotions, feelings, and ability to dramatize and promote. In this Edenic vocation (whatever it is) he can lose himself and escape to the fantasy land of creativity. His heart delights in this unreal world and in it he can forget about the harsh realities of the mundane world. If he does complete his goal he can make a great contribution to society as did the late Pisces-born Michelangelo. Encourage him, be understanding, and you'll be headed in the right direction to achieve success with him.

IF YOU ARE A PISCES

Because you worry about money you may ask, "What can I do to get ahead?" Success can be achieved faster if you adhere to the following advice when you deal with others:

When dealing with an employer don't be timid. If you hold back from expressing your ideas because you lack self-confidence, it'll be more difficult for you to get a promotion. When you speak up it shows that you're interested in the company's welfare — this endears you to your superiors. Your desire to serve can be utilized successfully in this direction.

Try to finish tasks. It's difficult for you to do because a good deal of your work time is spent in musing about things you'd rather be doing or places you wish you were at — like the beach, mountains, or a resort. If you don't concentrate your mental energies on your chores, you may not have any to tend to — especially when you're fired.

Your emotions can keep you exhausted, especially if you are not content with a job and thus worry about losing it. That's when you do careless and sloppy work that could lead to you're getting axed. If you want to be a permanent fixture, and advance, mentally talk to yourself while you are performing your job. This conversation should consist of your telling yourself each step of the job as you do it. By so doing, you won't allow your mind to slip off into fantasy land.

When dealing with partners, employees and coworkers guard against becoming too easily discouraged when things do not go as desired. Realize that success comes through persistence and not giving up on that illusion of utopia that spins around continually in your thoughts. Think about that popular adage, "Practice makes perfect." Stick with a project until you reap the rewards you've aimed for. Listen to the advice of your associates or those who are qualified, by license, to give it.

Your work will be adversely affected if you are in the same room with someone who is emanating discordant vibrations; it's because your system is extremely sensitive to every sound, tone, thought, and feeling. Therefore change the help (if you're the boss), job (if you're the coworker); or partner (if he's the one that's upsetting you).

Guard against impractically spending too much money on streamlining operations. You trust others implictly and thus your gullibility can lead you into the hole. Seek the counsel of an accountant before taking action. When job proposals come in you are either noncommittal (thus losing projects because you don't take action) or overcommitted (thus taking on so much you don't deliver what's promised). Let your partner take care of the propositions or hire an assistant who has sound judgment and can transact this part of the business for you.

When dealing with clients your main difficulty is that you devote so much time toward being a sympathetic listener that you lose sales. You can't stand to see others suffer; therefore when a customer has a problem you go out of your way to give solace. There's nothing wrong with helping others but you are too compassionate and tend to overdo it. If a client walks into your store who looks a little shabby, you feel sorry for her to such an extent that you might possibly give her free merchandise or some cash from your own pocket or the cash register, regardless of whether you're the owner of the shop or an employee. Of course, that's dishonest if you steal and do a "Robin Hood" act; keep in mind that when you do something wrong, it'll come back double to you — therefore it pays to be honest. It could get around that you're a soft touch, and you may have a whole flock of people who walk in and don't spend a dime but go out quite happily. Money isn't as important to you as helping others. That's fine and dandy; however, you are one person who has to be careful of being taken.

When a customer walks in the store, don't just sit there waiting for her to come to you. Get up! Move faster than your normal lackadaisical pace. Wrap the packages fast, especially if you've noticed the client is the impatient type. By being attentive and on the ball, she'll return to your shop — and that's being successful, isn't it?

To go one step further, once you as a Piscean know or can recognize the sign your partner, employer, employee, coworker, or client is, read that sign's chapter to know how best to deal with him as well as to understand his compatibility with you. If you wish to know what he thinks about you read the Sun-Sign Compatibility section starting on page 227. The remainder of this Pisces section deals with how others relate to you, what they can expect of you and how they should handle you. So let's go on an interview with your sign, okay?

AN INTERVIEW WITH A PISCES

A Pisces employer interviewing you: Your resumé will be scanned quickly — almost as if she didn't read it. This woman is psychic and can tune in to your entire personality immediately. She'll be very unassuming and friendly. Some personal questions may be asked; answer them with warmth. Pisces will be impressed with you if you are kind, affable, and sensitive. If you are cool, detached, and unemotional, you may not get hired.

You can tell she's a Pisces if she starts promising you the moon — large salary raises within short periods of time, promotions; profit-sharing and other benefits that are normal for most companies will be discussed — but when one thing is played up strong (whatever she promises you), that's a clue that Pisces is in her wheeling and dealing mood.

Speak slowly so she can absorb everything you are saying. If you have been doing volunteer work for charity, hospitals, the needy, etc., mention that you do this in your spare time — that will expedite your getting hired.

If you're interviewing a Pisces applicant: He may be fearful that you don't like his appearance or application, if you keep him waiting a long time. He's impressionable and if he gets a good feeling in your reception room he won't leave — instead he'll sit there and stare into space until you call him — that snaps him back to reality.

Once you start interviewing him, he'll be confident that you are interested in him. He will answer all questions pleasantly. If you ask him about his goal, he may tell you about his fantastic dreams (if he feels he can trust you) or he may startle you and say, "I haven't any as yet."

Pisces may inquire about the nature of the work and how often one can get a raise, as well as what size of an increase is normally given. This fellow likes big money without having to put forth much effort in getting it. He worries about security, although it's not his number-one priority — happiness comes first. If you ask him to start work right away, he may, depending upon his mood.

Now that the interview is over, let's first go to work for a Piscean and thus see how Pisces is going to fare as your employee, okay?

YOUR PISCES EMPLOYER
What Does Your Pisces Boss Expect of You?

If you were transferred from one department to another, regardless of the reason, Pisces will be understanding and know that you don't need any upsets in your new environment. Therefore, she'll have someone give you instructions and she'll leave you alone to adjust. She won't make any demands; you'll be given plenty of time to learn your tasks. If you make errors she may not tell you about them — they may just slip by, perhaps she won't even catch them. (Most of the time she doesn't, especially if her mind is wandering at the time she looks at those reports you typed.)

Once you've grown accustomed to everything, Pisces will expect you to keep your nose to the grindstone and work hard. Because she's not a slave to the job, she expects you to be the opposite. This woman wants you to use sound judgment and make logical decisions — something she lacks; usually she relies upon her ESP to give her the answers she needs — or she wants you and others in her employ to make progressive contributions.

Pisces wants you to organize her office and systems if you think she's disorganized. She wants you to take the responsibilities off her shoulders. Keep the business running smoothly while she naps and when you say you are going to do something, be reliable. If you come up with any fantastic and wild ideas, be sure and tell her; she'll be quite pleased, but even more so if your brainstorm is sound and practical, too. This woman doesn't always follow accepted business practices; therefore she expects you to give her wise advice if you've noticed that she's about to get into hot water because she wants to go on a money-spending tangent. The aid you give to her goes toward your own success.

How to Handle Your Pisces Boss

This is one boss who doesn't care how you dress unless a uniform goes with the occupation or she caters to a particular class of patrons. Pisces like comfort on the job, therefore she gives you the same consideration. She pampers herself, so why don't you do the same?

This woman doesn't like nine-to-five hours. Therefore she will rarely come in or leave at a set time. Try to be punctual because she'll want you to hold down the fort while she is away. If you do technical work, try avoiding mistakes like transposing figures. She won't bawl you out if you make an error, but if you do it often, she'll think that maybe you're dissatisfied with your job — because she goofs up when she's unhappy with her vocation.

Pisces wants you to use discipline and stick with all tasks until they are finished (not like she who abandons things when she's bored). This woman prefers the solid and stable individual who she doesn't have to worry about. If she thinks that you are dutiful, loyal, and the type who enjoys permanency, she'll keep you on her payroll.

Your boss often finds herself lost in chaos as a result of her own bungling, she can be negligent and careless when the job has become a drag. Therefore, when you see her looking helpless, rush to her aid. She needs your wisdom on important issues; otherwise she may find herself floundering around in a bottomless pit. If she's involved in a new venture, and it's risky, don't be afraid to explain to her the practical side — even though she doesn't want to hear it.

Pisces will listen to your advice and that of several other people. She keeps changing her mind as each person's views differ — she's like an actor playing a role with each individual she contacts. She may get to a point where she gets so confused, she can't decide who is right, and if she's a supervisor, may quit the job — if she's the boss, she'll turn it over to you or anyone else who she thinks is competent. Assist her so she doesn't do anything foolish; urge her not to spend so much money. But don't take her dreams away, help her make them a reality — but in a down-to-earth sense. As a result, she'll be thankful that you're in her employ.

Pisces has an uncaring attitude toward rank or power. She mixes with all of her employees, so don't be surprised if she sits with you in the cafeteria at lunchtime or socializes with you. (This woman believes she's one with all of humanity.)

During these little tête-à-têtes, she may listen to your ideas and suggestions. Pisces will give you the floor and let you do all of the talking. To keep her interested, use your imagination; weave a mental picture of how she can increase sales or expand. If you do it visually, she can see it in her mind's eye; otherwise, if you do it in a drab, matter-of-fact fashion, her mind will wander off into the clouds and she won't even hear a word you're saying. But she's a great listener if you are dramatic in your presentation. Pretend you're on stage; if you do, you'll appeal to her creative mind. If she's gung-ho over your idea, don't let it be just a fantasy; back your words up with action.

This is one employer who may promise you a whopping big raise and not deliver. More than likely it's because she forgot about it. Pisces goes to extremes; often she's fond of material possessions and likes the security that money brings as well as how she can give it away to those in need.

Then she goes the opposite direction and is on her spiritual kick. When she's in that frame of mind, money is meaningless. If you need that raise because of sickness in the family, a new baby being born, the Internal Revenue putting a lien on your property because you didn't pay your taxes or any other type of sob story —Pisces will give you the raise plus some money out of her pocket. What's more, she won't even ask for it back. In fact, she may forget that she loaned it to you. Even if you don't need help financially, and ask for a hike in your earnings, Pisces still has trouble rejecting you; however, if you don't keep after her, you won't get it.

If she owns a large corporation, she may not discuss raises with you because she's smart enough to know that she'll give in constantly. Therefore, it may be left to your immediate supervisor, who may be a tough nut to crack — Pisces will see to that. Or if she owns a small company, she may tell you to take up all financial matters with the accountant — probably someone who comes in once a month to take care of the books — that gets her off the hook. Usually Pisces is in debt and has the creditors knocking on her door; therefore, she doesn't always have the money in the bank account to afford to give raises as promised. Her firm may just have a big front. Generally, Pisces splurges and doesn't know where her money disappeared to; it probably went to those in dire circumstances. However, if you are working for the Pisces boss who clings to every penny, then she's got it locked up and hidden away; she pretends she's broke — it's her poverty role she's playing.

Your Pisces supervisor can be lazy and shiftless. Make her job easier by asking her if you can help her do anything; she'll keep you really busy. She adapts easily to change and won't mind if you take over; she's submissive.

Don't believe everything Pisces tells you because it could cost you your job. For instance, one day she may compliment you for being brilliant and needed in her organization. The following day, you could be so overconfident that you become careless and make a mistake. As a result, she could fire you. Therefore, let the Pisces words flow, enjoy them, but don't let them go to your head; if you fall for her lines, it may wind up being your own undoing.

Pisces doesn't always tell the truth for several reasons: *first,* she doesn't want to hurt your feelings, therefore, she believes a lie will spare you any suffering. *Second,* this woman sincerely believes that falsehoods sound prettier than the reality of the cold, hard, ugly truth; she thinks that you would rather escape to that lovely world rather than the earthy one. *Third,* if she tells you that you are going to be famous, rich, or do exceedingly well in her company, perhaps you will, because she put the thought out into the substance known as the ether — but it may be nothing more than a lot of hot air. So wake up!

Don't pay any attention to her fabrications, regardless of how awe-inspiring her words may be — and they are. Accomplish goals that you've set and try to live up to her flowery phrases, but you'll be better off considering them as a beautiful dream that you can make come true if you follow your own star — and do your thing to get to the top.

YOUR PISCES EMPLOYEE
What Can You Expect from Your Pisces Employee?
Pisces adapts easily to his new environment, just like a fish (his sign's animal symbol) does to water. He's eager to please and may be devoted to you. His career advancements come from his bright and sunny personality as well as the fresh imagination he gives an ad, a campaign or, anything else that is promotable. If he is working in a job that appeals to his emotions and feelings, he'll do splendidly. This man is at his best when he does things on an unusually large scale — anything with ballyhoo is right up his alley.

When he talks his conversation is rich; he bubbles like the finest sparkling water. If he's happy, you'll never know it. He's an actor and you'll never know what role he's playing. He's sensitive to his environment and picks up the vibrations of the place in general. Therefore, if it's cold, drab, and unfriendly, he may hide and be bored to tears. When he's in that state, you can expect him to just not show up the next day, or any day thereafter.

When he's in an office that is full of laughter and fun, he's found his niche.

He may tell a few jokes and join the merrymaking. And he can slip out of that role and into another guise. You'll never really know this fellow. What part is he playing today? Tomorrow? He'll never let you penetrate beneath the surface — that's his private world, his very own that he alone can spend his time in. And when does he retreat to this inner sanctum? Anytime. On the job, if it's boring. Don't expect Pisces to be interested in power, wealth, or a high position. He's intrigued with the dreams he can manufacture but he'll let you make them become a reality.

How to Handle Your Pisces Employee

Pisces tends to live in two worlds — one the land of dreams and the other a physical earthly existence — at home and in the office. If he seems a little vague when you give him instructions, that will clue you to where his mind is. In this make-believe world that Pisces escapes to, his misty fantasies are so real that he deludes himself about what is real and what is unreal. Thus you may be talking to him, and believe that he's listening to you because he's grinning. However, if he finds your conversation dull, his mind may drift to another place and time. It's as if Pisces is wearing a costume and attending the masquerade ball — which is your office.

You can get him back to reality if you ask him if he has any ideas that can help your business. Mention how you need his assistance along these lines. Appeal to his desire to create; he has an imagination that overflows like a water fountain that has been flooded by rain. He gets high discussing his dramatic ideas. But whether he comes up with a sales campaign, ad, promotional scheme, or whatever, it will be when he has the urge. Don't pressure him to have it finished on a certain day or at a set time; let him do it at his own leisurely pace. Pisces is flexible and can take on many different jobs. But don't give him so much to do that he won't get around to doing any of them —he becomes too confused and disoriented when he's loaded down with many projects.

Don't give him any work that requires him to be bogged down by detail, unless it's something that will absorb his imagination. He has a quick, clever mind and can grasp figures (he does it psychically, but may not realize it), but anything mathematical is like a game to him. He flees from heavy responsibilities because they are harsh and too down-to-earth when he wants to be up in seventh heaven. This fellow will procrastinate if you give him orders to do something. He can be indolent and undependable. Pisces will get around to it in his own time — when the mood strikes. Try to encourage him; get him all pepped up with compliments — it's the best way to get him into taking action; otherwise, if you push him, he may quit.

Avoid fussing with him if he's sloppy or his desk is a mess. That will hurt his feelings and he'll want to hide from the embarrassment, although he'll appear like he's letting your comments fly by. He may pop out with a witty remark; but that's just the actor in him on stage again. As soon as you leave the premises, he'll bury his head down so you can't see his eyes full of tears. You may not hear a peep out of him for days — that's a clue that he's suffering and in a despondent mood

222

because he's failed you. Therefore, bring him coffee and be cheerful — that is if you want him to remain in your employ. If you don't, give him one more day, and he may never show up for work that morning.

If you're a supervisor, you don't have to be afraid that Pisces is after your position, he's not. This fellow can't stand to be tied down to a job where he has to make decisions or be responsible for anything — those headaches are for others. Also he likes to change jobs until he finds the one that really turns him on. His right field also has to have an uplifting environment.

Don't give him work where he has to use discipline. Avoid routine chores for him — that's pure drudgery in his book. Keep him away from the files; everything may be misfiled and you'll search for a long time for the reports.

He's absentminded and transposes figures — that's his mind wandering again. He needs work that's not hard but fun. Let him serve and help you or others. Pisces is competent and efficient when he's in a job where he can wheel and deal — no one is better than he in this area; he's the master. He does his best when he's working with people because they can make him see reality and say kind and encouraging words that inspire him. Let him turn your business into an astronomical organization with his larger-than-life plans. He'll give you the ideas but you'll have to take them from there.

Pisces worries excessively about money. He wants to sock it away in the stock market so he can have dividends that pay for his spending sprees. Don't expect him to ask for a raise, although he may want an advance from his salary if he's broke. However, if it's a large corporation, you needn't be concerned that he'll be asking for a loan from you; he'll take one out if the company has a credit department. That money may not be for him, but to help someone else out. Most Pisceans don't care about money as much as they do about spiritual needs. However, if you've got the wheeler-dealer type of Pisces in your employ, then he's going to want wealth. You can expect him to ask for a large raise every time he does something he considers spectacular. If it's denied, he'll leave the firm in nothing flat.

Usually Pisces quits a job before he gets fired — he is psychic and can sense when the ax is coming down on him. Therefore, he'll take a quick departure before he chances getting his feelings hurt or being embarrassed by the other employees who may witness the scene. He prefers to be a beachcomber rather than not wanted on a job. His method may sound like madness, but maybe it's his way of being successful.

YOUR PISCES COWORKER
What Can You Expect from Your Pisces Coworker?
There are just a few basic facts to keep in mind when working with this woman she's easygoing, retiring, emotional, sensitive, unhurried, and isn't about to outdo you. Pisces doesn't care if she's not superior to you because she lacks confidence in herself — besides, she's not that career-oriented. If she didn't have to earn a living, she might not be working. Therefore, you don't have to concern yourself with losing that promotion due to Pisces outperforming you. If she has any acting talent and pursues a profession in that direction, don't be surprised if she winds up as famous

as Piscean-born Elizabeth Taylor.

Pisces may stay hidden behind the scenes — she's so quiet and peaceful that you may not realize that she's there. You may not even recall her name. You may find her difficult to comprehend. If you glance at her you may not be sure she's even working; it seems she has an odd way of going about things. Even when she's talking and promoting, you may be confused as to what she's up to. This woman doesn't want you to know her inner thoughts; thus she disguises her motives, appears deceptive, and keeps her true aims hidden.

Your coworker is sweet and eager to please, therefore she'll be cooperative on the job. She's weak-willed, adapts easily to changes, let's you be the boss and make the decisions, and takes life as it comes; nothing excites her that much. Pisces is broad-minded so you can tell her anything.

How To Handle Your Pisces Coworker

Don't try to pin Pisces down, she'll just slip through your fingers. She'll withdraw from you to live in a fairyland where everything is rosy and peachy keen. You may think she's listening to you talk but she's not hearing a word you say. This woman may come back to reality and join you in conversation. Don't be surprised if she tells you about her wonderful ideas to make a fortune — that maybe the two of you could do it together. Her fanciful notions may sound enticing, but keep in mind that Pisces is afraid of encountering frustration if she commits herself to a specific action; thus she may not follow through or ever realize her plans. If they aren't carried out, she'll wind up dreaming her life away. If you believe they are worthy of some effort, you can help bring them to fruition. If you have anything to suggest, most of the time she's receptive and will listen; however, if she switches characters (her dual nature — the two fish is her sign's animal symbol), she may refuse to hear your views.

Often Pisces has imagined fears or phobias; perhaps she may be under the impression that you'll give her wrong instructions on purpose so she'll get fired. She may think that some catastrophe is going to occur; for instance, the office is in an old building, is thus a firetrap and she may be burned if it is caught in flames while she's working there. Pisces may mention this impending doom to you, or some other anticipated disaster; therefore, try to make her see the bright side of life, pep her up and give her reasons why these events are not likely to take place.

Avoid thoughtlessness; think before you speak or you'll offend her sensitivity. She's easily moved to tears whether it's from looking at a beautiful sunset or because you said something upsetting. Pisces has little control over her emotions; however, outwardly she's smiling, but inwardly she's quaking. Be kind and apologize if you've realized that you shouldn't have been as candid telling her that she's lazy. Be hospitable. Praise her for her good traits and aptitudes, but mean it; she'll know if you are lying — she's got ESP.

Pisces has the capacity to receive impressions easily from external influences. She's tuned in to her surroundings; if the walls are in pretty, light, peaceful colors, she feels soothed; if bright red, her temper comes out (basically she's not temperamental); if dark shades, she's morbid, gets really blue and down in the dumps. Not only does she pick up from colors, but also from objects and people. If you are ill, she also becomes sick; if you are negative, so is she; if you are happy, she's joyful. Therefore, if you want an atmosphere that is conducive to performing your best, keep an uplifted mood as much as possible.

Not only is Pisces receptive to what's happening around her, but also she can sense when you are in need of a sympathetic ear. This is one woman who can't stand to see anyone suffer; therefore, if you are in distress, don't be afraid to seek her advice or to just get it out of your system by talking to a compassionate individual — your coworker. Pisces wants you to turn to her for help; it's important for her to be needed — it's her way of giving service. She is self-sacrificing and will help you financially or emotionally if you are in dire circumstances — she'll do her best whether it is little or much. This woman has the ability to understand you and has a great insight into your problems, even though you may find that hard to believe because Pisces doesn't exert herself much on the job. She has empathy and, after she's heard your story, she'll go home and worry about you.

If Pisces has to make a decision on the job, offer your assistance if she looks helpless; otherwise, she may quit. Once you've come to her aid, she'll be like a slave, devoted to you. She is a little shiftless when she's dissatisfied and disheartened with her occupation. If she has found she is behind, and your work is dependent upon hers, it's best you pitch in and help her — if you don't, you may run into difficulty with the boss when you hold up production. So if you want that raise and promotion, lend Pisces your assistance.

YOUR PISCES CLIENT

What Can You Expect from Your Pisces Client?

This woman may walk into your store so quietly that you'll hardly notice her. She'll touch objects softly and while holding them may get a faraway look in her eyes. Her mind is wandering and she's visualizing how this item could be part of her life. If she decides that it's irresistible, she'll buy it instantly.

Pisces may not ask the price; she's self-indulgent and enjoys parting with her money foolishly. She'll pay cash if she has it, otherwise she'll put it on a credit card. If her limit has been used up, she won't say anything—instead she'll pray that you don't check her out. If you do, she'll lie and say that the bank has not received her Master Charge payment yet—that she mailed it in days ago. Pisces will try to con you into letting it go through. If you don't give in to her, she'll cry a bucketful of tears that just might make you believe her story and accept her credit card. This woman's a great actress and when she's playing her dramatic role on you, you'll probably fall for her tale, hook, line, and sinker.

If you are a salesperson and go to her office, she may have forgotten that she had an appointment with you. If she seems vague you can chalk it up to that; nonetheless, you'll find her bright and smiling happily. She is an easy sale unless she's in her passive mood — that's when she doesn't pay much attention to what you're saying because she retreats from life into fantasy land. If she's really listening to you, she'll probably buy your product. Pisces isn't afraid to take a risk, regardless of how new and untried your equipment might be. If it's something she can sell to the public, she'll find a way to promote it from the rooftops of America. It's not difficult to be successful when you're dealing with a Piscean.

How to Handle Your Pisces Client
Because Pisces is fanciful, appeal to her imagination when trying to sell her your product. If it's electronic equipment, talk about it in a visual way so she can picture it. If you give her the facts, without visualization, she won't even hear your voice — she'll be so bored that she'll think about that sandy beach she wishes she was lying down upon. Regardless of the item you are selling Pisces, present it in as a dramatic and exaggerated fashion as is possible. Tell her how fantastic it will be for the company and how much money the firm will make because of it.

If you work in an antique shop and Pisces comes meandering in and stops at an ancient clock, go to her and tell her the history of the clock — from the past to its last owners. This is the technique that many oriental rug merchants spin to the potential customer in Moroccan Casbah (medina). They will tell of bloodshed, passion, thievery, and make up all sorts of wild tales that intrigue the imagination so the proud owner of the rug can tell everyone that steps upon it this same fable. It may not be the truth, but it's a surefire way to sell to a Piscean. Even though it is fabricated, this woman prefers to hear something exciting that may not be valid rather than something unexciting and valid.

Another angle that appeals to Pisces is your product making this earth a better place to live; perhaps it's for the environment, or will feed millions cheaply (like plankton in powder form), or can aid the handicapped or downtrodden. Inspire her with words of how she can do her part. Be honest because she'll know the difference — she tunes in to your thoughts even before you have spoken. However, she is gullible and falls for most lines that are dramatically presented.

An easy way to wrap up a deal with Pisces is to take her out to lunch. Go to a fancy restaurant, wine and dine her; this woman's been spoiled and loves the finest food and beverage. She enjoys an eating establishment that has soft music in the background and lights that do not glare. In this atmosphere use illusion with your sales pitch — again let her see her own mental screen of everything you are saying.

If you make a promise that her goods will be delivered by a certain date and they don't arrive, she'll imagine the worst catastrophe happened to them — they got lost, burned, or stolen or who knows what else she may surmise. Therefore, if you can't keep your word, call her and let her know; apologize and try to cheer her up because most likely she's disappointed. And when she reaches that state, she can get on a crying jag, especially if the item is a personal object that she had her heart set on. Be kind when talking to her and never be critical of her actions. When you use the proper approach and treat her correctly, you'll be on the right road to becoming successful.

YOUR PISCES PARTNER

What Can You Expect from Your Pisces Partner?

You are the driving force to turn his dreams into reality — and that's where you come in. In other words, he's the idea man who can capture the public's (and your) imagination with his sensational ideas or methods of promoting. His world is glamor and if you don't let him promote it, he'll confine himself to his dream world like a prisoner.

If you want to streamline operations at a plant, factory, showroom or in an office — go ahead, Pisces will go right along with whatever you desire. He's not going to be an argumentative partner; quiet and peace are necessary to keep his body and mind balanced. This fellow wants the business to run smoothly without any mishaps — that's when you'll see a contented man.

This is an associate who can inspire you to do great deeds. He has an innate understanding of his fellow man which comes in handy with all those people he's dealing with on a continual basis. These are traits that can make you both successful,

How To Handle Your Pisces Partner

Pisces is hopeless where money is concerned. He may keep the company in debt if you don't take control of the finances. Arrange to have all checks countersigned with both signatures. Try to maintain a budget for you company; this is difficult for Pisces to cope with, but a necessity if you want to be in the black instead of the red continually. This associate of yours is impractical when it comes to business; his judgment is off — he sees everything through rose-colored glasses so you'll have to take the glasses off of him and show him the naked truth. Pisces is generous because he likes the good things of life and to help others.

He may go to the bank and try to borrow money using the company, and its assets, as collateral — this may be without your knowledge. Therefore, make sure you have legal documents prohibiting him from such action. Contact all the banks and let them know that two signatures are needed on all financial transactions — he just may go to a bank other than the one your company deals with; perhaps the banker is a pal of his.

Your associate is given to fanciful and impracticable ideas or plans. He can be fooled easily and led into schemes by phony people. This fellow gets around and lacks discrimination when it comes to choosing his friends. His visionary ideas can be applied to business if they are made practical by you. (He's not the type to do it.) But don't be unwary and get caught off-guard. Have an accountant go over everything. If another person is involved in one of these speculative deals, have him checked out by a private detective. Because Pisces is trusting and wants vast sums of wealth without working too hard to attain it, he is often involved in fraudulent deals. A swindler may try to get Pisces to sell your company's stock, or some valuable shares in a large oil corporation. Perhaps the firm is a fly-by-night organization that disappears after the deception has taken place. Therefore, you should arrange that Pisces gets your approval on everything before he does a thing. If you don't, you could attract losses of all sorts. Therefore, take practical precaution from every angle of all business transactions that your Pisces associate might involve you and the company in.

This fellow would rather tell a lie than a truth, therefore you may attract problems in business. Perhaps he promises a client that your firm will deliver the goods on a certain date. Pisces may know that it is an impossibility but he wants to make the customer happy, therefore, he tells a fib. He can be dishonest with himself as well; often he believes that what he's saying is true — it's difficult for him to distinguish between actuality and the world of his imagination.

You should handle the practical side of the business, finances, routine jobs for employees, menial tasks, etc., and let Pisces promote large projects, deal with clients (successful people are delighted with him, he wins them over to his side easily), plan campaigns for politicians (if your firm is in public relations and has them for accounts), and travel (if he doesn't take a trip, he'll be so frustrated that he'll be on a mental one, and get less work done).

If you handle all the responsibilities, you'll have a gleeful partner. Leave the pressures away from Pisces, he can't hack it. Often he quits in midstream because he's afraid he'll fail along the way. His self-confidence keeps him mentally out of whack so he can't think straight. But he won't let you know; therefore encourage him as much as you can — daily will suffice.

You'll never know when he's not happy because he grins to cover up what's bothering him. He dislikes going through quarrelsome scenes and having to explain what's bugging him. If he's discontented with his job, don't expect him to tell you — that's something you've got to figure out for yourself. Any slight upset and he may be ready to dissolve the partnership. Thus keep him inspired and let him know you have faith in his abilities; this may be all he needs to hear — it may result in success for your business.

Sun-Sign Compatibility

This section deals with each sign of the zodiac in relation to a Pisces Sun sign. By knowing how your sign blends with a Piscean, you go one step beyond understanding his personality and one step closer to knowing how to handle him in any business situation. Greater insight is invaluable — it not only helps a business prosper, it encourages peace of mind on and off the job.

The following Sun-Sign compatibility summaries, with the exception of Pisces/Pisces, *are from the point of view of the person dealing with Pisces. Note:* For the Piscean's point of view, see the Sun-Sign chapter of the person Pisces is dealing with, i.e., Cancer — refer to the Cancer chapter explaining how Pisces thinks about Cancer.

ARIES/PISCES

Your Pisces employee bugs you when she gives you evasive answers to your direct questions. Her inability to relate to matters at hand and absentmindedness make you furious. She is subservient and tries to obey your commands but you want immediate action and don't get it from her.

You are in awe of your Piscean partner's ability to promote your ideas to wondrous heights. Her exaggerations don't disturb you as long as it is for your benefit. You dislike it when she makes promises that are not kept. One too many upsets the apple cart and that's when Pisces runs for shelter as you rant and rave.

This is not the greatest combination because you are opposite personalities. You (a Fire sign) tell it like it is and have a fiery temperament; Pisces (a Water sign) doesn't want to hear or tell the truth and has watery eyes that often spill tears because you've hurt her feelings with your angry words.

Both of you spend money as fast as it comes in so you'll be insolvent most of the time, with creditors pounding at the door. You pay bills immediately whereas Pisces forgets about it. Therefore if you're in business together, you need an accountant who can control the both of you.

TAURUS/PISCES

Your Pisces coworker is a delight to be around because he's so quiet. He never disturbs your concentration and when he does speak it's pleasantly and softly. He goes a little slower than you but you don't mind lending him a helping hand when he lags behind. He's so appreciative of every little favor that you do for him.

Your Pisces employee doesn't gossip on the job or waste time talking to his coworkers. Often his suggestions for sales are profitable although you have to make them practical; he's just too far up in the clouds with some of his pipe dreams.

It's a cinch working for Pisces. This is one boss who doesn't rush you. He lets you tend to the detail and work in your own methodical fashion.

The two of you are a good team because there's an innate understanding between you. You need his imagination and dramatic ability and he needs your dependability and practicality. Both of you are gentle, kind, and have a wide circle of friends — all aids to success.

You are a workaholic and Pisces can be shiftless, however if you keep him happy with tasks he can cope with — promoting on a large scale, wheeling and dealing — then he puts in lots of time on the job. When this occurs, it makes it easy to gain the goals you both desire.

GEMINI/PISCES

It's no picnic working with Pisces — she's slow and holds you back. She does laugh when you tell jokes but there aren't any of the intellectual exchanges so important to you. This woman just seems to be a little bit of a recluse. You enjoy working with someone who stimulates your mind — something your Pisces coworker can't manage.

Your Pisces boss is very inspiring with those fantastic praises she dishes out. You can't wait to get that raise she promised but you hope it's not like the last time — that one came a year late even though you reminded her about it each month. Luckily money isn't that important to you or you would have quit.

You are thinking of dissolving your partnership with Pisces because she's too lackadaisical about everything; except you've noticed she's got fantastic ideas, but she doesn't do anything about them unless you push her — and you're tired of doing that.

You two do not make a good business pair. You are frank and couldn't care less if you hurt Pisces with the truth. She will be in tears most of the time. You are full of action, she's full of talk; therefore, you've got to take your time to make sure she tends to business and doesn't goof off.

You care more for facts than you do fantasy; Pisces is the reverse. However, if you take care of the practical and technical end and let Pisces use her creative mind and imagination to promote projects, products, and the company, it could be a workable solution. However, you've got a great gift of gab and are also good with dealing with clients — so you'll have to take turns if you both want to drum up business by dealing with customers.

CANCER/PISCES

You feel very protective toward your Pisces coworker. He gets snowed under with the work and just can't seem to hack it like you can. You don't mind giving him a helping hand because he's so sympathetic to your personal problems. And you're glad that he can keep a secret, too.

It's a relief to work for Pisces because he doesn't push you to hurry and get your tasks completed. In fact he doesn't even look over your shoulder to see how you work. If he did he might criticize your oblique method of doing a job; however, you've found that it has been advantageous in the long run. He's never complained yet about anything that you turned in.

This is a good partnership; both are compatible and may do well together. You need encouragement and Pisces is the type who can inspire you to do great deeds. He seems to adore the way you handle the behind-the-scenes, menial, and routine part of the business while he's the front man wheeling and dealing.

Neither one of you have a lot of energy but you are both people who cling to your beliefs; therefore, if you persist with your individual duties and do everything to make the corporation a success, you might be able to bring in that million-dollar profit that Pisces dreams about and tells you is "just around the corner."

LEO/PISCES

This is about the laziest coworker you've seen. But Pisces is so complimentary every time you do something for her that you just can't help but like her.

Your Pisces employee brings your temper out because she's so slow and doesn't seem to care about her job. She never says a word so you don't know what she's thinking; perhaps she's not happy here. If she doesn't improve her job performance you may have to give her the ax.

This boss is someone you can wrap around your finger. Pisces acts so subserviently to you and doesn't seem to mind that you've practically taken over her supervisory job. She lets you make all the decisions and run the business your way.

This is not a bad combination if you are both performing tasks that you are best suited for. As long as Pisces is using her creative processes and you are in the management and responsibility end of the business, all is great; otherwise, you will have difficulty being successful.

You might get angry if she doesn't put action behind her flowery phrases; therefore you do all the hard labor. You both need an accountant or financial adviser because the two of you are impractical, generous to a fault with salaries, and splurge on expense accounts, risky ventures, new equipment, and may be in debt most of the time.

VIRGO/PISCES

Your Pisces coworker is so shiftless, inaccurate, and spaced out that you wonder at times if he's on drugs, pills, or has an alcoholic problem. You chide him for the least little thing and tears start flowing down his cheeks. If you were the boss he would have been fired after the first day.

It just seems like your Pisces employee doesn't use the brain God gave him. Most of your time is spent in correcting his errors, lecturing him, and trying to analyze him. He's not easy to figure out!

Your Pisces boss doesn't seem to be well informed about the overall business picture. He seems to know how to spend money foolishly and doesn't mind your telling him about it. In fact he welcomes your financial report although he doesn't seem too pleased when you try to explain that he has to go on a budget or the company will fold. When you are talking to him, he looks as if he isn't even listening to you — it's as if he's living in Shangri-La and doesn't have a care in the world.

Virgo and Pisces are a bad combination, although you both like to serve others. But your methods are opposite and not agreeable with one another. You are better working behind the scenes whereas Pisces is good dealing with people. Therefore if you could both be in your own little world doing your own thing and not bugging one another, perhaps you could make a go of it. But Pisces will not be able to live in the peace he needs and enjoys because you'll be too busy nagging him for his many faults. It's best you be friends rather than in a partnership together.

LIBRA/PISCES

It's delightful having Pisces as a coworker because she's harmonious, never argues, and just seems to drift through life the way you do. Often you catch yourself slipping into flights of fancy when you're working. You've noticed that Pisces daydreams too because on many occasions you've brought her back to reality with your questions. It sure is great to work with someone who doesn't rush you.

Your Pisces employee isn't as productive as you'd like her to be, but her warm-hearted and likeable personality makes up for her shortcomings. She is very cooperative and doesn't give you any trouble on the job like some of your other employees do. You are lucky to have someone so flexible in your organization — she doesn't mind shifting from one phase of an operation to another, in fact she seems to be joyous about it.

You've never had an easier job than this one working for a Pisces. She's so good-natured and easygoing that it's a pleasure coming in every day, even though you are a little late. But Pisces never scolds you — she just grins and says "good morning." This boss doesn't seem to mind it when you're a little slow getting those reports out.

This is an odd combination: both of you are gentle, dislike quarrels and thus give in to the easy way out; the two of you are lazy, take naps, enjoy the social scene although Pisces tends to be a little reclusive on occasion. Between the two of you there isn't enough gumption or energy to get things moving; to be a successful team you need action and persistence — which you tend to have when *you* are balanced.

Pisces dislikes making decisions and you get indecisive weighing the pros and cons, therefore this can hold up important projects, make clients angry and cause utter chaos. It's a weak twosome; however, in spite of it, happiness reigns.

SCORPIO/PISCES

Your Pisces coworker certainly isn't competitive. He won't interfere with your getting that promotion you've been plotting to get. You are glad that he doesn't yak and disturb your concentration, and also he doesn't meddle in your business. His dawdling on the job makes it necessary for you to do some of his chores for him. But you don't mind; it'll make you look good if the boss sees you handling both desks. Now maybe you'll get that advance quicker than you had anticipated.

This is one employee you'll have to fire if he doesn't become more meticulous. You really hate to do it because Pisces is such a nice and loyal fellow. He's one of the few people you do trust — you just wish he'd get his head together. He procrastinates too much and holds up production.

Your Pisces partner's ideas are illusions that could make you both rich if put into practice. He's excellent for dealing with the clients — that gives you time to tend to the managerial duties that are so necessary when you run an organization.

You make a great team, especially if you let Pisces do all the grandiose promoting. You will have to guard against being so caustic that you hurt your partner's feelings. You tend to have a hard personality whereas Pisces has a soft one. Perhaps these opposites are helpful in the business the two of you conduct.

Pisces is not as interested in finances as you are — unless you know a wheeler-dealer Pisces. If that's the case, then the two of you are out to make a fast buck. Watch get-rich quick schemes that Pisces may want to involve you in; use your innate intelligence and you'll win. Money can be made, lots of it — when you two put your heads together.

SAGITTARIUS/PISCES

You feel like giving your Pisces coworker a shove to get with it; she is slower than a snail crawling. She irritates you to no end and spoils your fun because she's so sensitive to every little thing: you can't even play a prank on her that she doesn't take it the wrong way. It's a real drag working with this woman.

You are anxious to please your Pisces boss because she's so lenient. It's wonderful working in an office where there are no rules or restrictions — lots of freedom to move about.

Your Pisces partner has many traits that you can't stand: laziness, procrastination, and dishonesty. You don't like deceptiveness and when she steals money out of petty cash and blames someone else, you see red — that's just not fair, especially when you've previously caught her in a few lies.

You two make a disastrous pair! You are honest and frank, therefore you expect Pisces to be the same. When she doesn't tell the truth, your words are enough to make Pisces dissolve the partnership — however, you are doing it when yelling at her but she's so embarrassed that she just stares into empty space making her plans never to see you again. Inwardly she may be weeping but outwardly she's got a grin on her face. Your extravagance, and hers, could also keep the corporation insolvent. Most of the time she won't oppose your spending plans but why should you both go for broke?

CAPRICORN/PISCES

Your Pisces employee isn't very ambitious, but he's pleasant to have around because he's quiet and retiring. He obeys your instructions; however, he's a little slow in performing them. You're glad he's not the type who's always asking for a raise — that way you can wind up with a better profit for yourself.

You are amazed at all the money-making schemes your Pisces partner comes up with; some sound a little far-fetched to try but a few in the past were fortuitous. His publicity campaign for your merchandise may go over really big — you'll give it a whirl next month.

Capricorn and Pisces make a good team. Pisces excels out in front whereas you excel behind the scenes. However, when it comes to negotiation, you should be the one who takes over this part of the operation; you are shrewd and patient, whereas Pisces will give in and give up too soon in this power game.

Both of you are people who will make sacrifices: however you are aimed toward a goal with your denials and Pisces toward helping people. Naturally you'll have control of the money and budget because Pisces gets too carried away with spending to be practical — he needs your guiding hand.

AQUARIUS/PISCES

Your Pisces boss seems to be very spiritual for someone in her position. Her philosophical comments are inspiring and give the entire office an uplifted feeling. When you come in late, she never says anything; you don't even think she notices. She doesn't mind that you take vacations at odd times of the year or in broken days rather than a solid week here and there.

Your partnership with Pisces is very satisfying because neither one of you tells the other what to do. There are no regulations or set schedules to maintain. Pressures are a rarity. Both work when you want and come and go as you please. You don't care that you aren't making a fortune, but you're making a living and also have some spare money to donate to your favorite crusades.

You may not accomplish much in this relationship but you'll be able to get along. However, you are a bit more ambitious than Pisces and move faster. There is an exception to this and that is if you have the type of Pisces who wants to strike it rich overnight. In either case she'll still try to make her wealth the easiest, and most effortless, way possible.

The money spent will be enormous, unless you're the conservative Aquarian. If not, the profits will be spent in both of your humanitarian causes: Pisces leans toward helping the poor, hungry, and handicapped, whereas you are interested in the ecology, conservation of lands, gun control, and changing the laws of the land through reform movements.

PISCES/PISCES

Your Pisces coworker is a real gem. You can cry on his shoulder when the boss hurts your feelings by insulting you for being lazy. His sympathy is just what you need and then he turns around and tells you a joke that makes you forget your woes. This fellow is uncanny with the way he can sense when you are upset.

It's a pleasure working for Pisces. He lets you contribute your ideas for those ads the company's planning to take out in a trade magazine. There isn't any conflict or frustration on this job except when you have to complete those boring tasks that you'd rather give to somebody else to finish.

Your Pisces employee tends to procrastinate just like you do. But you understand it — he's probably bored with his job or is confused; therefore you'll change him to another department where there's more variety. Maybe he'd be good in assisting you on those promotional projects that are pending.

For the two of you to be a success in a business partnership, you'll need to hire efficient help who can take care of the menial tasks, finances, and other areas that both of you deplore. But with this setup, there will be two wheeler-dealer's with the grandest brainstorms in the world working twenty-four hours a day — but you need the other people in your firm to make them become a reality.

Both are extremely extravagant and use money like it's water going right through your hands: it's something that will bring you both the high-roller type of life you love to live — but please listen to your accountant so you'll have something stocked away for that rainy day, okay?

Made in the USA
Middletown, DE
09 January 2023

21725624R00136